Cities OF THE IMAGINATION

VIENNA

A cultural and literary history

Nicholas T. Parsons

Signal Books
Oxford

First published in 2008 by
Signal Books Limited
36 Minstèr Road
Oxford OX4 1LY
www.signalbooks.co.uk

ISBN 978-1-904955-45-0 Paper

Cover Design: Baseline Arts
Production: Devdan Sen
Cover Images: Herbert Kratky/istock; Baseline Arts
Photographs and Images: p.i © Karl Thaller/istockphoto; p.xvi © Lebrecht Music and
Arts Photo Library/Alamy; p.xx © Dave Zilla/dreamstime.com; p.2 © Frantisek
Staud/Alamy; p.10 © Lebrecht Music and Arts Photo Library/Alamy; p.16 ©
Georgianrevival/dreamstime.com; p.36 © ÖNB/Wien, NB540.008-B; p.40 © Mira
Janacek/istockphoto; p.56 © D12/dreamstime.com; pp.62-3 © bpk/Hermann Buresch;
p.70 © Karl Thaller/istockphoto; p.82 © Private Collection/The Bridgeman Art
Library; p.90 © bpk; p.98 © Bridgeman Art Library; p.113 © HfxP/dreamstime.com;
p.114 © bpk/Hamburger Kunsthalle/Christoph Irrgang; p.132 © bpk; pp.150-1©
ÖNB/Wien, L56918C; p.168 © Gudella/dreamstime.com; p.172 © Private
Collection/The Bridgeman Art Library; pp.174-5 © bpk; pp.182-3 © bpk; p.189 ©
Doktora/dreamstime.com; p.190 © Hulton Archive/istockphoto; p.197 © ÖNB/Wien,
31876B; p.204 © bpk; p.209 © ÖNB/Wien, 284094B; p.218 © Peter Barritt/Alamy;
pp.232-3 © ÖNB/Wien, LW72226C; p.236 © Digitalpress/dreamstime.com; p.238 ©
Art Kowalsky/Alamy; p.249 © bpk; p.256 © Karl Thaller/istockphoto; p.258 © bpk.
Printed in India

VIENNA

Cities of the Imagination

Contents

Foreword

When I first came to Vienna in 1972 as a rather naive graduate student it was without the benefit of a work like the present volume by Nicholas Parsons. Instead, I arrived armed with knowledge acquired from an earlier and more formal observer of things Viennese, Ilsa Barea, What I learned from her was supplemented by a young scholar's immature understanding of imperial Austria augmented by an appreciation of Viennese pastry and music to which was added a scant acquaintance with Austrian wine. In short, I really knew next to nothing about the place where I was about to spend the next ten months of my life.

The reason for my presence in Vienna was to pursue the research for my dissertation on the Viennese Secession. Sustained by a Fulbright Fellowship, I was an historian in search of not only the meaning of avant-garde art in *fin-de-siècle* Austria, but also a kind of time traveller who hoped to find a city in which at least part of its urban identity was still vibrant with the atmosphere of a world as it was before the realm of the Habsburgs had come to an end. My rather romantic expectation came to be realized, but not exactly as I had imagined it. The past was still alive in Vienna; however, what it had to offer was more akin to the love-hate dichotomy experienced by so many Viennese rather than the uncomplicated life in three-quarter time of my imagination. As a result, my life in Vienna, although not devoid of the experiences redolent of the past I had been looking for, instructed me in the realities of how history can preserve the good and not so good as the ingredients of the present and future of a great city.

In the early 1970s Vienna was just beginning to move out of the phase of post-war reconstruction into that of restoration. Despite the gradual reappearance of colour here and there as in the rehabilitation of Otto Wagner's famous Majolica House, Vienna was a city dominated by shades of grey courtesy of decades of accumulated dirt and soot. This monochromatic cityscape was further reinforced by a fall and winter of overcast skies and a bone-chilling dampness that remained until the untimely arrival that year of a late spring. Aside from archives, museums, and the national library, my chief refuge from the inclemencies of Viennese weather was the salon of a nineteenth-century haut-bourgeois apartment that served as my residence. While both the building and the apartment had seen better days and the indifference of the family from whom I rented allowed me to experience how one could freeze to death from the warmth of a Viennese heart, I was living just off the Ringstrasse within a stone's throw of the Hofburg and the Kunsthistorisches Museum. In other words, greyness, bad weather, and unsociable landlords aside, I was in the middle of the old world for which I had longed.

Outside the faded splendour of my rented room daily life was still carried on in the midst of that world. Except for the socialist public housing of the 1920s and early 1930s and some uninspired modern architecture from the 1950s and 1960s, Vienna was physically dominated by the eighteenth- and nineteenth-century imperial and domestic architecture of its golden age. Habsburg double-headed eagles and the name and image of Franz Joseph were (as they still are) omnipresent. With the subway just in the early stages of excavation, streetcars and Wagner's art nouveau Stadtbahn constituted the bulk of public transport and in the absence of pedestrian zones the centre of the historic inner city was a bustling hub of traffic. Fortunately, along with the physicality of the past came some of its amenities. Vienna's coffee houses were beginning to emerge from the long night of alien espresso bars and indifference that had darkened the 1950s and 1960s. As they had in the good old days, they offered shelter from the outside world along with coffee and cake. If, however, all you really needed to escape from the cares of the day was a taste of whipped cream, chocolate, or marzipan, places like Demel's, Gerstner's, and numerous lesser establishments showed that the Viennese tradition of fine baking and confection had lost none of its vitality. Finally, if it was simply the spirit that needed refreshing opera, the theatre, and a seemingly endless supply of concerts were available in abundance. Yes, the preservation of the past had its pleasures, but there was a price to be paid for them.

The museum-like character of the city was sustained by a fundamentally conservative political and social atmosphere in which notions of hierarchy and deference were the common currency of everyday life, not only in Vienna, but in Austria as a whole. From the obsequious attitude of clerks to the insistent use of titles, the past had laid its dead hand on a city of nearly two million people. Thus, at a time when most of Europe west of the Iron Curtain was experiencing a lively, urban-based youth culture, life in Vienna was under the sway of generations born before the two world wars. It was their memories, their experiences, their tastes, and their anxieties that dominated to such an extent that young people with ambition and a desire for change often felt compelled to go abroad. What was pleasant, charming, and stimulating about the Vienna of my student days represented the cumulative legacy of its imperial culture at its peak just before the First World War. To be sure, it was a legacy worth preserving, but, at the time, the act of preservation seemed to be at the expense of the city's ability to recreate the kind of innovation that had made its reputation as a centre of cultural activity. When I left Vienna at the end of my fellowship ossification seemed to be what the future had in store for the city and I felt like I was escaping from a pool of amber before it hardened.

Fortunately for us all, I was not alone in making good my escape—Vienna itself had done the same. In 1973 I had overlooked the historical fact that generations pass away and when they do their place in the sun is taken by those who had been kept in the shade behind them. When I returned to Vienna in 1981 as a fledgling professor I found a city transformed. My own post-war generation had finally come of age and was everywhere in evidence. The physical character of the city had also benefited from the passage of time. The efforts at urban renovation and improvements that had barely begun nine years earlier had resulted in a cleaner, brighter city complemented by a modern subway and a pedestrian-dominated inner city. Of course, the generations that had been newly displaced deserved a good deal of the credit for creating this revitalized urban scene, but those populating it with energy and expectations were the submerged youth and the temporary émigrés of the 1970s who were now claiming their birthright. In its way a kind of revolution had occurred, but one that was uniquely Austrian.

No guillotines, either literal or figurative were set up by this revolution nor did any Jacobins step forward to call for a "republic of virtue". Rather, the double-headed eagles of the Habsburgs were polished, the likenesses of their imperial masters made more visible, the coffee houses became more inviting, and the opera house, theatres and concert halls grew more alive.

All this signified that the revolution was integrative rather than destructive. The secret of old Austria's success before the tragedy of 1914 and the inter-war calamities had been its ability to marry continuity with change as a creative union in which what had been past became not merely prelude to the present, but a nurturing part of it. The trick in all this, however, is not to mistake a stifling conservatism for genuine continuity as had been the case for the first thirty odd years after 1945. Contemporary Austria has relearned this lesson and its fruits can be seen on display in Vienna where a cosmopolitan atmosphere has returned to its core and even debates over preservation versus new construction can remind one of the creative ferment associated with the city's famous *fin de siècle*. So too does the self-absorbed carping of Thomas Bernhard, Peter Handke, and Elfriede Jelinek as representatives of the new Viennese literati emanate from an older, if more profound, tradition of complaint represented by the likes of Johann Nestroy, Franz Grillparzer and Karl Kraus. Indeed, the very iconoclasm of these writers and architects , as well as the critics who invoke the past to remind them of their shortcomings follow in the footsteps of a Viennese creative dialogue that has been interrupted, but never silenced.

Returning to Vienna almost every year since the early 1980s and with a much more diverse circle of contacts than I had as a graduate student, I have been able to experience at first hand the process just described, but so has Nicholas Parsons and that constitutes the great strength of what he has written. In the pages of his cultural history the reader will experience not only the results of distilled research, but also the insights of someone who has spent much of his adult life in the city about which he writes and has learned to discern the essentials in its past and present that make it what it is today. All this adds up to a cultural history of Vienna that, although brief and often witty, is never superficial or condescending in presenting the long life-span of this city. Nicholas Parsons has combined a fine sense of discernment with fine writing to produce a volume that rewards the reader with profit and pleasure.

James Shedel
Georgetown University

Acknowledgements

I would like to thank Bob Dent, the author of an excellent volume on Budapest in this same series, for first suggesting that I might consider tackling the subject of Vienna, and James Ferguson, the series publisher, for allowing me to do so.

All my Viennese friends have contributed to such knowledge, understanding and appreciation of Vienna as I have acquired over the last twenty years. I owe them a great debt of gratitude, but it would be impossible to name each of them and invidious to pick out just a few. However, I make an exception in the case of Wolfgang Bahr, an eagle-eyed *Lektor* who corrected many errors of fact, cleared up confusions or misconceptions and patiently argued me out of some of my more doggedly clung-to prejudices. Most of the text was also read by my art historian wife, Ilona Sármány-Parsons, who likewise saved me from a number of errors and stupidities that would otherwise have crept into it. Neither of them, however, is responsible for any errors that remain, still less for the opinions expressed.

The publisher asked for a personal response to the culture and history of Vienna, which is what I have endeavoured to supply. Such a brief inevitably means that the text is somewhat more opinionated than a conventional guidebook or a history aimed at professional historians. I hope, nevertheless, that even when the knowledgeable reader is in disagreement with my viewpoint, he/she will at least find it thought-provoking. Vienna is nothing if not a thought-provoking environment, so my final acknowledgement is to the city itself that has provided me with such intellectual, aesthetic and emotional stimulation over the years.

Vienna, May 2008

To Ilona, a *Wahlwienerin*...

Introduction:

VILLAGE AND WORLD CITY

The ordinary Viennese apartment house in which I live (architect, date of 1910 and "Secessionist style" meticulously recorded in Dehio, the Pevsner of Austria) looks across the street at low-level late Baroque and neoclassical houses. We gaze on their picturesque roofs and chimney stacks from our upper-floor window. The street itself was formerly the western border of the village of Penzing, now (with slightly altered parameters) one of Vienna's twenty-three administrative *Bezirke* (Districts). On an outside wall on the corner where our road merges with Penzinger Strasse, which was once the village's main street, perches a beautifully restored Baroque pietà bearing the date 1632. You would hardly notice it, of course; such things are to be seen all over the city. Turn up our street in the other direction and you soon encounter a mysterious octagonal column of carved white stone with an open lantern at the top. It has a Late Gothic relief of the crucifixion on its eastern side. I nurture the conceit that our Viennese existence is thus poised between the Crucifixion at the top of the road and the pietà at the bottom—between the universal symbol of Christ's suffering on the one hand, and an altogether private image of family mourning on the other. It reminds me of the way that historical Vienna was simultaneously universalist and intimate, one of the two capitals of an empire on which the sun never set, yet always preserving a stubbornly vernacular civic identity. The Viennese were imperial subjects, but they were hardly citizens of the world.

The aforementioned column, located by a zebra crossing, attracts only a passing glance from motorists and pedestrians, but the Office for the Protection of Monuments sent two experts to restore it a few years back, and it occupied them for three weeks of loving attention. Dehio explains: "the *Lichtsäule* ("Light Column") stood at the edge of the cemetery (dissolved 1854) for St. Jakob's Parish Church; an eternal flame burned in its little tabernacle in memory of the dear departed." In truth, the column is not especially beautiful, and of course no light burns in it now. Yet it is a romantically pleasing marker for the past, the light for the dead that is now a small memento vivere, celebrating, however modestly, the survival of the city's material fabric and its people. Once it had a significant symbolic and actual function. Now it is a simply a memorial of those func-

Stephansdom (St. Stephen's Cathedral) combines elements of Romanesque, Gothic, Late Gothic and (in the interior) Baroque. Like no other building in Vienna it is emblematic of the city itself, the richness of its culture and the resilience of its people.

tions. That idea also can be projected onto a wider canvas. Vienna was once the symbolically vital Christian bastion against insurgent Islam in Central Europe; more recently (and more cautiously) it was a last outpost of the Christian capitalist and liberal West, rescued by the skin of its teeth from the clutches of atheistic communism. It no longer fulfils such portentous roles, but their memory is woven into the city's understanding of itself, preserved and cherished, just as the Office for the Protection of Monuments preserves and cherishes the Lichtsäule.

Across the road stands the Church of St. Jakob, a not untypical architectural palimpsest, its successive makeovers reflecting layers of Viennese history. Founded in 1267 as a dependency of the then St. Stephen's Church (later St. Stephen's Cathedral, or Stephansdom, and the focal point of the city), it was badly damaged in the Turkish siege of 1683. (It claims to preserve part of a Turkish tent among its treasures.) In 1758-59 a leading Baroque master, Matthias Gerl, barockized it. It was damaged again in the French occupations of 1805 and 1809 and the tower caught fire at the end of the Second World War. But it is still there, living testimony to the vicissitudes of history and the continuity of faith.

Penzing itself is still there—just—although its two main streets are now busy traffic arteries with a bus route. A map of 1840 shows it as a picturesque village completely surrounded by meadows and vineyards to the west, north and north-east. On the southern side it is bounded by the River Wien, across which can be seen the vast park of Schönbrunn and the village of Hietzing. Both are about seven minutes walk from my flat.

In theory Vienna became a modern metropolis when its bastions were demolished in 1857, and an elegant boulevard (*Ringstrasse*) with grandiose Historicist buildings was built along the perimeter of the medieval and Baroque city. In practice it has retained a village-like quality, both on the macrocosmic scale of metropolitan politics and intellectual life, and on the microcosmic scale of my parish church in Penzing. Although it is changing now, there used to be families who lived in the same Bezirk for generations. Actually Greater Vienna is an agglutination of villages (known as *Vororte*, and lying outside the *Gürtel* or Ring Road) and suburbs with distinctive identities (*Vorstädte*), lying between the Gürtel and the Ringstrasse. The *Innere Stadt* (First District), the old core of the city, is where the tourist inevitably spends most of his or her time. A Viennese says he is going *in die Stadt* ("into town") when he is going to shop or to eat in the old city. It sounds like a journey from the provinces, but in reality it is only ten to twenty minutes in the tram or U-Bahn from somewhere in the *Vororte* or *Vorstädte*.

Vienna—it is one of its charms—combines the intimacy (occasionally claustrophobia) of a provincial city with the accoutrements and aspirations of an international one. For centuries it was the *Residenzstadt* (seat) of the Habsburg dynasty. It is to the latter and its aristocratic adherents that the city owes its vast *Hofburg* (court) and grandiloquent palaces, while the Catholic Church (in periodically ambivalent alliance with the Habsburgs) raised buildings to the glory of God that rivalled those advertising the glory of individual princes and generals. Yet bombast and elegance has always co-existed with the intimacy and homely tastes that most Viennese share. So it is that you leave an Inner City church dripping with Baroque luxury (the Jesuitenkirche perhaps) and soon find yourself in a mesh of narrow streets with curious shops, modest *Beisls* (traditional Viennese eateries), a faded coffee house or two… It is the juxtaposition of antinomies that gives Vienna its particular flavour both on the ground and in the mind. The writer Egon Friedell caught this flavour in his essay on Vienna as a "Theatre City": "The Habsburgs' distinctive trait," he wrote, "was that they had no sense of reality."

> The world was supposed to pattern itself on them, not they on the world. Therefore they could only make use of creatures who had no will of their own, and so arose the "Nation of Privy Councillors." Then came the Baroque with its double reversal of the idea of worldliness. It first rejected the world as mere dream. But since at the same time it affirmed dream as the only reality, it again returned to the world by a roundabout way. Thus it became the philosophy of the most worldly worldliness, since it rejected every accountability on the grounds that the world is just a dream. So arose that odd mixture of withdrawal from life and love of life, of submissiveness and pride, of incense and musk.

Theatre city, music city, *Residenzstadt*, village, melting pot of ethnicity, crucible of intellectual genius, provincial backwater of complacent philistinism, "experimental laboratory for world endings" (Karl Kraus), an oasis of piety, a breeding ground for racial hatred, a city of hedonism and frustrated artists, of easy-going pragmatism, of *Schlamperei* (muddle), of bureaucratic obsessions—these are just some of the perceptions of Vienna that have materialized through the ages. Of course, while all or any one of these characterizations may have been true at a particular point in time, they cannot all be true at the same time or all the time.

People who like a city to announce itself in clear-cut terms will have a hard time of it in Vienna, not least because the locals offer competing versions of the reality they inhabit. The temptation is to take refuge in reassuring clichés emblematized by Sachertorte, Lipizzaners and the New Year's Day Concert of the Wiener Philharmoniker. Marketing itself is rather the city's strength, and the guest conductors of the New Year's Day Concert play along with this, wrinkling their features in simulated ecstasy for the close-up camera as the Philharmoniker jog through some exceptionally banal polka. But Vienna is a lot more interesting than that. As Friedell pointed out, it is a city perpetually arguing with itself and this argument hovers between dream and reality. In this book I have tried to trace the lineaments of this argument through Vienna's complex and fascinating history.

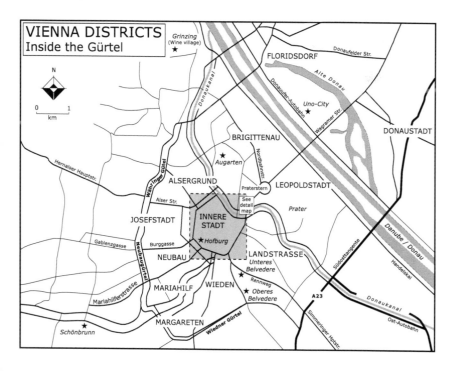

The Vienna Rathaus (City Hall) built in magnificent neo-Gothic style by Friedrich Schmidt and completed in 1883. Modelled on the medieval city halls of Flanders, the new *Rathaus* expressed the political aspirations of increasingly prosperous Liberal burghers in the Ringstrassen era from 1861 to the turn of the century. Vienna became an Austrian Federal State in 1922 and democratic Socialist administrations have been returned at every free election held since then.

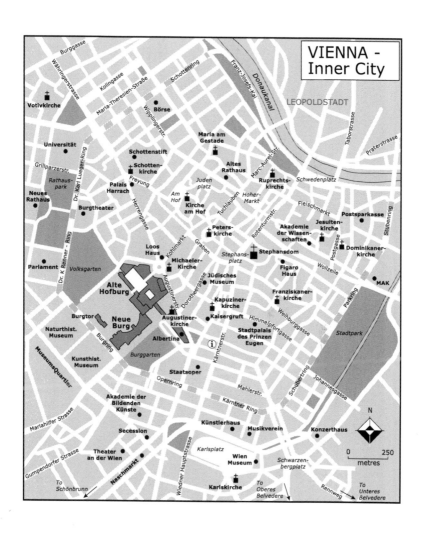

VIENNA - Inner City

LEOPOLDSTADT

Burggasse
Wahringerstrasse
Kolingasse
Maria-Theresien-Straße
Wipplingerstr.
Schottenring
Franz-Josefs-Kai
Donaukanal
Taborstrasse
Praterstrasse

Votivkirche

Universität

Grillparzerstr.
Rathaus-
park
Dr. Karl Lueger-Ring

Börse

Schottenstift

Schotten-
kirche

Freyung

Palais
Harrach

Herrengasse

Maria am
Gestade

Juden
platz

Am
Hof

Kirche
am Hof

Altes
Rathaus

Marc-Aurel-Str.

Ruprechts-
kirche

Schwedenplatz

Fleischmarkt

Hoher-
Markt

Tuchlauben

Rotenturmstr.

Postsparkasse

Stubenring

Akademie
der Wissen-
schaften

Jesuiten-
kirche

Neues
Rathaus

Burgtheater

Peters-
kirche

Loos
Haus

Kohlmarkt

Michaeler-
Kirche

Graben

Stephans-
platz

Stephansdom

Postgasse

Dominikaner-
kirche

Pariament

Volksgarten

Dr. K Renner - Ring

Augustinerstr.

Dorotheergasse

Jüdisches
Museum

Figaro
Haus

Wollzeile

MAK

Alte
Hofburg

Kapuziner-
kirche

Franziskaner-
kirche

Burgtor

Neue
Burg

Augustiner-
kirche

Kaisergruft

Himmelpfortgasse

Weihburggasse

Parkring

Naturhist.
Museum

Burgring

Albertina

Stadtpalais
des Prinzen
Eugen

Kärntnerstr.

Stadtpark

Kunsthist.
Museum

Burggarten

Schubertring

Johannesgasse

MuseumsQuartier

Staatsoper

Opernring

Mahlerstr.

Akademie der
Bildenden
Künste

Mariahilfer Strasse

Kärntner Ring

Secession

Künstlerhaus

Musikverein

Konzerthaus

N

Gumpendorfer Strasse

Theater
an der Wien

Naschmarkt

Wiedner Hauptstrasse

Karlsplatz

Wien
Museum

Schwarzen-
bergplatz

0   250
metres

To
Schönbrunn

Karlskirche

To
Oberes
Belvedere

Rennweg

To
Unteres
Belvedere

Part One

THE CAPUA OF MINDS:
"OUR BELOVED AND HATED VIENNA"

"Whether Vienna is a city of dreams (*Träume*) or of trauma (*Traumas*) is a moot point."

> Gottfried Heindl (theatre manager and cultural critic)

A night-time view of the Michaelerplatz seen from the Michaelertor of the Hofburg. The Michaelerkirche is directly ahead, while the Kohlmarkt leads off to the Inner City from the left of the church.

Chapter One

VIENNA PRESERVED:
THE PALIMPSEST

The Michaelerplatz is not the most beautiful square in Vienna, but it is one that most poignantly evokes the restless spirits of the past. Here at the interface between the Hofburg (the Habsburg court) and the Stadt (the city), between the rulers and the ruled, the visitor who allows himself a moment's reflection can glimpse the variegated layers of Viennese history. Stand in the arch of the great Michaelertor and you are looking down a street that runs closely parallel to one which led to the south-western gate, the Porta Decumana, of the Roman camp of Vindobona. The military road running along the Roman Empire's northern fortified boundary (the *limes*) issued from the Reitschulgasse to your right, joined the road running from the legionaries' camp into the square and then curved north-east of the Herrengasse on your left. The junction must have been significant, since it was marked by a monument over thirty feet high, but we do not know to what or to whom.

In the middle of the square the fourth-century remains of downtown Vindobona (the *canabae*) and the camp's red light district have been laid bare—together with other remains from some eighteen centuries of continuous civilization. The Viennese palimpsest here includes fragmented medieval houses and Baroque cellars, as well as the outline of the Habsburgs' "Paradise Gardens" of the sixteenth and seventeenth centuries (it was a vegetable patch rather than a latter-day Eden—*Paradeiser* is the local word for tomatoes).

Another cultural memory of the Habsburgs is hard on your right (see the plaque on the wall), namely the site of the old Burgtheater. In 1776 Joseph II gave it the remit of nurturing "national" German drama to replace the lightweight French and Italian plays or musical comedies that had dominated the repertoire for much of the eighteenth century. He hoped thereby also to purge the theatre of dialect productions and improvisations which were so hard for the censor to monitor, but which the

Viennese loved as an outlet for their frustration with authority. Unfortunately decent dramas in German proved at first hard to come by and harder still to make popular, so the preferred Viennese fare of operas soon established hegemony. As an opera house the old Burgtheater was the venue for many a controversial and historic premiere, including those for *Orfeo ed Eurydice* and *Così fan tutte*. "Madness, tumult and noise", complained the court poet, Pietro Metastasio, of Gluck's masterpiece; "an insult to womanhood" was Wagner's later verdict on Mozart and Da Ponte's scintillating operatic jewel—and it is true that Mozart's view of womanhood was not exactly Siegfried's. Ironically *Così fan tutte*'s central conceit of a "fiancée swap" is derived from the French tradition of comedy that the Burgtheater, with its Teutonically earnest mission statement, had been set up to replace. One could also say that the stylized German speech long nurtured by the Burgtheater, which has made it the Mecca of theatre-lovers in the German-speaking world, is akin to the same tradition in the Comédie Française. Like the Comédie Française, too, a more or less permanent troupe of actors and actresses still keeps the traditional repertoire alive, nurturing the canon and projecting a cultural identity: "This is who we are; this is what we do. Accept no imitations."

In Vienna one was never, and is not now, neutral where theatre and music and the visual arts are concerned; people are passionate and partisan about the new or the reinterpretation of the old, praising, disputing, condemning, as they did in the Brahms-versus-Bruckner conflict of the 1880s, or when Mozart overturned their notions of Salierian rectitude. Their rulers were often somewhat indifferent to all this passion, evincing the stolid philistinism of Franz Joseph, or Joseph II's generally benevolent, but occasionally bemused, support for the arts. It was he who famously complained to Mozart that *Die Entführung aus der Serail* contained "an awful lot of notes," which puts one in mind of the Duke of Gloucester's restrained enthusiasm on receipt of Volume II of the *Decline and Fall of the Roman Empire*: "Another damned thick square book! Always scribble, scribble, scribble! Eh! Mr Gibbon?" The admirable Maria Theresia regarded (carefully censored) theatre and Baroque "spectacles" as useful and generally harmless diversions for her peoples, but was also wont to refer to comedy actors as *bagage*. Her cultivated advisor Sonnenfels was a connoisseur of the theatre, but Maria Theresia was not impressed, telling him that he "should have better things to do with his time than writing theatre reviews." Like Mrs. Thatcher, she was incapable of irony, a figure of speech on which the Viennese thrived. She dismissed her liberal censor's defence of irony as an instrument "for criticizing and improving humanity," remarking that it "only embitters," and that writing or reading such matter wasted valuable time that could be so much more profitably employed. She had no hesitation in interrupting a performance in the Burgtheater when weightier matters required the audience's immediate attention: for example, she once burst into the imperial box dressed only in a nightgown, and startled the audience with a joyful bellow in Viennese dialect: *Leutln, freut's eng, der Poldl hât an' Buam kriagt!* ("People, rejoice! My Poldy's had a boy!") In this way was the birth of the future Emperor Franz I communicated to the world.

The Baroque Burgtheater is no more, replaced in 1888 by the neo-Renaissance Burgtheater on the Ringstrasse; looming over its former site is the gilded and green dome of the majestic Michaelertrakt of the Hofburg, the residence of the Habsburg dynasty. Although this part of the Hofburg is a neo-Baroque edifice, it closely follows the original plans of the younger Fischer von Erlach, who (with his father, Johann Bernhard) left such an enduring footprint on late seventeenth- and early eighteenth-century Vienna. If you turn back towards the square, its varied architecture of Baroque, Gothic and Modernism unfolds layers of Viennese history before your eyes. On the right may be seen the Gothic Michaelerkirche, with its finely wrought Baroque portico, topped by Lorenzo Mattielli's dramatic sculptural group of the Archangel Michael expelling a rebel from heaven. It could be a scene from Milton's *Paradise Lost* recreated in stone. Above it soar the slender and graceful features of the earlier Gothic church, whose crypt provides the last resting place of many loyal servants of the Habsburg court. Only a few yards away, on the other side of the junction where the Kohlmarkt meets the square, your gaze encounters the recently restored Loos-Haus (1912). The latter's uncompromisingly plain façade (it was dubbed the "house without eyebrows") so upset Franz Joseph that the curtains of the Hofburg windows opposite it were kept permanently drawn. Architecture in Vienna always arouses fierce passions.

The burden of press complaint about the Loos-Haus was that "from the lowest point of the threshold to the bridge tiles on the roof, there [isn't] a trace of anything *Viennese* about the new building. The ground floor and mezzanine [are] of proud marble, the lofty street facades, which fill the spaces between the huge planes of glass, [are] all made of the noblest material, costly marble, and above it all, a bare plaster wall without the shadow of an ornament, pierced by tasteless window openings, a desolate poverty above all this marble splendour... " To which onslaught Loos replied as follows: "I did indeed design the building so that it might harmonize as far as possible with the square on which it stands. The style of the church [Michaelerkirche], which forms the pendant to my building, acted as my point of departure... I chose real marble because any form of imitation is distasteful to me. I kept the plaster surfaces as simple as possible, because the burghers of Vienna also built in a simple style..." Loos' mixture of puritanism (he was after all the author of a famous diatribe against the eclectic excesses of Historicism entitled "Ornament and Crime") and his insouciant arrogance (the Michaelerkirche has already become a mere pendant to the Loos masterpiece!) cut no ice with the nostalgic votaries of *Alt-Wien* ("Old Vienna"), who pined for a cityscape set in aspic. Their Vienna, in the view of the modernizers, existed as an imagined and inviolable agglomeration of periods and styles, even if its individual elements must themselves have replaced an even older "Alt-Wien". With characteristic acerbity the critic and campaigner Karl Kraus, who was an ally of Loos, slapped down the sentimentalists: "I have devastating news for the aesthetes: Old Vienna was once new."

It is not only architectural controversy that raises the blood pressure of the Viennese; generally well-informed arguments over music and theatre are likewise a staple of metropolitan life. In any dispute, both sides of the argument bolster their case with an appeal to the notion of what is, or is not, "Viennese". The relatively new Haas Haus on the Stephansplatz (completed in 1990 to a design by Hans Hollein) provoked reactions which were in some respects similar to what Loos had to endure—not surprisingly, when one considers that it was being built alongside the very symbol of the city's survival and its cultural identity, St. Stephen's Cathedral (Stephansdom). Hollein's response to his critics combined chutzpah and arrogance in true Loosian style, but the critics may have had the last word, since the original concept of placing numerous small (and very expensive) boutiques in the interior foundered on landlord rapacity and the scepticism of potential customers. By day the Stephansdom is moodily reflected in the plate glass of the Haas Haus and by night fairy lights draped across the façade give it a picturesque quality. It is a great improvement on the hideous post-war building (filling a bomb hole) that it replaced, but that is not enough to mollify its fiercest critics, who seem to regard Hollein as little more than a latter-day Vandal who should leave the Viennese in peace and go back to Germany where he originally made his career.

The conservationists, while they do not have it all their own way, are always a force to be reckoned with by the *Stadtregierung* (municipal government) and developers itching to get their hands on desirable sites. For many years an architectural historian produced an annual illustrated catalogue of (in his view) valuable buildings that had been more or less surreptitiously demolished, a publication designed to cause maximum embarrassment in the relevant political departments. Then again, the public showed its determination to protect the city and its traditions in a referendum held on the issue of whether Vienna should host a "World Exhibition" (in collaboration with Hungary) in 1995. The result, a resounding "no", seemed to surprise the politicians, though probably not the people themselves. The more historically minded might have recalled that Vienna's World Exhibition of 1873 had been an unmitigated disaster for the city, although this was admittedly due as much to a cholera outbreak and the first great stock market crash of modern times, as to cultural factors or poor planning. The Viennese of the 1990s seemed to feel that the city had plenty of tourism already, and were unenthusiastic about turning it into a gigantic exhibition centre to be trampled over by the world and his wife for an entire year. Unfortunately this admirable stubbornness was overriden by the decision to hold the final of the European football championship in Vienna in 2008, but that did not last long and the substantial money to be made was a powerful consolation…

The pride that the Viennese take in their city becomes ever more understandable as the visitor widens his field of exploration, striking out in different directions on foot from the Michaelerplatz. Vienna's beauties are many and varied—the Gothic and Baroque churches, the noble Baroque palaces, the numerous pleasant parks with their meticulously tended allées, flower-beds and gravel paths, the grandiloquent Historicist edifices of the Ringstraße: all of these reflect phases of the city's past that have left their mark on the Viennese character. Throughout its history, the town was not only engaged in a continual political and environmental argument with its rulers, but also with itself. Often the landowning class or the dynasty simply imposed its will, as when medieval houses were demolished on a large scale to make way for the nobility's boastful Baroque palaces. They were in a strong position to do so since, as Elisabeth Lichtenberger has pointed out, the nobility, clergy and court personnel owned seven-eighths of the area within the city walls by the end of the Baroque era in the mid-eighteenth century. We do not know to what extent the ordinary Viennese were able to object, if at all; but probably they had a few well-chosen remarks to make about the megalomania of princes, just as a later generation delighted to point out the deficiencies of the Ringstraßen architecture's grandiose Historicism or Loos' "house without eyebrows." One can imagine the sheer delight in the *Beisln* (cheap restaurants) and coffee-houses when it was discovered that the elegant new Burgtheater auditorium (Gottfried Semper and Karl Hasenauer, 1888) not only had terrible acoustics (rectified in 1897), but actually contained boxes facing away from the stage. This simply confirmed what the cynics had long been saying. Did not the grandeur of Theophil Hansen's Classical Parliament on the Ringstraße deaden the speakers' voices so that they could scarcely be heard? Was not the interior of Friedrich Schmidt's huge neo-Gothic Rathaus opposite the Burgtheater permanently plunged in Stygian gloom due to hopelessly inadequate lighting and narrow Gothic windows? And now this! As the contemporary joke had it: "In the Parliament you can't hear anything, in the Rathaus you can't see anything, and in the Burgtheater you can *neither hear nor see anything.*"

Chapter Two

VIENNA LIBERATA:
CIVIC PRIDE AND THE METROPOLIS

On the day of German reunification (2 October 1990) the socialist Mayor of Vienna ordered a German flag to be hoisted on the City Hall, immediately provoking a characteristic Viennese row by his action. At a press conference, Bürgermeister Zilk, a shrewd self-publicist with a gift for the flamboyant gesture, was vigorously attacked by (mostly) young people, who complained that the last time someone hung out a German flag from the Rathaus, it was the swastika. But it is precisely because it is *not* now the swastika that we should fly it, was the gist of Zilk's tart and skilful reply. Still, Zilk knew that Austria's tortured love-hate relationship with Germany had deep historical roots and that German reunification was a deeply sensitive issue for many of his fellow-countrymen. The real significance of the incident, however, was the way it underlined the political and symbolic weight of Vienna, firstly as the seat of federal government, and secondly as one of the nine *Bundesländer* (Federal Provinces). Nobody would have paid much attention if this row had erupted in St Pölten or Graz. Vienna indeed generally supplies the international profile of Austria to less travelled foreigners, who are not altogether sure if Vorarlberg is part of Austria or Switzerland, and are rather surprised to discover that Südtirol (South Tyrol) is in Italy.

Bürgermeister Zilk was no Ken Livingstone given to solipsistic gestures, such as declaring parts of the city a nuclear-free zone; as Mayor of Vienna he was not only the chief executive of a city with more than one and a half million inhabitants, he was also a Provincial Governor (*Landeshauptmann*) with extensive powers. While he did not go as far as the Governor of Lower Austria, who was wont to refer to his "foreign policy" when opening regional exhibitions, Mayor Zilk frequently took an independent line on controversial matters, sometimes to the manifest discomfort of his socialist colleagues in the federal government. His conciliatory statements on such delicate matters as immigration policy (where

Dr Karl Lueger.

the government was constantly under pressure from an insurgent right-wing "Freedom Party") were notably courageous. Indeed the issue of immigration has always been extremely sensitive in Vienna, home to the majority of migrants, where socialist working-class voters fearing for their jobs desert to the extreme right in times of economic uncertainty. The centre-right People's Party has never been able to make much headway in the fully democratized city, despite being the (much purified) successor to the Karl Lueger's Christian Social administration, which modernized the infrastructure and embarked on a popular programme of municipalization around 1900.

The civic pride of Vienna, in its modern, middle class form, emerged in the Ringstrassen era (1857-1900). In the heyday of the *Gründerzeit* (the so-called "Founding Period", 1850-1914, when Vienna was rapidly expanding economically and territorially) liberal mayors presided over the city. They owed their position to an extremely limited franchise and their entrenched financial power, a good deal of the latter derived from corruption. But the aspirations of the less wealthy classes, and eventually of the working class itself, could not be denied indefinitely. A political milestone was reached in 1897, when the Emperor Franz Joseph was forced against his will (and after several refusals) to accept the election of the aforementioned Karl Lueger as mayor. In this anti-semitic Christian-Social politician the Viennese petty bourgeoisie had discovered a local hero, one who represented their interests instead of enriching himself at their expense like the liberals; and one who stood up to the imperial government. Alarmingly for the court, the strikingly handsome Lueger attracted more applause at the annual Corpus Christi processions through the city than did the emperor himself.

The Christlichsoziale Partei was peculiar to Vienna, and was founded in 1893 as the politically active arm of the Catholic-oriented movement of the same name. Spurred by the increasingly efficient socialist organization of the working class, but also responding to a religiously based suspicion of monopolistic capitalism, party and movement adopted a voter-friendly stance on social issues. Lueger legislated for better working conditions, in particular introducing health and safety controls on employers, and taking rapacious foreign utility companies into municipal ownership. Based on the ideas of the Catholic social and political reformer, Karl Vogelsang, *Christlichsoziale* politics aimed at governing through a form of corporate state that nevertheless (and unlike socialism) left intact the fundamental principles of private property and enterprise, while seeking to curb the latter's anti-social elements. It appealed therefore to small landlords, tradesmen, artisans and the like, whose existence was threatened by unbridled liberal capitalism and who were resentfully dependent on credit whose source was the "Jewish" banks.

The same perception of a primarily "Jewish" conspiracy against their interests fuelled the petit-bourgeois distrust of financiers, developers and speculators. The full-blooded corporate state (*Ständestaat*) became the reality of the authoritarian and Catholic (so-called "clerico-fascist") regime of the inter-war period. And even Austria's famous "Social Partnership," established *after* the Second World War, retained elements of corporatist government artfully disguised as "Chambers" representing specific economic, political and (effectively) class interests. The influence of the Chambers acting in the *Sozial Partnerschaft* was, however, unofficial and deals on wages were struck in negotiations held away from the limelight. Yet this system was the main reason for Austria's long post-war period of social and economic stability, with time lost annually through strikes often being counted in minutes or even seconds. In 2007 the Chambers (Employers, Workers, Agricultural etc.) were suddenly and unexpectedly incorporated into the Austrian Constitution, a defensive measure by the "welfare state" (*Sozialstaat*) against the more aggressive tendencies of contemporary neo-liberalism. While this move represented the *de facto* position long obtaining, it provoked furious protests from neo-liberals, one of whom wrote to *Die Presse* claiming that not even Hitler had gone so far! Corporatism, even if it is under more democratic control, therefore remains part of the Austrian political architecture.

Once the *Fünf-Gulden-Männer* (those who only paid five Gulden in tax) acquired the vote in 1882, the large class of the economically active petit-bourgeois in Vienna backed Lueger as their champion. He was seen as the one politician who would not only put a stop to liberal misrule and corruption, but also represent fundamental Christian values against the looming atheism of socialism and the nationalistic posturing of those who favoured a "Greater German" political solution for Austria. Lueger's mixture of populist eloquence and genuine support for the little man gradually seduced a large part of the Viennese bureaucracy as well, and he even made inroads into the strongly anti-socialist agricultural vote. His political use of anti-semitism attracted the cautious admiration of Adolf Hitler, a penniless visitor to Vienna between 1906 and 1913, though Hitler complained that Lueger was far too pragmatic and insufficiently racialist. This was true—Lueger's anti-semitism was carefully calculated to weaken his (frequently Jewish) opponents among the liberals and their corrupt cronies; but it was also not dissuasive to his more pious supporters, since the Austrian Church had an almost unbroken tradition of theologically justified anti-semitism. But he aimed to make his support as broad a church as possible and was not much interested in the politics of race for its own sake. As he famously remarked, *Wer a Jud' ist, bestimme ich* ("I decide who is a Jew").

The increasingly *de facto* autonomy of Vienna before the First World War was made *de jure* by the establishment of Wien as a *Land* (Federal State) in 1922 under the First Republic. At this point it was detached from Lower Austria, of which it had previously been the capital. The divorce was convenient for both sides, since the largely agrarian Lower Austria was firmly in the hands of the conservatives, while the vast *Wasserkopf* ("hydrocephalus") of post-war Vienna was equally firmly in the hands of the social democrats. This preponderance was due to the combined demographic weight of a large working class and numerous left-wingers in the middle class. Vienna was full of deracinated individuals coming from former Habsburg territories, jobless officials and a frustrated intelligentsia. The unflattering tag of hydrocephalus referred to the accumulation of "fluid" (the unemployed and now unemployable) in a city that had lost its function as the heart and brain of a great empire. Meanwhile, the universal franchise for men had been won in 1905 (though Lueger outrageously managed to postpone its application to the elections for the City Council) and this was soon to change the political landscape of Vienna permanently. In fact the Social Democratic Party (under various slightly different names since its foundation in 1888) has won every free election for the Stadt Wien since 1922. It was only dislodged by fiat under the clerico-fascist state from 1934, and of course by the Nazis.

It has been said that Vienna, with the achievement of federal status in 1922, finally won back the independence it had once enjoyed in the Middle Ages before the Habsburgs suppressed the city's ancient rights. In the endless tug of war with the dynasty that runs like a leitmotif through Viennese history, the burghers usually came out on the losing side. The

Habsburgs indeed executed no fewer than three mayors: Konrad Vorlauf in 1408 and Wolfgang Holzer in 1463 (both for backing the "wrong" (i.e. losing) side in a conflict between opposing branches of the dynasty); and Dr. Martin Siebenbürger in 1522 for his open rebellion against a further reduction in the city's rights and privileges. It was after this last revolt that Archduke Ferdinand put the city council back into the hands of the nobility and landowners, shutting out the craftsmen and limiting the influence of burghers to an "outer" council. The so-constituted 100-strong council retained this division of powers until modern times. Many have remarked how a long history of stifled aspirations has left its mark on traditional Viennese attitudes and behaviour.

Chapter Three

HOW TO BE VIENNESE

But what are traditional Viennese attitudes and who are the Viennese? Much ink has been spilled—chiefly by people born or brought up in Vienna—in attempts to answer these questions, which have a way of changing themselves just as a solution to them appears to have been reached. To answer (albeit somewhat imprecisely) the second question first, the chroniclers trace German Austrians back to an original Germanic tribe stemming from Bavaria (hence *Bajuwaren*) that formed a single ethnic unit under Frankish hegemony in the mid-sixth century. (The anti-immigrant letter bomber who injured several prominent Austrians, including Mayor Zilk, in the 1990s claimed to represent the *Bajuwarische Volksfront*, an organization whose membership turned out to consist solely of the bomber himself.) The original Bajuwaren had settled most of what is now Austria by Carolingian times (early ninth century). The Bavarian Babenbergs were made margraves of "Ostarrichi" in 976 and became dukes when Heinrich II moved his court to Vienna in 1155. Thereafter, however, Vienna was subject to constant influxes of other nationalities at all levels of society throughout its history.

In the Middle Ages Vienna attracted merchants who travelled down the Danube (known as "the dustless highway") and traded with their counterparts from the east. The Regensburger Hof at Lugeck in the Inner City recalls where the Regensburg merchants stayed and stored their goods, while the Ungargasse (3rd District) derives its name from the cattle, horse and hay merchants from the Great Hungarian Plain who lodged there in the Middle Ages. As late as 1548, Wolfgang Schmeltzl published a eulogy of Vienna, in which he likens Lugeck to the Tower of Babel, so many languages did he hear being spoken there ("Hebrew, Greek, Latin, German, French, Turkish, Spanish, Czech, Slovene, Italian, Hungarian, Dutch, Syrian, Croat, Serb, Polish and Chaldean"). The Babenbergs—and Vienna—grew rich from the staple right applied to Danubian commerce, which obliged traders to offer their goods for sale in the city. But trading was only one aspect of Viennese cosmopolitanism: both the Babenbergs

The neo-Baroque monument to Maria Theresia (Caspar von Zumbusch, 1888) situated between the Kunsthistorisches Museum and the Naturhistorisches Museum.

and the Habsburgs saw themselves as rulers with a religious mission. The Middle Ages witnessed the arrival of Benedictines (from Regensburg), as well as Augustinian canons and mendicant friars (from Italy), who built their churches and convents in the Inner City from the thirteenth century. The Renaissance saw further stimulation of city life by incomers; on the eve of the Reformation, Vienna experienced a boom in academic learning, literature and drama due to the influence of the great humanist scholar, Konrad Celtis, who was summoned to his court by Maximilian I. Like Celtis, another distinguished scholar, Johannes Cuspinian, came to Vienna from Germany, was rector of the university in its most flourishing humanist phase and wrote a seminal history of Austria published posthumously in 1533.

After the turmoil of the Reformation, which resulted in a net outflow of population due to the repression of Protestantism, academic and artistic life began to recover under the influence of the Jesuit-led Counter-Reformation. In the sixteenth century the strongly Catholic Habsburg court introduced a retinue of Spanish nobility which left its imprint on the upper echelons of society in manners and etiquette. The less than overwhelming enthusiasm that the Viennese evinced for these arrogant killjoys is preserved in expressions such as *das kommt mir spanisch vor* ("that seems odd to me"). At the same time there was a further influx of Italians, partly clerical (members of the religious orders) and partly secular (artists, architects, composers and musicians). The artistic incomers were attracted by the career opportunities arising out of the sensual display and religious propaganda that the Habsburgs required to celebrate the triumph both of their dynastic power and of the true Catholic faith.

More modest in numbers, but perhaps more influential in moulding the city, were the Frenchmen who either made Vienna their home or contributed to its culture. The gardens of Prince Eugene of Savoy's Belvedere Palace and imperial Schönbrunn owed their initial splendour to the work of Frenchmen. The park for Schloss Belvedere was the work of a Bavarian of French descent, Dominique Girard, who had been a pupil of Le Nôtre, Louis XIV's landscape architect. The formal Baroque gardens of Schönbrunn were laid out under Leopold I by Jean Trehet, likewise trained by Le Nôtre, while the smaller Kronprinzengarten (1750) in the park was the work of Nicolas Jadot de Ville-Issey (or possibly Louis Gervais). De Ville-Issey also designed Franz Stefan's menagerie, the predecessor of

Schönbrunn's celebrated zoo. He was actually from Lorraine and was brought to Vienna by its ruler, Franz Stefan, when the latter, following his marriage to Maria Theresia, was elected Holy Roman Emperor. De Ville-Issey's most important architectural gift to Vienna is the elegant Academy of Sciences (1755) on Dr. Ignaz-Seipel-Platz, although he left the city shortly after its construction, partly because he was unable or unwilling to learn German.

Another Frenchman made a major contribution to Viennese culture without even visiting the city. Louis XV's master of the horse, F. R. de la Guérinière (1688-1751), systematized the "gentle" method for horse training already developed to some extent by predecessors such as Pluvinel and the English Duke of Newcastle. His *École de la Cavalarie* (Paris, 1732) had a major influence on the techniques that are still used for shaping the magnificent Lipizzaner performances in the Spanish Riding School, one of the city's greatest tourist attractions. Last but not least, one should mention the Prince de Ligne (1735-1814), who came from an ancient "Belgian" aristocratic family based in Hainaut in Wallonia, which in his day was part of the Austrian Netherlands. He has gone down in history as the *Maître de plaisir* for the Congress of Vienna at the end of the Napoleonic War, and for his therefore rather disingenuous complaint that the "Congress doesn't progress—it waltzes" (*Le Congrès ne marche pas, il danse*).

Like the Spaniards, largely aristocratic was the Hungarian contingent that began to arrive in Vienna from the eighteenth century, cosmopolitan nobles who occupied palaces in streets like the Herrengasse ("The Street of the Lords") in order to be close to the Hofburg, and who often had no more Hungarian than was sufficient to give orders to their Magyar retainers. Maria Theresia, who had successfully appealed to the Hungarian nobles for their support against her Prussian enemies by appearing before the Pozsony Diet in 1741 with the infant Joseph in her arms, founded the honourable company of Hungarian Lifeguards in 1760. Its seat, which still exists, was the Baroque jewel of the Palais Trautson (1712), facing the back of the Palace of Justice on the Museumstraße. Designed by Johann Bernhard Fischer von Erlach, it was inspired by the Stadhuis of Amsterdam (1661), but shows to magnificent effect all the qualities of monumentalism and grace that made Fischer von Erlach the leading architect of Central Europe in his time. The Lifeguards were disbanded when Hungary revolted and temporarily dethroned the Habsburgs 1848, but were refounded and restored to the palace following the historic compromise between Franz Joseph and the Magyars in 1867 that created the Austro-Hungarian Empire. The Hungarian Cultural Institute owned the palace between 1924 and 1963, when the communists sold it back to the Austrians and built a characteristically hideous modern Collegium in the Leopoldstadt. Palais Trautson now belongs to the Ministry of Justice.

The other layers of Viennese citizenry (artisans, craftsmen, small entrepreneurs and merchants) have also received steady infusions over the centuries from neighbouring or near-neighbouring countries—southern Slavs, Poles, Czechs, Slovaks, Greeks and Armenians, to name but a few. The Jews came, were expelled, returned and were expelled again, before their last great wave of immigration between 1867 and 1918. At that time too the Czechs arrived *en masse* (a glance at the telephone book reveals the impact that nineteenth-century immigration from Bohemia has had on the Viennese population) and by 1900 constituted an astonishing twenty-five per cent of the Viennese population. These were for the most part the raw human material of industrialization—the construction and factory workers who settled in the 3rd, 10th, 16th, 17th and 20th Districts (*Bezirke*); especially in the 10th—Favoriten—where (it is claimed) that locally posted policemen were required to be Czech speakers up to the 1930s. For many years the newcomers preserved their own culture and entertainments, and there was always the Böhmische Prater (an amusement park, originally so named with condescension) for the family outing on the few holidays allowed them. Today, some 10,000 Viennese speak Czech (as a first or second language) and there are quite extensive Czech cultural activities for native speakers in the city. To promote Czech culture more vigorously (principally to non-Czechs) a new Czech Cultural Institute was opened in the Herrengasse after the fall of communism.

The immigrant Jews of the nineteenth century came from the eastern borders of the Austro-Hungarian Empire (Galicia) and Moravia (Sigmund Freud's father was a Moravian merchant), or were refugees from discrimination and frightful pogroms in Poland and Russia. They settled in the Leopoldstadt, between the Danube Canal and the Danube itself, where they eked out a living as traders, pawnbrokers or shopkeepers. The well-to-do assimilated Jews (mostly of western Sephardic origin), who originally established themselves in Vienna in the eighteenth century, did not look with favour on these newcomers, who were unattractively poor and, worse still, Orthodox. The Jews of the Leopoldstadt indeed constituted an embarrassment to the type of Jew who had largely submerged his origins and emerged as a liberal industrialist, a member of the professions or a maker of modern culture. He saw himself first and foremost as an "Austrian" rather than a "Jew" and was invariably a staunch supporter of the emperor, who reciprocated by guaranteeing the position of Jews and frequently ennobling successful ones. Anti-semitic conservatives indeed derided Franz Joseph as a *Seeadler*, a word which literally means "Sea-eagle" but contained a complicated pun implying that the emperor only needed to see (*sehen*) a Jewish entrepreneur and he would at once ennoble (*adlern*) him. But Franz Joseph valued this conspicuous loyalty among some of his most prosperous citizens and was well aware of its political and economic value. Indeed, the main reason why he kept vetoing the election of the above-mentioned Karl Lueger as Mayor of Vienna in the 1890s was his fear that Lueger's open anti-semitism would result in a flight of capital from the Habsburg metropolis to its would-be rival, Budapest. The political, economic and increasingly cultural influence of the Jewish elite in Budapest was, if anything, even greater than in Vienna, so the emperor's fears were perfectly well founded.

Before the Second World War there were between 180,000 and 200,000 Jews in Vienna, making up some ten per cent of the population, the majority of them concentrated in the Leopoldstadt. The name of their district was itself grimly ironic, since the area (formerly on the Danube flood plain and known as the *Werd*) had contained a Jewish ghetto founded by Ferdinand II in 1623. However, Leopold I, prompted by his overly pious Spanish wife Margarita Teresa and her confessor, Bishop Kollonitsch, expelled the Jews in 1670 and erected the Leopoldskirche on the site of their demolished synagogue. The entire area was then renamed "Leopoldstadt". Nobody knows exactly how many of the twentieth-century's Leopoldstadt Jews were hidden in the city and survived the Second World War; a handful certainly did because the Nazis, conscientiously working through their bureaucratic system, never got as far as actually dissolving the Jewish hospital, or sifting through all the borderline cases of classification of "Jewishness". Other Jews were given asylum by Christian Viennese at great risk to themselves. According to the Nazis' own meticulous reckoning, there were still 5,799 persons classified as Jews under the Nürnberg laws (through mixed marriage or on confessional grounds) in December 1944. Adolf Eichmann's boast that he had made Vienna *judenrein* (clean of Jews) was therefore not strictly accurate. Some 60,000 Viennese Jews were slaughtered in the Holocaust, and most of the rest were expelled or managed to escape to the West. Today's population of around 8,000 consists substantially of new immigrants, refugees from the Eastern European countries under communism (primarily the Soviet Union), although Jews of Viennese origin tend to dominate the *Kultusgemeinde* (religious community).

Vienna's latest—though it is unlikely to be its last—major influx of foreigners are the southern Slav and Turkish *Gastarbeiter*, the majority of them living in the capital. Here an old pattern repeats itself: just as the Czech men were employed in factories or in construction in the nineteenth century and their wives or daughters found work as domestics, many wives and daughters of today's Slavic Gastarbeiter earn money as dailies or baby-sitters and are indeed a virtually indispensable part of the domestic work-force, as their menfolk are of the labour force. Austria had reached full employment by the early 1960s, and the subsequent labour shortages compelled the government to import workers, despite the initial hostility of the unions. Employers were still finding it hard to fill all the unskilled and semi-skilled jobs in the new millennium, despite a recent rise in the un-employment figures, a phenomenon that hard-line conservatives attribute to the unwillingness of Austrians to undertake menial jobs after years of rising prosperity. Figures for 2006 published in *Die Presse* show that some 19 per cent of Viennese hold a non-Austrian passport and a staggering one in three of them have a *Migrationshintergrund*, meaning that at least their parents were not born in Austria. *Plus ça change...* The ethnicity ranking of these incomers in terms of numbers puts the Serbs (with Montenegrins) on top, followed by Turks, then Poles and then Germans. The size of the last-named group is significant, because it shows that Austria weathered the last mini-recession better than its big neighbour, thus to some extent reversing a tradition of Austrian jobseekers migrating to Germany.

Immigration has presented Austria's coalition governments with some delicate political choices; just how delicate may be seen from the fact that Chancellor Schüssel was attacked in the run-up to the 2006 election, when it was alleged (it later emerged, untruthfully) that care was provided for his aged and ailing mother-in-law by an "illegal" (i.e. someone working in

Austria without the necessary permit). This smear (as it turned out) was in any case largely ineffective: synthetic outrage rapidly turned to embarrassment as politicians and propagandists on all sides of the political spectrum suddenly recalled that practically everyone of even modest means in Vienna has engaged "black" labour at one time or another—to fix the flat, look after the dying, babysit or clean.

Although on a far lesser scale, Austria has similar issues with immigration as larger EU countries, in that mass cheap labour can be a social burden when economic circumstances change—in 2005 foreign workers drawing benefits were already double the number of natives, a new and potentially divisive situation. While the city does not yet have immigrant "ghettoes" like Paris, it still has areas of heavy concentration of foreigners, e.g. in the 15ᵗʰ District to the north of the Western Railway Station, where there are several excellent Turkish restaurants. There are some schools in Vienna with ninety per cent of pupils whose mother tongue is not German. The author of the study citing these figures also has a few sharp observations about Vienna's hypocritical liberals who are quick to raise the alarm about *Ausländerfeindlichkeit* ("hostility to foreigners")—but are often able to send their children to private schools, or schools with relatively few immigrant pupils. He points out that the lower classes bear the brunt of any difficulties of integration, both in terms of housing, schooling and stress on social services, while eloquent (and mostly well off) liberals usually live in areas inhabited by relatively few foreigners.

Although there are some Arabs and Africans in Vienna, immigration has traditionally been from the Eastern European hinterland and the Balkans; the previously quoted figures show that is still largely true. A heterogeneous mix of Viennese inhabitants has therefore always existed, excluding calamitous times like the Reformation and the Nazi period, and has resulted overall in a more balanced population spread in the city than (for example) exists in Paris or London, which have been subjected to shock waves of post-colonial immigration. Dialects, gastronomy and other aspects of urban culture also reflect this heterogeneous tradition. On the other hand, the enlargement of the EU in 2004, and particularly its further enlargement in 2007 bringing in Bulgaria and Romania, has produced louder than usual grumbling about the country's capacity to absorb more job seekers. The politicians reacted by erecting temporary barriers to entry (in stark contradiction to the entire *raison d'être* of the EU) and are zealously anxious to demonstrate that they share the voters' hostility to the prospect of Turkey joining the EU.

Behind opposition to Turkish membership of the EU there probably lurks something more atavistic, namely a residual distrust of Islam. Such might be said to be traditional in Vienna since the Turkish siege of 1683 and before, but has acquired connotations of terror in the early twenty-first century. Yet very little Islamic extremism is observable in Austria (and Austrians were almost unanimously opposed to the Iraq war), although recent investigations (2007) by the authorities into the radical preaching of a much fêted "moderate" imam seem to suggest that Vienna is not entirely immune to Jihadism.

In reality the presence of Islam in the city remains discreet, mosques and prayer houses usually being located in former industrial buildings or inconspicuous cellars. The exception was a mosque with a minaret erected near the UNO-City in 1979, when both the then chancellor (Bruno Kreisky) and the Austrian President (Rudolf Kirchschläger) were conspicuous by their presence at the opening. Today, however, a large mosque with a minaret planned for Bad Vöslau, near Vienna, has attracted opposition from locals, ostensibly on aesthetic grounds, but probably reflecting anxiety about the footprint of Islam becoming more conspicuous in Austria. The Turkish body behind the plans has had to capitulate on the minaret and heed the local council's insistence that the building shall not be allowed to "dominate the landscape." (All this recalls Emperor Joseph II's 1781 Edict of Tolerance, which forbade the Protestants from building steeples on their churches, for fear of inflaming Catholic opinion...) Certainly more mosques will be needed: in 1991, two per cent of Austrians were Muslims, but ten years later the figure had more than doubled to 4.2 per cent. Current estimates suggest there are now some 400,000 Muslims settled in Austria, the vast majority in Vienna.

Quite apart from its ethnic immigration of a mass character, Vienna was always a place that attracted gifted men who managed to make a career in the Habsburg residential capital, the first city of the Holy Roman Empire. Many of the greatest names that we associate with Viennese history and culture were "foreigners" in the sense that they were neither born nor bred in Vienna, although it could be said that many of them became so Viennese in their outlook that the distinction was subsequently lost. Of the great preachers who made such a dramatic impact on their contemporaries in Vienna, Capistran (Giovanni Capistrano, 1386-1456) was a Neapolitan (and not even a German speaker), and Abraham a Sancta Clara (Johann Megerle, 1644-1709) a South German. Klemens Maria Hofbauer (1751-1820), who led the influential Catholic reform movement in the *Vormärz* period (i.e. from 1814 up to the March revolution of 1848) was from Southern Moravia. In 1914 he was made the patron saint of Vienna. Count Salm, the defender of the city against the Turks in 1529, was born in what is now Belgium. Financiers, administrators, generals, industrialists and scholars were drawn from such far-flung and diverse lands as Portugal, Holland, Ireland, Lorraine, Bohemia, Hungary and Macedonia, not to mention the Jews from the west and east. Prince Metternich, who oppressed the Viennese for thirty-three years, was a Rhinelander.

Except in the earliest periods, a similar pattern may be observed in the cultural and visual formation of Vienna. Romanesque architecture in the city was originally influenced by Cistercians from the west, who subsequently turned to the Gothic style and built the stunning Romanesque church at Heiligenkreuz in the Wienerwald. Of a once substantial native tradition of the Romanesque, only fragments remain. The most visible of these is the Ruprechtskirche, occupying a site which, according to the early chroniclers, dated back to the Carolingian era. Much more has survived of the German masters of Gothic in Vienna, men like Hans Puchsbaum, Peter von Prachatitz, Hans von Prachatitz and Anton Pilgram who worked on the Stephansdom, or Michael Knab, who designed the graceful Maria am Gestade church. These masters were either native Viennese or came from neighbouring regions (Pilgram from Brno, then a largely German city, Knab from Wiener Neustadt). However, as the influence and territory of the Habsburgs expanded, but also following the influx of Italian religious orders to Vienna, non-native masters (chiefly Italians) increasingly held sway in the arts and architecture.

The non-Viennese element dominated visual culture and the performing arts from the Renaissance through the early Baroque period, until Haydn and Gluck broke the stranglehold of the Italians on music, while Fischer von Erlach, father and son, together with Lukas von Hildebrandt, broke their dominance in architecture. Even so, none of the above, except the younger Fischer von Erlach, were Vienna-born, although Haydn was bred there; Beethoven, Viennese by choice, was from an originally Flemish family settled in Bonn. One has to wait until the nineteenth century to find a native genius of the city like Franz Schubert, whose life and work have been taken to express something quintessentially Viennese—lyricism combined with melancholy, a personal modesty coupled with a stern devotion to his art. Next to him might be placed the dramatist Franz Grillparzer, who was born and died in Vienna, seldom leaving in between, and when he did so, feeling like a fish out of water. As with two other theatrical geniuses, Johann Nestroy and Ferdinand Raimund, Grillparzer's life and his grumbling commentary on it illuminate many of the contradictory elements in that shadowy concept, the native "Viennese character". Here is the slightly self-satisfied modesty of the little man and his ambivalent attitude to authority (outwardly obedient, inwardly often resentful or irreverent); also his melancholy, his scepticism and his self-irony. "The Viennese," remarked Grillparzer characteristically, "hold greatness to be dangerous and fame but an empty play."

Nevertheless the Viennese lived in a symbiotic relationship with the great and the (theoretically) good, who may have periodically oppressed them, but also cared for them. An interesting example of aristocratic survival and resilience in the city is the great family of Schwarzenbergs, who even have a statue and a square (Schwarzenbergplatz) just off the Ringstrasse named after one of their illustrious military forebears. They can trace their line back to 1155, and had branches or noble connections in Bavaria, Franconia, Swabia, Bohemia and Hungary, as well as Austria. Their association with Vienna runs through four centuries. The present prince is descended from the soldier honoured with the above-mentioned statue and square, Field Marshal Karl Philipp (1771-1820), and seems to have inherited some of the latter's diplomatic skills (as Austrian ambassador in Paris, Karl Philipp arranged the strategic marriage between Napoleon and Maria Luise, daughter of Emperor Franz I). At any rate, the Czech-speaking Prince Karl VII has had a remarkable career as senior adviser to Václav Havel, President of the Czech Republic after the fall of communism, and then as Czech Foreign Minister. He is a true survivor of the Austro-Hungarian Empire, combining German, Czech and Viennese identities.

Nor is the current Prince Schwarzenberg the first of his line to be significant in Central European politics. The Viennese of the nineteenth century would have had decidedly mixed feelings about his ancestor, Prince Felix, who took over the reins of power when the eighteen-year-old Franz Joseph became emperor during the 1848 revolution. Together with the "enlightened absolutist" Alexander Bach, Prince Felix erected a neo-absolutist regime which, while it reversed many of the revolution's achievements, retained others and pushed through an effective reform of the Vienna administration. All in all, the Habsburg emperors owed a lot to the Schwarzenbergs—possibly even their throne; but the Viennese also owed a good deal to them in terms of endowments and job creation. Three Schwarzenbergs were made honorary citizens of Vienna, while Ferdinand Prince Schwarzenberg (1652-1703) earned the sobriquet "Plague King" for his efforts on behalf of the citizens in the frightful plague epidemic of 1679. The social-democratic and Marxist tendency to smear the aristocracy of the past indiscriminately meets a powerful counter-argument in the Schwarzenbergs' record of service to the city. The family share one thing at least with the humble ranks of Viennese citizenry, a talent to survive and the flexibility to adapt to changing times.

Chapter Four

MASTERS AND SERVANTS:
A TALE OF COGNITIVE DISSONANCE

Grillparzer's suspicion of "greatness" is still prevalent and takes an interestingly Viennese form. In stark contrast to the Anglo-Saxon preference for kicking a politician when he or she is down, the grumblers of the Viennese *Beisln* and coffee-houses prefer to administer the kicking while the charlatan is riding high, but lament him after he is gone. It is possible to get the impression that the more successful and efficient their leaders are, the greater the efforts of lesser Viennese mortals to knock them off their perches. But when they have succeeded in this (or death intervenes), the mood suddenly changes to unctuous condolence. There is even a phrase for such crocodile tears, which are dismissed as *Friedhöflichkeiten* ("graveyard courtesies"), a pun on the words for cemetery (*Friedhof*) and courtesy (*Höflichkeit*). When the recent President of Austria, Thomas Klestil, expired before his term of office, his fiercest critics, who had hitherto not spared themselves in character assassination, appeared before our wondering eyes in mournful interviews given outside the Stephansdom after the funeral. Even the Catholic establishment, which had denied communion to the divorced Klestil, could hardly restrain the tears that fell into its purple handkerchiefs and discommended the harshness of its own sanctions, while carefully avoiding any bankable commitment to change them.

Democracy has put a new spin on attitudes whose origins lie deep in the past. The bitter experience of history had taught the Viennese to show exaggerated respect for an established authority which in private many despised. Now that the freedom to show disrespect for authority is guaranteed by democracy, the disrespect too can be exaggerated. That is, until death and the opportunity for Baroque obsequies have their sobering effect, like the arrival of the skeletal figure with his sickle in Hugo von Hofmannsthal's *Jedermann* (Everyman). But even though disrespect may be the order of the day, there remains a residual love of pecking orders in every Viennese, which probably accounts for the almost comical obsession with ranks and titles in academe and the bureaucracy that has survived the official abolition of all the noble ones under the First Republic (1918-34).

In 1988 Paul Hofmann, in his book *The Viennese*, pointed out that there were nineteen titles in the bureaucracy listed in the Civil Service Directory of 1910, and fifteen were still in use. The practice of calling bureau chiefs in the civil service *Hofrat* (Aulic Councillor) began in 1765 and in the nineteenth century titles such as *Ministerialrat*, *Regierungsrat* and *Oberregierungsrat* proliferated. Even now (wrote Hofmann) a ministerial chauffeur, after a few years service without a major accident, will be promoted to the dizzy rank of *Fahrmeister* (Master Driver). Meanwhile, people with noble titles going back several hundred years are not allowed to use them, although this rule would not apply to the current Prince Schwarzenberg since he is, ironically, a Czech citizen with a Swiss passport. Nevertheless, he tactfully eschews his rank when appearing on Austrian television, the rubric under his name reading picturesquely *Forst- und Landwirt* ("farmer and forestry consultant"), or even "hotelier", since his Viennese palace is a five-star hotel run by his son. If he had a higher degree (which he does not), he would obsequiously be addressed as *Herr Doktor* at every possible opportunity. For the older generation, the wife of a *Doktor* also qualified for the title by a process of social osmosis; sadly, the present author can vouch for the fact that the downtrodden husbands of female *Doktoren* are offered no such courtesy.

Obsequiousness—often concealing an underlying dislike—is a legacy of the sclerotic system of privilege, tenure and *Protektion* (patronage) in the Austro-Hungarian monarchy. Right to its end, real and substantially unaccountable power rested constitutionally with the emperor, his ministers and the bureaucracy answerable to them. The theoretical basis of such a system went back to the enlightened absolutism instituted by Joseph II (ruled 1780-90) and the idea that the state alone enjoys the competence to limit its own authority—a notion expressed in the surreal and self-referential bureaucratic phrase *Kompetenz-Kompetenz*. For *normale Sterblichen* (ordinary mortals) the best way to operate such a system to one's own benefit was to have a patron, from whom one would receive Protektion, and know whom to bribe and in what manner (the use of *Hintertürln* or "back doors"). An interesting example of the way it all worked is provided by the case of Freud, on behalf of whom petitions requesting that he be made an Extraordinary Professor (lower-ranking than *Ordinarius*) were for long of no avail. In the end an influential patient, Baronin Marie Ferstel, told the Minister of Education that she would donate a picture to the newly founded Modern Gallery if he obliged her in the matter of the professorship, which he duly did.

The bureaucracy occupies a unique place in Viennese consciousness. Although in reality many officials are conscientious, courteous, efficient and honest, almost nobody can bring himself to speak approvingly of them. In one of Austria's most popular TV shows the *Volksanwalt* (the "people's lawyer") brings up cases of bureaucratic mismanagement on behalf of its victims. Usually the show ends in unproductive acrimony, with the officials, who have been invited to give an account of themselves, passing the buck between them and on to others, or disputing arcane legal points with the Volksanwalt and his assistant. To an outsider, the show sometimes has the reverse effect to that presumably intended, since it often arouses sympathy for the bureaucrats, who are virtually subjected to trial by television. On the other hand, the Volksanwalt is a valuable and valued institution, and behind the scenes it often successfully defends the little man against the arrogance and might of officialdom. This being Austria, however, the people's lawyers are nominated by the political parties according to their parliamentary strength.

Fencing with the bureaucracy is also a game from which a sort of perverse pleasure may be derived. The struggle can take on farcical aspects, as when a Hungarian was appointed director of Vienna's Museum of Modern Art in the 1980s. Although he arrived and took up his post, forces opposed to his appointment (or perhaps just waging an obscure battle against colleagues in another ministry) contrived to bog down his contract in the Ministry of Finance for five months, at the end of which time the unfortunate director received a letter from the police Aliens Department instructing him to leave the country immediately, on the grounds that he had no contract of employment to support his residence permit.

Yet bureaucracy has also impregnated Viennese culture in a positive way, many of its perhaps not hugely overtaxed functionaries in the nineteenth century also being writers of note. It remains a constant source of fascination, envy (relatively better pensions entitlement after fewer years of service than in the private sector), frustration and—this being Vienna—

entertainment. While it may appear viciously Kafkaesque to some (and, after all, Kafka's tales were inspired by the Byzantine workings of the Franco-Josephin bureaucracy), to others it appears as a product of Viennese self-irony, a gentle and usually harmless absurdity, as described by the writer Jörg Mauthe. "On the Minoritenplatz in Vienna," he writes:

> [are to be found the combined] Ministries of Education, Science and Research. In the old Starhemberg palace that houses them are many dimly lit corridors. At the end of one such corridor is a permanently closed door on which has been placed a notice with the legend: "Entry for all persons is strictly forbidden!" Such a form of words on a door, which, so to speak, embodies the notion of entry and access by its very existence, is in itself rather bizarre. However, it is rendered completely incomprehensible by the fact that this absolute and total prohibition on entry is followed by the sentence: "Mind the step!"

The bureaucratic dispensation depicted so deftly by Mauthe and beloved of cabaret artists has, however, recently been subjected to some rude shocks by the Schüssel reforms (2000-2007). *Inter alia* these substantially (but not completely) removed what had hitherto been the sheet anchor of a bureaucrat's existence, namely the *Pragmatisierung*, or tenure. The latter had ensured that it was impossible to dismiss officials (or indeed academics) after they had served a qualifying number of years, although obvious incompetents might be denied promotion. This was supposed to ensure that the bureaucrats served the state, in an abstract sense, rather than party political interest, and were therefore less likely to be corrupt. Chancellor Schüssel's (in this respect, iconoclastic) government was rather successful economically, which added further insult to the injury that Vienna's intellectuals and bureaucratic elite felt they had suffered when his People's Party allied itself with the erratic right-wing Freedom Party of Jörg Haider in 2000 (and thereby initiated the near-destruction of the latter as an electoral force over the following five years.) This high-minded grievance provided effective cover for a far more deeply felt one—the diminution of privilege and (potentially) loss of income.

Nevertheless a highly developed sense of self-irony is something that redeems even the most self-important Viennese intellectuals. No outsider will ever be able to depict the local character with such hilarious ruthlessness as the Viennese themselves. The dramatist and comedian Johann Nestroy (1801-62) made them laugh at their own unflattering portraits, and the cabarettist Helmut Qualtinger (1928-86) drew large audiences for his sharp depiction of the genially unscrupulous survivor, "Der Herr Karl", eternally looking after Number One through the whole period of the Nazi regime and afterwards. However, the laughter provoked by Herr Karl's un-amiable mixture of lick-spittle obsequiousness and latent bullying is more than a little uneasy for many who see him as embodying at a particular social level the characteristics of the national psyche of which they are least proud. The political scientist Anton Pelinka's bitter characterization of the controversial Austrian President (1986-92) Kurt Waldheim has more than an echo of "Der Herr Karl" about it when he writes: "Herr Waldheim [is] Herr Österreicher... always to be found as a faithful, humble and obedi-ent servant in the ranks of the majority."

Waldheim was deemed to have been less than frank about his career during the war, especially in his campaign biography. His protestations that he "just did his duty," adequate for an earlier generation, no longer sufficed as a "get-out of-gaol-free card" for a more sceptical audience, most of it too young to have had anything to do with the war. It was meant to be a dignified riposte, but it sounded like Herr Karl's self-serving apologia claiming to be patriotism. The issue that the Waldheim affair brought into the open was an especially painful one for older Austrians. Unlike in West Germany, the political and psychological purging of the national psyche after the horrors of the Third Reich had been diluted by the allies' strate-gic decision to treat Austria as a victim of the Nazis, instead of their co-bel-ligerent. At best this convenient choice of roles bolstered the claim that most Austrians were simply unwilling participants in the Nazi totalitarian machine—or, Waldheim-like, "just doing their duty"; at worst it meant that the hysterical jubilation with which Hitler was acclaimed on Vienna's Heldenplatz, or the viciousness with which Jews, gypsies, homosexuals and the handicapped were hunted down and liquidated with the zealous or passive support of many Austrians, could be quietly forgotten. In fact, unlike Germany, Austria paid no reparations to Israeli citizens until 1988, the 50th anniversary of the *Anschluss*, when it was deemed politic to make a gesture in the wake of the Waldheim rumpus. Inevitably such a denial of any obligation of *Wiedergutmachung* (reparation), even when the country had become financially strong enough to do so, had placed

Austria's official line uncomfortably close to that of the late and entirely un-lamented German Democratic Republic, which simply asserted that East Germans had had nothing to do with Nazism and were free of any obligations or responsibilities in the matter.

Restitution and reparation fell (ironically) to the controversial right-of-centre coalition formed in 2000, whose adjudication committee has so far returned some 700 artefacts to the heirs of expropriated Jews. The most dramatic (and costly) restitution was that of five pictures by Gustav Klimt in the Austrian National Gallery, with an estimated worth of $150 million. (In fact, they fetched $280 million at auction.) After protracted litigation led by a New York lawyer, who just happened to be the grandson of Viennese composer Arnold Schoenberg, the pictures left Austria for the United States in 2006; the most famous of them (Klimt's portrait of Adele Bloch-Bauer) ended in up in New York's Neue Galerie. The Austrian bureaucracy had placed every possible obstacle in the way of this particular restitution and no doubt felt it was just "doing its duty" thereby. In the end, however, it submitted to independent arbitration and thus set a precedent for similar cases, which it would be nice if (for example) Russia would follow...

Chapter Five

LOVE-HATE AND AUSTROMASOCHISM

Vienna has inevitably been the focal point for the clash between those who feel it is best to "move on", or even draw a veil over the recent past, and those who feel it must be examined as necessary lustration of the Austrian psyche. The theatre is one of the obvious places to conduct such a debate. According to a long tradition, Viennese theatre—all of which is subsidized by the state—both reflects and challenges the Austrian's self-image. This is especially true of the Burgtheater, which has a status approximately equivalent to that of Britain's National Theatre and the Royal Shakespeare Company rolled into one. It was here in November 1988 that Thomas Bernhard's play *Heldenplatz* was staged, provoking a scandal that was at least in part shrewdly orchestrated by the theatre's management for maximum publicity value. The plot (not that there is much plot in Bernhard's plays) concerns a Jewish professor's family who return from English exile to their Viennese flat in March 1988. The flat has a view of the Heldenplatz, where Hitler was celebrated by perhaps 200,000 Viennese in 1938. When the play opens, the paterfamilias has recently thrown himself to his death from one of the flat's windows. The family are all disgusted by their experience of the contemporary city and the piece is full of characteristic Bernhard tirades against the whole Austrian nation in general and specific targets such as Waldheim, anti-semitism, socialist corruption and Catholicism, in particular. It was designed not so much to touch a raw nerve as to take a sledge-hammer to it. The politicians and press commentators duly obliged with outraged squawks of condemnation and a packed house was assured from day one.

Whether or not *Heldenplatz* was a positive contribution to the *Gedenkjahr* (the fiftieth anniversary of the Anschluss), as its supporters claimed, may be open to doubt. Characters were given lines such as: "Hatred of Jews is the purest, the absolute, unadulterated nature of the Austrian." These Baroque exercises in abuse make Jimmy Porter's whingeing tirades in *Look Back in Anger* seem rather tame, but they stem from something rather similar, a love-hate relationship with the author's homeland and a frustration with it that has aptly been described as *Austromasochismus*. Like John Osborne, Bernhard makes drama out of the pure word, rhetoric and elaborately honed hyperbole filling the vacuum left by historical decline and spiritual sterility. That he can have become the leading playwright in Austria during his own lifetime is in itself a demonstration that his fellow-countrymen, at least some of them, are not actually living in the state of ethical denial that his characters so mordantly condemn.

At the same time, Austromasochismus has always been highly marketable in Vienna. "If there is a wall of silence round me I will make the silence audible," said the coruscating critic Karl Kraus defiantly at the turn of the century; but the fact is he became a celebrity; his readings were often packed out and his magazine *Die Fackel* sold, as the Viennese say, like *warme Semmeln* ("warm bread rolls"—admittedly to a rather select clientele). Likewise, Thomas Bernhard "knows that... his primarily middle-class conservative public is titillated by his grudge-filled rage," as one critic has written of him, "partly because of masochism and partly because of *Schadenfreude*." As was the case with Karl Kraus, Bernhard's very success was in danger of becoming an embarrassment, since he held the view that most Austrians believe the only good author is a dead one. It is after an artist's troublesome spirit is safely elsewhere that the citizens rush to erect a tombstone to the man they persecuted or neglected during his lifetime.

This is an old accusation endlessly repeated in countless books about Vienna (including this one), but one should also record that the hyperbole of *Austromasochismus* is not the whole truth, and there is plenty of evidence to counter it. Innumerable architects, musicians, painters and writers made a very good career here, although we tend to recall all too readily the exceptions like Vivaldi, who died penniless in Vienna in 1741 after being blocked in his musical ambitions by the intrigues of the *Hofkapellmeister*, Johann Joseph Fux. Of the supposed *causes célèbres* adduced by the case for the prosecution, it is true that Mozart and Schubert were not widely appreciated in their lifetime, yet both received much private support from Viennese friends, Mozart being lent large sums of money from a fellow mason and Schubert being treasured and cosseted in a circle of artists, intellectuals and performers. The nobility even induced Beethoven—an eccentric and difficult character—to stay in Vienna by supplying him with a pension free of all conditions. Bruckner, it is true, was bullied and attacked—but he was also given a grace and favour residence in the Belvedere at the end of his life. Moreover, an American scholar has recently pointed out that both the positive and the (often violently) negative judgements, for example, of Bruckner's Seventh Symphony, were printed in an advertisement put out by the publisher of Bruckner's music (Gutmann.) This was evidently seen as good publicity and one could argue that Bruckner actually benefited from his unwilled status as figurehead for the besieged (and besieging) Wagnerian faction, since it kept his music in the public eye. Gustav Mahler may have finally tired of intrigue against him at the opera, but his work as a conductor was certainly appreciated by many during his tenure. Yes, Kokoschka and Schönberg met with hostility, but so did Expressionists elsewhere. The objections to their work on aesthetic grounds did spill over into personal abuse, but Kokoschka at least was always ready for a scrap.

Thomas Bernhard left instructions in his will that none of his works were to be performed in Austria for the term of copyright (seventy years) and those currently in production at the Burgtheater were to be withdrawn at the end of the contracted period. With this parting shot he hoped to prevent his transmogrification into a plaster saint of Austrian culture. Probably this is a disappointment to Austromasochists, but no doubt it came as a relief to that well-known guardian of the nation's conscience, Kurt Waldheim, who described *Heldenplatz* as "a great insult to the Austrian people". Mayor Zilk added his own splendidly Viennese insult to those already available: "*Heldenplatz*", he said, was "a paranoid self-display of a man who throughout his life has never come to terms with himself." If this is true, it would seem to place Bernhard in distinguished company—that of Nestroy, for instance, who once observed: "I believe the worst of everyone, including myself, and I have seldom been wrong."

One of the enduring images of Vienna: a Lipizzaner makes a leap at a high point in an elaborately Baroque equestrian ballet.

Chapter Six

CLICHÉS AND THE ART OF
SELF-IRONY

Austromasochism seems far divorced from the clichés with which the tourist is instantly bombarded when he or she arrives in Vienna. One tourist brochure, and it is not an especially grotesque example, begins the assault thus in Viennese argot: *G'schamster Diener! Küss d'Hand und Servus! Gehn S', bleiben S' a bisserl bei uns!* An excruciating English translation follows: "Humble servant! Kiss your hand and servus! Go on, stay a bit with us! We'll show you our Vienna, your servant, and what goes on here with us." This opening blast of bloodcurdling bonhomie is followed by references to the Viennese character ("the friendliest misanthropes"), and a promise that the "legendary ill humour" of the inhabitants is compensated for by "Viennese charm"—and, of course, the famous *Schmäh*, which may roughly be translated as "blarney". The only thing the reader is spared is a reference to the "golden Viennese heart" celebrated in *Wienerlieder* (Viennese songs) —but that may be found in almost every other tourist publication.

The golden heart of the Viennese has been so relentlessly marketed that it has saddled them with an image that any city would find it hard to live up to (nobody, for example, has ever accused the Parisians of having golden hearts). As usual, the Viennese are mocking themselves, even when busily stressing the warmheartedness and *Gemütlichkeit* of their city. Daniel Spitzer, a nineteenth-century feuilletonist, records the following exchange between two Viennese: "In Vienna everything's pleasant, except the wind," says a coffee-house sage to his friend. "Yes, and that comes along just because it's so pleasant here," the friend replies. Another rhetorical claim for the city is that "the angels themselves take their vacations here" (the idea is taken from a Wienerlied and subsequently prompted the title of a book of witticisms about Vienna). But if you are five minutes in the company of a Viennese, at least an intellectual Viennese, he/she will be sure to disabuse you of any romantic notions you may be harbouring about

VIENNA

the city and its inhabitants. As Max Winter dolefully remarked: "The saying that 'all that glisters is not gold' is never more applicable than to the 'Golden Viennese Heart'...." And the composer Richard Strauss came up with a typical back-handed compliment to the "golden-hearted" Viennese, drily observing that "people are two-faced everywhere. But in Vienna they are so pleasantly two-faced."

Schmäh, Gemütlichkeit, Raunzen, Schlamperei: these phrases meaning respectively "blarney", "cosiness", "whingeing" and "muddle" or "slovenliness", will soon be encountered by anyone who spends some time in Vienna. Although they are important constituent parts of the Viennese self-image, an outsider sometimes gets the impression that the inhabitants are playing up to their own self-created roles, just as in the nineteenth century, it was said, they slipped into the roles that their favourite actor, Alexander Girardi (1850-1918), had created for them. Girardi was the cult figure of the Viennese stage in the "golden age" of operetta and brilliantly played such roles as Frosch in Strauss' *Die Fledermaus*, an archetypal representation of the genial, idle and drunken types to be found in the lower grades of public service. Girardi appealed to the narcissistic trait in the Viennese, who had always, as writers like Hermann Bahr and Felix Salten pointed out, tended to take their cue from the theatre. Salten wrote of him:

> After he invented the Viennese character [*Wienertum*] it was relentlessly imitated. People learned from him in the theatre how to be "typically Viennese" and copied it. Hundreds of his inspired ideas, his sudden perceptions of Wienertum, were assiduously put into practice and embellished... in the end every second young man one met in the street was a Girardi role—every "cab-driver", every "messenger", every "Babbitt" or "petit-bourgeois".

And Bahr added: "Theatre is not a representation of life [in Vienna]. Life is an imitation of theatre."

Chapter Seven
BACKING INTO THE FUTURE

Perhaps the least obviously justified accusation that the Viennese continually level at themselves is that of *Schlamperei*, which implies general inefficiency and muddle. Even in the days when the founder of the Social Democratic Party in Austria contemptuously dismissed Franz Joseph's regime as "absolutism mitigated by muddle", its bureaucracy was quite efficient and scarcely corrupt if measured against its Mediterranean counterparts. Today, the achievements of the Viennese administration look even more impressive measured against other metropolises. Compared with London's collapsing infrastructure and chaotic administration, Vienna is a remarkably well-run city, exploiting to the full the advantage of having had a stable (in the 1970s falling) population until the fall of the Iron Curtain in 1989. The underground is modern, clean and quiet. The trams are similarly environment-friendly and provide a reliable service that largely by-passes the traffic jams. Heavy investment is still being put into the whole public transport network and into the restoration of buildings.

The success of the shrewd socialist Chancellor Bruno Kreisky in luring some of the organs of the United Nations to Vienna in the 1970s has also brought new life (as well as some grandiose modern architecture) to the city. Preservation of the old in architecture has gone hand in hand with some interesting (post-) modern experiments. The most celebrated (and bizarre) is the Hundertwasserhaus, an early attempt at "ecological architecture" in the form of a multi-coloured apartment block (Löwengasse, 3rd District) designed by the painter and amateur architect, Friedensreich Hundertwasser; then there is the beton fantasy of the Wotrubakirche (completed in 1976—another building designed by an artist rather than a trained architect). One might feel that the Bundesamtsgebäude on Radetzkystrasse (Peter Czernin, 1986) carries the mannerisms of postmodernism to extremes, but is notable for the fact that the state has, in this case as in several others, taken an obviously bold architectural initiative.

The earlier and more rational modernism that preceded such extravaganzas is an acquired taste, but admired by the cognoscenti. It includes

The Haas-Haus, a modern multi-purpose building (Hans Hollein, 1990), has aroused considerable controversy due to its position opposite the lovely western façade of the Stephansdom.

such Viennese landmarks as Karl Schwanzer's Museum des 20. Jahrhunderts (1958-9) in the Schweizergarten (3rd District), Roland Rainer's Stadthalle (1962, 1994) in the 15th District, and his broadcasting house (ORF-Zentrum, 1968, Würzburggasse, 13th District). Then there is the Millennium Tower (1999) in the 20th District, by Gustav Peichl, Boris Podrecca and Rudolf Weber, at 662 feet Vienna's highest building, and Wilhelm Holzbauer's interesting modelling of the U-Bahn stations (1971). These are works by home-grown architects, but some distinguished foreigners are gradually making a mark, a novelty for Vienna in modern times, however much it follows an ancient Viennese tradition. Norman Foster is involved in the ambitious Eurogate regeneration project (planned completion 2016) in the Landstrasse area (3rd District). It has been described as a "Central Park idyll" reflecting the *genius industrialis loci*, but its proposed skyscrapers have attracted opposition. A residential building (2005) by Zaha Hadid, the flamboyant Iraqi architect, spans Otto Wagner's Stadtbahn arches to the north of the U4 Friedensbrücke. Unfortunately no one wants to live in it.

Despite the changes wrought by modernization and the political and economic impact of the European Union, Vienna remains a deeply conservative city. Modernity is welded onto to the past, yuppiedom onto traditionalism, producing a southern German lifestyle the *Financial Times* once characterized as "*Lederhosen* and laptops". Its inhabitants remain attached to the mysterious virtues of such things as *Tafelspitz* (a rather unexciting piece of boiled beef which was Franz Joseph's favourite dish), of sharp and *pétillant* Heuriger wine diluted with soda water, of Sunday walks among the lowering arboreal shades of the Wienerwald that recall the outings whimsically depicted by Carl Spitzweg in the so-called Biedermeier period of paternalistic conservative rule between 1815 and 1848 (see pp. 191-202), and much else that the non-Viennese only slowly learns to appreciate. The German composer Brahms, however, loved precisely the pleasures of the small man and the quasi-provincial nature of Vienna, and there are many ways in which the city has not lost the quality of "small is beautiful." The city centre may play host to international concerns with their faceless accountants, computer culture and yuppie executives, or to such bodies as UNIDO and the CSCD, but there are still as many as 330 families occupied in growing small quantities of wine in the villages on the city's border and selling it cheaply in the Heurigen.

The charabancs park in rows outside the Kunsthistorisches Museum, the tourists are expertly sold ready-made experiences of the "golden Viennese heart", or of Habsburg nostalgia, and willingly fork out the money for Sachertorte, *Kaiserkitsch*, *Mozartkitsch*—even, alas, *Klimtkitsch*. The Viennese play their parts splendidly, even if they lack a Girardi today to remind them of the finer nuances of their roles. It is easy to sink into a haze of unreality in a city where, as Karl Kraus waspishly remarked, "the streets are surfaced with culture as the streets of other cities are surfaced with asphalt." The dangerous haziness of the borders between the real and the imagined world, between *Sein* and *Schein* (appearance and reality), is something the Viennese are well aware of, in their self-mocking and self-deprecatory way. Franz Grillparzer expressed their ambivalent feelings and his own in his *Farewell to Vienna*, the city so many found it hard to love but impossible to leave:

> Beautiful art thou, but dangerous too
> To the pupil as the master;
> Enervating wafts thy summer breeze
> Thou Capua of minds.

Part Two

THE SPIRIT OF PLACE

"One dies in Vienna, but one never grows old here."

Baron de Montesquieu

This monument to the writer and diligent bureaucrat, Adalbert Stifter, appropriately shows him reclining on a rock and shrouded in greenery. A "Viennese by choice", Stifter's writings evoked the yearning for harmony and peace in the countryside around the city that was shared by so many Viennese, especially when such experiences represented an escape from authoritarian politics in the Biedermeier era.

Chapter Eight

WIEN:

A PHYSICAL AND SPIRITUAL

TOPOGRAPHY

Vienna (48° 13' N, 16°20' E) is a city poised on a climatic, geopolitical and cultural divide, one that has determined both the character of its people and its historical fortunes. In the Danube Valley at Vienna, and in the dried out triangular sea of the Neocene era lying to the south of it (the Wiener Becken), weather conditions can change abruptly and dramatically. Such unsettling days are a reminder that the local micro-climate marks a transition between the oceanic macro-climate of the Atlantic rim and the continental macro-climate of the Carpathian basin and its hinterland.

The weather mostly comes from the west or south-west, warm winds (*Föhn*) stimulated by Alpine air streams, and cooler, wetter winds blown along the Danube Valley. But you also feel the influence of the great Pannonian Plain to the east, where the heat boils up over the dusty *puszta* in high summer, or the freezing fog swirls across a ghostly landscape in seemingly interminable winters. The Föhn, in particular, is a significant component of Viennese folklore and actuality, though its influence is less pronounced in Vienna than in the towns in the northern lee of the Alps. Even so, the sober *Österreich Lexikon* is moved to point out that the Föhn is everywhere malevolent, leading to "spiritual malaise, as well as psychosomatic and physical problems, with a consequentially higher incidence of motor accidents and suicides." You can usually tell if it is a bad Föhn day, if not from your own irritability, then from the ambulance sirens in the Viennese streets...

Blustery but mild, warm but insidious, the Föhn is a recurrent and unpredictable phenomenon, especially in the transitional seasons, the otherwise tangy, blossomy springs and long, mellow autumns. Just as Vienna embodies the notion of transition climatically and geographically, so the transitional seasons are the time when the city seems to be most itself, exuding an air of contentment and intellectual alertness. In April, the windows of the Music Conservatory in the inner city are already open, encouraging the *flâneur* to linger along the street as the sound of Schubert's *Trout Quintet* conjures the plashing waters of the Wienerwald streams and the trout that glide therein. In September the flâneur moves to the gardens of the innumerable wine taverns (known as *Heurigen*) on Vienna's periphery. As the young wine (the *Heurige*, or wine of the last vintage) begins to flow, the heat of the day recedes and a velvety warmth descends with the shadows on the flushed faces of the *Stammgäste* (regulars). The conversation becomes wittier—or more maudlin. The Schrammel quartet under the pergola plays numbers from the repertoire of *Wienerlieder*, each one more flattering than the last to the city's image of itself. For an hour or two the world is in order and each has found his place in it. It is an idyll recycled in songs and illustrations from at least the early nineteenth century, the so-called Biedermeier period, when the Viennese were ruled paternalistically and consoled themselves for limited freedoms with the little man's "happiness in a quiet corner".

The alternation of the seasons in Vienna has its own iconology and liturgy. The sense of an existence grounded in the biorhythmic cycle of days and years has often been captured by the city's writers and poets, for example in a quintessentially Viennese novel like Heimito von Doderer's *Die Strudlhofstiege*. The title refers to a celebrated Jugendstil flight of steps dropping from the seventeenth-century Strudelhof towards the Liechtenstein Summer Palace in the 9th District, a spot that the novelist chose to embody the *genius loci* of Vienna, at least in the eyes of his middle-class characters. There are of course many other places he could have chosen for a different set of characters—for example, the Stephansdom for the clerisy and Vienna's many practising Catholics, the Prater and the trotting racetrack at Freudenau for the *Kleinbürger* and working classes, or the now ethnically mixed *ur-Wien* of Ottakring. Just as the Strudlhofstiege acts as a backdrop for the passage of time, so also the year's cycle plays a fundamental role in another famous novel that has had a great impact on the Viennese, though it is not set in or around the city. Adalbert Stifter's *Der Nachsommer* (Indian Summer, 1857) presents a topography both spiritual and physical, an Austrian version of the *Bildungsroman* that was handled so masterfully by Goethe or Thomas

Mann. Here the rhythm of the seasons marks also the stages of a life opening out, the slow ripening into manhood of the novel's naively realized boy-hero.

Although Stifter lived in Vienna for some twenty years, his work is chiefly remarkable for its idealization of life in the countryside as contrasted to the "depravity" of the city; and this sentimental hankering after rural simplicity and unblemished morality, even if brief weekends and summer holidays are sufficient to assuage it, was and is a marked feature of the Viennese middle class. Like one of those all too perfectly glowing Biedermeier paintings of Alpine scenes, Stifter's novel conjures a world where "the wind speaks more wisely than man," what Claudio Magris has called his "projection of a desire for peace and patriarchal political harmony." Beneath the workaholism and remarkable capacity for intrigue of many a Viennese lies this archetypal longing for a world unsullied by precisely the worldly things that otherwise attract him—fame, success and the appetites of the flesh.

Mutatis mutandis the turning year is reflected in the music of Beethoven's Pastoral Symphony, the songs of Schubert, or even the chamber music of an inveterate country rambler like Brahms. It has been said that Beethoven's Sixth Symphony is

> the expression, in Beethoven's own language, of his reaction to the natural beauties of the Viennese countryside, the villages (not yet suburbs at that time) of Heiligenstadt, Nussdorf, Döbling, Grinzing and Sievering on the northern and north-west periphery of the city, set at the foot of the vine-clad slopes on which he loved to wander for hours on end... It may well be that the beauty of the landscape, especially of the Vienna Woods, was one of the factors that induced him to settle in Vienna in the first place.

His biographer, Anton Schindler, recalls that they walked in the Wiesenthal between Heiligenstadt and Grinzing some time after the onset of the composer's deafness and Beethoven (perhaps romanticizing somewhat) revisited for him the composition of the Pastoral: "This is where I composed the scene by the brook [2nd Movement], and the yellowhammers and quails, the nightingales and cuckoos all around me played their parts."

These examples may serve to show how hard it is to divorce the physical environment from the Viennese psyche, or indeed Vienna's culture from its topography. It was always a place that sucked in influences from all four points of the compass, yet turned them into something specifically Viennese, localized and self-contained. For much of its early history Vienna lay on a border, but then became a centre from where the Habsburgs struggled to police their own distant borders. It has endured everything, yet retains something provisional and tentative about it, like the uncompleted building projects of the imperial dynasty. Even geologically, it is a little (but not seriously) insecure, lying in the Wiener Becken over a fault from which warm springs bubble up from their pristine reservoirs beneath Baden bei Wien, Bad Vöslau, Oberlaa and elsewhere. Occasionally it has small earthquakes, with nobody injured, which is how the rest of the world perceives what happens in Vienna, a place they mostly associate with the saccharine New Year's Concert, Sachertorte and a somewhat dodgy past.

But actually there are many small "Viennas", comprised of villages (as in London) that once were *Sommerfrischen* (summer retreats), whose romantic names linger along or at the end of public transport lines: Hietzing, Penzing, Hernals, Sievering, Währing, Döbling and so forth. These were the Vororten (*banlieues*) that lay outside the Linienwall erected on the orders of Leopold I in 1704 after serious attacks by the rebel Hungarian *kuruc* bands (see p.160). Between the Linienwall and the bastions of the Innere Stadt (Inner City) were other settlements known as Vorstädte (*faubourgs*) where much of the land belonged to monastic foundations or the nobility (two of them, Josefstadt and Leopoldstadt were named after Emperors, the latter now Vienna's 2nd District across what is today the Danube Canal). In 1861, after the demolition of the city fortifications, the Vorstädte became districts of the Stadt Wien. The line of the eighteenth-century Linienwall can still be followed—only now it is the traffic Ring Road known as the Gürtel (built 1873). Because a consumption tax was levied from 1829 on food and other commodities brought into the Innere Stadt, life in the Vororten was considerably cheaper. Industries and eventually massive substandard apartment houses (*Zinskasernen*) for their workers were erected there. In 1890-92 these outer suburbs, too, were amalgamated with the administration of the city. In 1904 Mayor Karl Lueger added the substantial community of Floridsdorf on the Danube's left bank and Vienna assumed the form that it retains in all fundamental aspects today.

LANDSCAPE AND ITS INFLUENCE ON THE VIENNESE

Just beyond the northern periphery of the Wiener Becken, the Danube surges through a gap that opens up between the last spurs of the Alpine foothills in the west and outrunners of the Carpathians to the north-east. Small wonder that the life of the Viennese has developed symbiotically with the majestically flowing river and the nearby mountain peaks. In the nineteenth century summer retreats became popular in the nearest Alpine resorts of Reichenau and Semmering, a region from which Vienna also takes much of its wonderfully pure water. It is this water that explodes into the air at the Hochstrahlbrunnen in front of the Russian War Memorial on Schwarzenbergplatz and is brought from the first Alps that can be seen on the south-western horizon (the Rax and the Schneeberg). Like the frequent windy blasts that both refresh and chill the city's inhabitants, this limpid and icy flow from the Alps delivers its 220,000 cubic metres daily to purge and refresh the city. In so many ways water has made Vienna what it is. The mountains deliver their water to it, as the karst plateaux and the rivers and the Wienerwald streams deliver theirs, and all are gathered into the multitudinous waters washing through Vienna and away down the Danube to Black Sea oblivion.

The Hippocratic author of *Airs, Waters, Places,* writing in the third or fourth century BC, set great store by climate and environment in determining both health and character, and has, moreover, much to say about the beneficial and harmful effects of different types of water. When he remarks that "Climates differ and cause differences in character; the greater the variations in climate, so much the greater will be the differences in character," one wonders what he would have made of Vienna; for Vienna manages to combine and maintain so many climatic and other variations that the Hippocratic writer would necessarily have treated as discrete and contradictory. At any rate he would surely have found a way of relating the physical and mental health of the Viennese to their environment, a task that has otherwise been left to writers, artists—and Sigmund Freud. Thanks to him (but also long before him), the Viennese soul knows its own peaks and valleys, an ubiquitous and paradoxical combination of lust for life coupled with the pessimism, despair and angst that we associate *inter alia* with the characters in a novel by the much-translated Arthur Schnitzler. The great literary miniaturist Alfred Polgar described the Viennese intellectual's existentialist angst (long before such things became fashionable on the Parisian left bank) in the context of a legendary coffee-house where the literati foregathered. He identified thereby a sophisticated psycho-geodesy for Viennese intellectuals which is still valid today:

> The Café Central lies on the Viennese latitude at the meridian of loneliness. Its inhabitants are, for the most part, people whose hatred of their fellow-human beings is as fierce as their longing for people, who want to be alone but need companionship for it. Their inner world requires a layer of the outer world as delimiting material; their quavering solo voices cannot do without the support of the chorus. They are unclear natures, rather lost without the certainties [derived from the feeling] that they are a little part of a whole (to whose tone and colour they contribute).

Vienna's coffee-houses still offer the comforting companionship of loneliness, catering equally to those who come to meet their friends or associates and those who sit alone, toying with a *Großer Brauner* (one of many possible coffee types on offer for the cognoscenti) and reading the daily press for an hour or more. Like the Heuriger, the coffee-house offers *Gemütlichkeit*, a consoling aspect of the "inner emigration" of the Viennese at a time when Metternich presided over a police state (1815-1848). There were many who appreciated such a life-style and its implied philosophy, not all of them complacent fools. Three decades after Metternich had been driven out of the city, Johannes Brahms described Vienna as a "village" in which he found it more congenial to work than in a typical industrializing metropolis of his time. As in a village, the people lived close to nature, and indeed made it their study and adapted their life-style to it. Their excursions—to the Alps, to the Danube Valley, to the edge of the *Böhmische Wald*—traditionally had a ritualistic, emotional, and even scientific character, as in this passage from the previously mentioned *Der Nachsommer*, where our hero's mentor is planning an autumn day's excursion in the northern uplands:

There has never been such a beautiful late autumn as this year. My weather books do not record anything like it since I was born; all the signs are that these conditions will last for several days. Nowhere are such late autumn days more beautiful than in our northern highlands. The morning fog often lingers in the low-lying areas, and the flowing river carries patches of swirling mist into its valley every day, yet the cloudless sky looks down on the peaks of the highlands and radiant sunshine spreads over them, lasting for a whole day. And that is why it is relatively warm up here at this time of the year: while the cruel fog has already curled around the leaves of the fruit trees in the low lands, above them there still glitters resplendently many a birch grove, many a blackthorn, many a stand of beeches with their red and golden sheen. Usually the view over the entire lowland is clearer than at any time in summer.

Stifter, who was born in the Bohemian uplands, and lived in Vienna between 1826 and 1848, was one of many *Wahlwiener* ("Viennese by choice") who have both moulded and reflected different aspects of its culture (Mozart was another such). The above passage is hardly reminiscent of the romantic scenes of nature painted by Caspar David Friedrich in the Erzgebirge or evoked by Wordsworth writing of the Lake District, even though it is written a good half century after Romanticism began to influence European taste; rather it reflects the quietist tradition of reflection and sensibility resting on Enlightenment notions of reason, harmony and the painstaking accumulation of knowledge. Stifter developed this tradition into a philosophy that he called *das sanfte Gesetz*, or "gentle law," which bracketed the ineluctable evolution of the natural world with the peaceful change that he saw as the only viable and fruitful way for society to evolve. Like his contemporary, the dramatist Franz Grillparzer (1791-1872), Stifter was traumatized by the failed revolution against Habsburg absolutism in 1848 and horrified by its violence. His "gentle law", formulated in the preface to *Bunte Steine* (Coloured Stones, 1853) was in part a reaction to those frightening events, just as Franz Grillparzer, foreseeing the likely result of the forces unleashed by nationalism, was to formulate his famous dictum: *Von der Humanität über die Nationalität zur Bestialität* ("From humanity via nationality to atrocity").

In both authors the link between landscape, character and history is a constant factor. It was Grillparzer who wrote the quintessential patriotic celebration of Austria, put into the mouth of Ottokar von Horneck in *König Ottokars Glück und Ende* (The Rise and Fall of King Ottokar, 1825). Nowhere is the identification between land and character more clearly emphasized and idealized than in this Austrian equivalent of the eulogy of England as an "other Eden... a demi-paradise" by the eponymous Richard II in Shakespeare's play. In von Horneck's similarly patriotic speech, Austria is hailed as a "good land!... Lying like a red-cheeked youth between the German man and the Italian child"—occupying therefore yet again a transitional space that Grillparzer defines in his own curious psychocultural terms. In Grillparzer's day, the Germans had a manly (for which read "militaristic"and "Prussian") presence, while the Italians (still partly governed by Austrians) preserved a rich culture that was both ancient and forever young. The two civilizations, on both of which Austria drew so deeply, sometimes appeared as complementary, sometimes as antithetical. Grillparzer, here as elsewhere, is quintessentially the poet of cultural ambivalence, of unresolved antitheses, of longed for harmonies that slip beyond his reach, expressed also in his ambivalence about Vienna itself. Nonetheless, in a rather feeble (but subsequently famous) couplet written in a friend's album, the Viennese born and bred Grillparzer also evoked that rootedness in the physical environment, the interaction between a physical landscape and the *genius loci*, which was and is such a conspicuous feature of his fellow Viennese and their city:

> If what I write, and what I am, you'd understand,
> Climb the Kahlenberg and view the land...

The Kahlenberg, formerly called the Schweins- or Sauberg after the wild boars that roamed its ancient oak forest, rises above the north-western purlieu of the city. From here and from its neighbouring peak the Leopoldsberg, which was home to Vienna's prehistoric Celtic settlers and the point from which the imperial armies launched their rescue of Vienna from the besieging Turks in 1683, the view encompasses the great sweep of physical and historical Vienna from its first Neolithic settlement. Ilsa Barea, who has written one of the best intellectual and spiritual biographies of Vienna, relates the contrasting (sometimes conflicting) elements in Grillparzer's quintessentially Viennese soul to the variegated aspects of land and city that the view from the Kahlenberg affords:

To the south, on the far rim of the shallow basin, are Alpine peaks so distant that their grey limestone looks smoke-blue, so near that their patches of perpetual snow glitter in the sun on dry clear days. The ancient roads to Styria, Carinthia and Italy lead in this direction. From there the land of the Mediterranean civilisation was brought to Vienna by Italians who, once they had made their new home in the German-speaking but wine-growing town, quickened its sluggish pace. Yet there is another, more elusive message spelt out on the southern horizon: the presence of high mountains within sight is a reminder of solitude and grandeur. A glimpse of the distant Alps had the power to open a gap in the snug, smug enclosures of Old Vienna.

To the south the mountains, to the east the plain. On both sides of the Danube with its islets and tangled waterside copses, the lowlands stretch eastward to Hungary, disappearing in a haze that never lifts. Out of it rose wave upon wave of invaders from Asia, Huns, Avars, Magyars, Turks, till the Magyars settled in these rich plains and the Turks were thrown back from the walls of Vienna, never to return to the attack on western Europe.

River, Stay Away From My Door...

Ah yes, the Danube! Perhaps no city is more romantically associated with its river(s) than Vienna, not Prague with the Vltava, nor London with the Thames, nor Rome with the Tiber.

Even Budapest, whose cityscape is determined more by the river than any of the above-mentioned cities, has not derived such imperishable associations with the Danube as has Vienna. It is Vienna that appropriated to itself the appellation "Danubian Metropolis," the focal point therefore of the *Donaumonarchie* ("the Danubian Monarchy," i.e. the Austro-Hungarian Empire). Ironically, since the great regulation of the river in 1875, much of Vienna (including the old town that most interests visitors) is well isolated from the main channel of the Danube. The waters that used to wash the walls of the Altstadt and regularly flooded the land-strip and islands of the Oberen and Unteren Werd (now the city's 2nd District, the Leopoldstadt) are led through the fast-flowing Donaukanal in a semi-circle from Nußdorf in the west to the Praterspitz in the east (just over ten miles). This paradoxical situation of the Danube being, as it were, of the city but not in it, extends to the River Wien itself. As the architectural historian and dialect poet Friedrich Achleitner has observed: "Vienna, unlike Budapest or Paris, has never quite known what to do with its rivers." In 2007 the Stadtregierung discussed, not for the first time, the possibility of instituting a *Wasserstraßenbahn* (water tram) on the model of the Venetian vaporetto and of initiating water taxis to ply the Danube Canal and the Danube itself in time for the European football championship held in Vienna in 2008. But Vienna is not Venice and the project had a somewhat implausible air about it.

Actually the river has historically been as much of a threat as a benefit for the Viennese, whose reaction to it has been correspondingly ambivalent. The intermittent flood catastrophes caused by the Danube before its regulation in the 1870s were vividly evoked by the seventeenth-century preacher Abraham a Sancta Clara in his ranting eschatological sermons. His Danube is a terrifying external power, like Grendel in the pre-Christian *Beowulf*, an unpredictable monster arbitrarily devouring humanity. But behind the nihilistic implacability of a natural force lurks (for Sancta Clara's audience) another image drawn from Christianity's lexicon of vindictiveness, the Old Testament's vengeful God, or the terrifying Christ Pantokrator of Byzantine iconology bringing retribution for the sins of the Viennese:

> Look on the Danube's flood, how great, how wide, how deep, how rapacious, how rampaging it is! It has no teeth, yet seizes whole regions of fallow in its jaws. It has no hands, yet it grabs entire fields and pastures. It has no axes or shovels, yet it can demolish palaces and houses. It has no gullet, yet swallows up entire ships with their loads. It is but water, yet its roaring is the roaring of drunkenness. Who can fathom its depths? Who can bind its might? Who can cut it down to size? Who can hold back its current? Great and cruel, cruel and great is the Danube!

This is a far cry from Johann Strauss Junior's "Blue Danube" (1890), a prettified *salon-fähig* (socialized) icon of the city, rippling and gliding like a Viennese waltz, redolent of nostalgia, eroticism and the bitter-sweet pleasures of the *belle époque*. Nowadays the Danube that Abraham a Sancta Clara saw as a metaphor for divine retribution is as likely to suffer from too little water as too much in some seasons, though climate change keeps it as unpredictable as ever. On its northern shore lies the Donaustadt, the

22nd District of the city, the second most recent to be founded. It contains the UNO-City, and with it most of Vienna's still scarce skyscraper architecture (skyscrapers are banned in the Altstadt, though some are now planned in the Landstraße area, provoking furious opposition from residents and conservationists). High above the city, in plate-glassed eyries of the Donaustadt skyscrapers housing the United Nations Development Organization and International Atomic Energy Authority, are performed the ritual dances of the international bureaucracies and their *Spesenritter* (expense account fiddlers), so-called because our taxes pay for their generous perks and privileged pensions. This rather inward-looking world of international civil servants often seems curiously detached from the real life of the city, even though (or perhaps because) it is located on the very shores of the Danube, which the "real" Vienna is not.

Although it is still a traffic artery for pleasure cruising, city to city hydrofoils, and 350-foot-long barges laden to the gunwhales, the Danube today is not quite the "dustless highway" that it was to medieval Vienna, when salt from Gmunden and Hallein was floated down to the old city and unloaded at the terminus that is preserved in the street name "Salzgries". Then the river was truly the foundation of the city's prosperity and culture, bringing not only granite and wood for building, or vegetables, fruit and fish to feed the Viennese, but originally also Christian missionaries, the founders of monasteries—in 1155 even the court of "Austria's" first dynasty, the Babenberg dukes.

Although no waltzes have been written for it, Vienna has of course another iconic "river" (but actually a mountain torrent), namely the Wienfluss (River Wien). It rises in the Wienerwald and joins the Danube Canal close to Max Fabiani's Urania building on the north-east edge of the Altstadt. Although it can still be seen dashing along its sunken channel at Hietzing, it enters thereafter a series of covered aqueducts built partly to accommodate Otto Wagner's celebrated Stadtbahn (1897-1906), before re-emerging in the Stadtpark. This usually undistinguished-looking stream (Fanny Trollope was astonished that the "black and vilely smelling" River Wien at Schönbrunn had been allowed by Maria Theresia "to flow between the wind and her regality") nevertheless gave Vienna its name, appearing first as *Wenia* in a document of 881. This nomenclature is claimed to be of Celtic-Illyrian origin, a corruption of *vedunja*, meaning "woodland stream". The later appellation of "river" is sheer hyperbole.

In this way continuity with Vienna's *ur*-inhabitants has been maintained, specifically with the Celtic tribe after whom the Romans had ominously named the *deserta Boiorum*, and whose loosely defined territory probably included much of the Wiener Becken. These Boier Celts of the Iron Age had their main fortress on the Leopoldsberg, until they were almost wiped out by Dacians around 50 BC. Their domain then fell under the control of Noricum, a superior Celtic kingdom to the south centred on what later became Carinthia, which had become wealthy from its iron-ore deposits. Noricum subsequently became the first Roman province that incorporated substantial parts of modern Austria. But the Roman name for Vienna itself, Vindobona, was also (as already remarked) of Celtic origin and traces of a parallel Celtic existence under Roman hegemony survive in burial sites uncovered in the Wienerwald.

The Wienfluss is our imagined link to this distant past, flowing, as it were, from pre-history into the present, and as unpredictable in its way as Abraham a Sancta Clara's drunken Danube; its flood waters, when swelled by melting snow, reach a volume two thousand times greater than its trickle in the droughty late summer. After such a fickle waterway, gathering within itself not only the previous winter's snows but metaphorically also the *neiges d' antan*, did the Viennese of the ninth century choose to name their city, reverting thereby to a pre-Roman nomenclature. By the time they did so, the Celts of the La-Tène culture, like the Romans, were long gone and waves of Huns, Avars and Langobards had swept over the vulnerable settlement that had once played host to Marcus Aurelius.

Half-drowned trees of the Danubian Aulandschaft (water meadows) recall the state of the river before its regulation in the 1870s.

Chapter Nine

NOTES ON *WIENERISCH* DIALECT AND
WIENERLIEDER

Linguistic researchers trace the famous *wienerisch*, a colourful and witty step-sister of High German, to a widely distributed *oberdeutsch* (Upper or Southern German) of the medieval period. The speech of the countryside, which gradually splintered into numerous regional dialects, became increasingly distinct from urban speech during and after the twelfth century, when the Babenberg dynasty of margraves (later dukes) was established in the Austrian territories (then called the "Ostmark"). Indeed some maintain that the Babenbergs brought this *ur*-wienerisch with them from their native Franconia, where the regional dialect treats the "a" vowel in a similar way to the Viennese. If it is true that ur-wienerisch was heavily influenced by the rulers' form of speech, it is also worth noting that many subsequent Habsburgs were happy to employ dialect informally and spoke it quite naturally themselves, something which the English, with their obsessive anxieties about social class betrayed by language, find almost incomprehensible.

Maria Theresia's unselfconscious use of wienerisch has already been mentioned, but the other rulers of the Enlightenment (Joseph II, Leopold II), freely employed the Viennese dialect. The same was true of Franz I (1792-1835) in the Biedermeier period (1815-48), who liked to portray himself as a benevolent *Volkskaiser* (or "People's Emperor", a less plausible Austrian version of the Princess Diana patent.) From Maria Theresia's time a slightly up-market version of wienerisch was spoken in her intimate circle at Schönbrunn Palace (hence its name: *schönbrunnerdeutsch*). According to Paul Hofmann, this type of quasi-demotic speech was "imitated in the palaces of the Vienna nobility and in army officers' mess halls throughout the Empire."

Anyone spending some time in Vienna will soon begin to distinguish the salient characteristics of wienerisch, even if the meaning remains impenetrable: for example its frequent use of *schwa* to replace other vowels, or even whole words (*geh' ma* for *gehen wir*—"let's go"); or its vivid palatal "l" (an absolute giveaway, even if a Viennese is not speaking in dialect); or its fondness for picturesque word combinations to give emphasis (for example *hautschlecht, sündteuer, blunz'ndumm, pumperlg'sund*, where images of flesh, sins, blood sausage and a thumping heart are paraded to emphasize the notions of badness, expensiveness, stupidity and good health.) Like most urban dialects, wienerisch also delights in diminutives (often with "l" or "n" endings, Vienna's equivalent of Italian *-ino* or Greek *-aki*). As in Italian or Greek, such diminutives are typically used for comic and deflating effect or for denoting affection.

Reference has already been made to the critical and ironic spirit of the Viennese, to which wienerisch is perfectly adapted. Max Mayr remarks in his study of it that the tendency of language in general to have more expressions for the bad and the unpleasant than for the good and the agreeable is multiplied in wienerisch, and often taken to risible extremes. The very intonation frequently sounds like a litany of complaint to the untutored ear, which indeed it may well be, since *raunzen* (grumbling) and *nörgeln* (carping) are staples of Viennese intercourse. Many of the *Raunzer* and *Nörgler* ingesting beer and sausages at street-corner stands, or sipping their *Große Braunen* in the coffee-houses, have brought the art of abuse to a degree of refinement seldom achieved elsewhere in the civilized world. Good abuse requires real artistry, and the lower orders of Vienna have their own skills that mirror the inventive coinages of Nestroy (see p.200-1), the incisive but intellectually complex satire of Karl Kraus (see p.234) or the splendidly contemptuous tirades of Thomas Bernhard.

Like all dialects, wienerisch has, of course, incorporated dozens of words and expressions that are not of German origin at all. A strong influence is French; *Bassena*, for instance, means the corridor washbasin of the old, unmodernized apartment blocks (from which is derived *Bassenawohnung*, designating an apartment in such a block), and comes from French *bassin*. *Bassenatratsch* implies malicious and voyeuristic gossip of the most lurid type that was swapped by the flatdwellers over the house's running tap. *Flanieren* comes from the peculiarly French notion (but adopted also by English) of the *flâneur*, although it must be said that the Viennese prefer to use their own magnificent word *bummeln* for this (non-) activity. Other French imports include *Melange* (coffee mixed in roughly equal proportions with milk), *antechambrieren* (from antechambre) to seek an audience, therefore to lobby, *Pompfinewerer* (from *pompes funèbres*) for the uniformed coffin bearers at burials, *schafu* from *je m'en fous* ("I don't care," and *lescheer* (carefree) from *léger*.

Even greater is the Slavic and Magyar impact on wienerisch. Words like *Mulatschag* (meaning a festivity, from Hungarian *mulatság*), or *Busserl* (a kiss, from Hungarian *puszi*) are typical of the Magyar contribution. Slavic imports include *Jause* (an afternoon repast from Slavic *jižní*) and several words of Czech origin that can be seen on the menu at a typically Viennese restaurant or Konditorei (e.g. *Buchteln*, *Golatsche* and *Ribisel*, respectively the words for two kinds of yeast pastry and red currants). The offensive word *Tschusch*, referring to persons of Balkan origin, is said to have come from the way southern Slav foremen confirmed instructions to their compatriot co-workers building the southern railway by shouting *čuješ?* ("Have you understood?"). A *Tschuschenkoffer* ("Balkan suitcase") is the humorous but politically incorrect phrase for a plastic shopping bag. Viennese dwelling houses with windowed galleries attached to an outside wall are known as a *Pawlatschenhäuser*, from the Czech word *pavlač* meaning a balcony. Words from other languages are normally quite easily recognizable (e.g. *fesch*, meaning smartly dressed, from English fashionable; or variants of Italian such as *Gusto* or *strapaziös*, although it would take a linguist to work out that the dish of rice with peas known as *Risipisi* takes its name from *riso con piselli*).

Like braid Scots, wienerisch has its own literature, a particularly vivid one that was chiefly centred on comedy and satire, leaving aside the *Wienerlied*, which we will come to shortly. It has its origins in the irreverent Hanswurst comedies of the early eighteenth century, a form of entertainment based partly on the Italian *Commedia dell'arte* and developed by Josef Stranitzky (1676-1726), who played at the Kärntnertortheater. In fact, Stranitzky's idiom was the peasant dialect of Salzburger Lande, which he deftly exploited to counterpoint the pretensions of *hochdeutsch*. His successors adopted wienerisch and made liberal use of puns and linguistic absurdities. It has been pointed out that in Mozart's *Zauberflöte* solemn passages spoken by Sarastro are in High German, while Papageno and Papagena often lapse into wienerisch. However, the greatest heirs of this tradition were Ferdinand Raimund (1790-1836) and Johann Nestroy (1801-62), the latter brilliantly using improvisation not only to introduce topical jokes, but also to circumvent the ever-vigilant censor by wrapping his satire in Viennese wordplay and subtle coinages. While Raimund peddled a naïve Biedermeier comedy of allegory, magic, romanticized characters and "happy-ends", Nestroy wrote and performed pieces packed with coruscating political and social observation, mixing farce, satire and realistic elements. He is the *fons et origo* of the modern Viennese satirical tradition, as Karl Kraus (1874-1936), the greatest social and cultural critic of his age, was quick to recognize. Like Kraus, he was a master of linguistic pyrotechny, but whereas Kraus identified purity of linguistic expression with ethical behaviour, Nestroy bent language to his purpose by coining hilariously improbable names for Viennese types and by the subversive use of Viennese dialect.

Vienna in Words and Music

Most great cities have a musical heritage through which the inhabitants market themselves to themselves and to outsiders, but most also are of comparatively recent origin. The Greek *rembetika*, for instance, is a blues-like urban genre with oriental elements that dates from the expulsion of Greeks from Smyrna after the disastrous attempt to re-establish "greater Greece" in 1922. Full of colourful complaint, it celebrates the lives and milieu of small-time crooks, dope addicts, the dispossessed and the unemployed or unemployable. Paris has its modern *chansons* which, by comparison with London's *soi-disant* cockney songs, are decidedly middle-class, even at times intellectual. And New York also has its own songbook, largely a by-product of Broadway and the recording industry, and one which hesitates between brassy Sinatra-like blandness and the self-conscious urban pastoral of Greenwich Village.

Unusually Vienna has a native tradition of popular song stretching back to the late seventeenth century, specifically to a collection of student songs published in 1686 and entitled the *Ehrliche Gemüthserquickung* ("An Honest Refreshment for the Soul"). This student effort was supplanted over the years by a broadly based lower-class culture that was in turn sentimental and subversive, reciprocally inspiring and inspired by the heritage of popular Hanswurst comedy already mentioned. The musical and verbal elements of Vienna's growing song culture elided with, and extended, a medieval tradition of wandering minstrelsy and balladry, a precarious profession until at least the nineteenth century, when the available venues for performance increased, as did the rewards for performers. The genre, in all its richness, was finally given scholarly recognition in the celebrated Kremser Albums of *Wiener Lieder und Tänze* (1913-14), compiled by the musicologist, composer, choirmaster and conductor Eduard Kremser (1838-1914).

Before Kremser erected his monument, however, there were significant writers and performers who were instrumental in building the unique Wienerlied tradition. Johann Baptist Moser (1799-1863) and his contemporaries established it on a somewhat higher level of cultural and social acceptance, making the texts more sophisticated in terms of human observation and aphoristic wit, but also less subversive than hitherto. Typically one of his songs even borrows from Shakespeare ("The world is a comedy theatre/We humans are the actors"), although it also dovetails with a commonplace of Baroque theology, the notion of *spectaculum mundi*, where the world is seen as a theatre with every man playing his allotted role. The genre now developed an *Urwiener* stock character who was homespun philosopher, melancholic introvert and eternal survivor. It posited the indestructible nature of the true Viennese (notwithstanding that many of the songs bordered on necrophilism or a pronounced death wish) who negotiated with wry humour the storms of life, the malignity of the authorities and the hubris of the rich.

In fact, the classic instance of this type is found in one of the supposedly earliest Wienerlieder falsely claimed to date from the plague year of 1679. It celebrates a drunken singer and bagpipe player named Marx or Mark Augustin. He makes a fleeting appearance in Abraham a Sancta Clara's fire and brimstone sermon *Merck's Wien!* ("Take Heed Vienna!"), which presented the plague as a visitation of a vengeful God upon the sinful Viennese. Augustin was a street balladeer, bagpiper and extempore poet who consoled the Viennese with (often obscene) songs during the plague. He was also a serious drinker and one evening, as he slept off a heavy session curled up in a side-street, the men charged with clearing the streets of plague corpses mistook the bagpiper for such, and carted him off to the open mass grave near St. Ulrich's Church. When they came to throw lime on the bodies in the morning, they found a hung over but obviously alive Augustin playing his pipes to alert passers by to his plight. Extracted from his insalubrious night quarters and none the worse for wear, he ambled off homewards to continue his riotous living.

Augustin's fatalism in the face of the grisly horrors of the plague was immortalized in a famous song entitled "Ei, du lieber Augustin". One

"That is my Vienna, the city of song..." Vienna has the richest songbook of any European city and the genre has accommodated extremely diverse musical influences and subject material.

Stadt der Lieder...

could imagine the attraction for Sancta Clara in the verses that gloat over the levelling effect of the plague ("Now the rich of Vienna are as poor as Augustin") and the punishment meted out to the heedless citizens:

> Once each day was like a fair.
> Now plague has stripped us bare,
> Naught but corpses everwhere,
> Naught remains but care!

Despite Sancta Clara's evident intention to frighten his audience, "Lieber Augustin", as the epitome of hedonistic obstinacy, was to become an encrusted barnacle of Viennese self-mythologizing. However, it has been pointed out that the ditty was probably not Viennese at all in origin, but a contemporary hit song (*Gassenhauer*) written to cash in on the overthrow of the Elector of Saxony and would-be King of Poland, Augustus II, in 1700:

> Oh my dear Augustin, everything's gone!
> Saxony's gone, Poland's gone,
> Augustin lies in the shit.
> Oh my dear Augustin, it's all up with you!

The tune for this appeared in Vienna with an altered text about a century later, thereby converting Saxon *Schadenfreude* into Viennese self-irony. "Lieber Augustin" has indeed proved a more enduring figure in popular consciousness than the unfortunate Elector of Saxony, no doubt because he represents a sort of Viennese Everyman.

This hedonistic and stoical Viennese type was refined and popularized by Edmund Guschelbauer (1839-1912), whose song celebrating the life of pleasure-seeking and drinking of the "Alten Drahrer" ("The Old Night-Owl") had many imitations in the second half of the nineteenth century ("I'm Just An Old Soak", "There Will Always Be Wine for the Drinker"). This was the golden age of the Heurigen (open-air taverns) on the city's periphery with their *Schrammelmusik* (so-called from a combo formed by a family of that name), and the protagonists of the Wienerlied became the pop stars of their day. One of the most famous of these, the louche *Fiakermilli* (Emilie Demel, 1848-89—she was married to a Fiaker driver) found her way into Richard Strauss's opera *Arabella* (1933) via Hugo von Hofmannsthal's libretto.

At the turn of the nineteenth century, the musical sub-culture of Wienerlied also crept into operetta, where its elements were more easily assimilable by an international audience. Yet its development since the end of the First World War has generally been seen as a decline, and ruthless marketing for the benefit of German-speaking tourists to Vienna certainly has not helped its reputation. But even while purists were lamenting the degradation of the form into "Heurigen Hits", it was showing surprising resilience. This was partly due to the interest shown in it by the Wiener Gruppe of experimental poets in the 1950s, especially H. C. Artmann, who revived dialect verse as part of his radical programme for revitalizing and democratizing Austrian literature, but it was also due to the fact that classical singers of the stature of Walter Berry, Angelika Kirchschlager and Heinz Zednik have preserved an archive of the Wienerlied in a series of CDs issued by the Austrian Broadcasting Service (ORF).

Last but not least, from the late 1970s onwards, performers like the great Roland Neuwirth have restored authenticity to performance of Wienerlieder and themselves enlarged its repertoire in the social-satirical tradition. Their Wienerlieder are often parodies of the genre's excesses, but a parody is also a kind of back-handed compliment to the original, which must be strong enough to be worth parodying.

Looking back on the history of the genre, musicologists recognize that the Wienerlied, like wienerisch, has promiscuously enriched itself with any number of influences, be they ethnic, stylistic or performance-oriented. Indeed, a 1994 CD dedicated to rare recordings made between 1906 and 1937 speaks of the "melting-pot" of Wienerlieder (appropriately enough, since the same phrase is applied to the assimilative power of Vienna itself throughout its history). It cites, among others, eleven influences: medieval ballads and the material of later folk singers from the Residenzstadt's (Vienna's) incrementally incorporated villages; the repertoire of singing harpists (traditionally blind like the antique or Celtic bards, they were a widespread phenomenon until 1848, though frowned upon by the authorities due to their coruscatingly obscene or politically subversive texts); Bohemian polkas, together with the gypsy laments of the Pannonian plain; the traditional music of the Alpine rivermen and the Styrian yo-dellers; market cries from all over the Austro-Hungarian monarchy and the march-tempos of the old *Kaiserlich und Königlich* ("Imperial and Royal") military; likewise dance music from the Austrian Crown Lands and beyond (especially *Ländler*, the ancestor of the *Wiener Walzer*). One could think of several other influences, but suffice it to say that this richness of input has ensured the vitality of the genre and accounts for its colourful diversity.

But what of the content of these beguilingly sentimental songs, gently satirical commentaries on city life and nostalgic encomia for Vienna and "the golden Viennese heart"?

A recently published representative sample of sixty-four "classic" Viennese songs (out of an estimated 60,000-70,000) reflects the clichés of the genre quite well, although it thereby obscures the great variety of themes handled in the corpus as a whole: seven songs offer homespun philosophy, with the emphasis on stoicism and resignation before death; seven deal with love and sex; eleven are drinking songs, some decidedly reminiscent of the "drunkard" music hall turn of the Glasgow comedian Will Fyffe, and all with a distinct air of *carpe diem*; no fewer than thirty-six are encomia of Vienna, or its various districts, or of Viennese characters and characteristics. At the end of the collection the compilers have added a handful of contemporary examples, which might better be described as anti-Wienerlieder, since they mercilessly satirize the kitsch sentiments and self-absorption that critics most object to in the genre. The late Gerhard Bronner has a song about the much-loved Viennese types so typical of the Wienerlied tradition, which gradually reveals itself to be about an abortionist, while Georg Kreisler parodies the cliché about the angels taking their holidays in Vienna with his less flattering take on the city ("Death must be a Viennese, just as Love is a French maiden.") Kreisler is also the inspiration for Tom Lehrer's agreeable ditty celebrating the joys of "Poisoning Pigeons in the Park."

It has been said that the patrimony of the Wienerlied is a "psychogram" of the Viennese, and certainly many of the characteristics we have already sketched in this book loom large in the songs. Recurrent is the "happiness in a quiet corner" of the Biedermeier era, Biedermann's contentment with his lot and likewise his resignation before the divine will ("If God doesn't allow it", "I need no paradise/ For Vienna's my paradise!"); this despite the insertion of sly couplets that undermine the apparent benevolence of the sentiments. The drinking songs celebrate the revellers who spend their nights like Augustin in the taverns and judge the congeniality of others by their drinking powers ("The man who's never been tipsy,/That is a bad man"). Gerhard Bronner's contemporary parody of boorish drinking in the Heurigen and of the supposedly comic elements of drunkenness celebrated in Wienerlieder is wickedly accurate, conjuring the Viennese version of the saloon bar bore. The difference is that his protagonists actually realize that they have drunk their brains away and do not care.

The love element in Wienerlieder is usually more coy than erotic, celebrating the charms of rosy-cheeked girls and *ingénues*, though again some songs ("You see, I'm so inexperienced") hint at a more blatant erotic subtext. The exceptions are the *Spittelberglieder*, named after a Red Light district that is now respectable, which constituted an openly indecent element in the genre, the musical and verbal equivalent of under-the-counter pornography. Two collections of them have been published, but even in the liberal climate of today they tend to be avoided in favour of merely ambivalent, but cleaner texts. However it is in the hundreds of mainstream songs celebrating local patriotism that the Viennese character is most vividly portrayed—self-indulgent yet self-ironizing, fatalistic yet hedonistic, self-pitying yet generous-hearted.

Around the world there exist many musical love letters addressed to romantic cities, and some ("I Left My Heart in San Francisco" or "J'ai deux amours," for example) have become immortal through iconic performances (Tony Bennett, Josephine Baker). There is, however, no tribute so genuinely moving as that to Vienna written and composed in 1912 by a civil servant called Rudolf Sieczynski. "Vienna, City of My Dreams", with its sophisticated three-part (sonata-like?) structure and beautiful flowing melody, has set the standard against which all other city serenades (not excluding "Come Back to Sorrento") must be measured.

In the classic performance by Richard Tauber, its famous refrain *Wien, Wien, nur du allein/Sollst stets die Stadt meiner Träume sein…* is made to sound like a Viennese dove gently cooing in her nest, an unforgettable musical phrase delivered with consummate artistry. The song can be seen as a portfolio of the Wienerlied's elements: local patriotism, topographically precise nostalgia, celebration of drinking and of Vienna's pretty girls; last but not least, a reminder of the transience of earthly pleasures. The song ends with its protagonist sitting in Heaven, from where he contemplates the city of his dreams, which prompts a final reprise of the melodic refrain. This was a one-hit wonder—Sieczynski never repeated his success—and its author spent the rest of his career as an official in the agricultural section of the Lower Austrian Provincial Government. The nostalgia of his song is all the more poignant for being written on the eve of the First World War, which was to sweep away for ever Sieczynski's world of "happiness in a quiet corner"—and with it the cautious ecstasy of a minor bureaucrat with with a poetic soul.

Chapter Ten

THE DEATH CULT IN VIENNA: OF JOYFUL MOURNING AND MACABRE PLEASURES

The Wienerlieder are full of references to death; indeed, many are devoted entirely to this topic of enduring fascination for Viennese, who seem to derive an almost erotic titillation from contemplation of their demise and the rituals attending it. *Der Tod, das muss ein Wiener sein* ("Death himself has got to be a Viennese") is one of the most famous lines in all Heurigen songs. Picturesque metaphors for kicking the bucket abound, often achieving a morbid sophistication and inventiveness. Roland Neuwirth's *Ein echtes Wienerlied* ("A Genuine Viennese Song") satirizes the sepulchral glee of popular tradition by offering sixteen images of the death state, including "putting on wooden pyjamas" or "viewing the potatoes from underneath." A famous nineteenth-century Wienerlied by Karl Rieder, and set to music by Josef Strauss, may stand as a classic evocation of the quasi-jocular stoicism of popular tradition:

> When I die one day,
> The cabmen should carry me,
> And zithers should be playing,
> For that's what I love, love, love;
> A dance they should play, loud and clear,
> *Toujours gai!*
>
> Oh lovely people, people, people,
> Tell all the vagabonds
> To beat out the rhythm on their bundles
> And sing it with joy, joy, joy,
> At my graveside,
> *Toujours gai!*

The pretty girls from Wien, Wien, Wien
Will dress themselves in mourning
And stand around my catafalque.
He is gone, gone, gone
Who was truly a genius,
And *toujours gai!*

"He who would understand how a Viennese lives," wrote Hermann Bahr, "must know how he is buried; for his being is deeply bound up with his no-longer-being, about which he is constantly singing in countless bitter-sweet songs." The theatrical approach to burials has its roots in the Baroque age and is a reflection also of the ritual and pomp that had attended the demise of Habsburg rulers, magnificent spectacles which the populace generally anticipated with undisguised enthusiasm. For their part, the Habsburgs were determined not to disappoint their subjects in this regard, laying on obsequies that ingeniously combined opportunities for the complementary display of religious and dynastic pieties.

Dynastic funeral and burial arrangements became elaborate in the mid-seventeenth century when the young King Ferdinand IV (of Bohemia and Hungary) predeceased his father, Emperor Ferdinand III, in 1654. In his will he had expressed the wish to have his heart buried "at the feet of our dearly beloved Lady of Loreto". This was a reference to the Loreto Chapel in the nave of the Augustinerkirche, one of several chapels in European churches replicating the house of the Virgin Mary at Loreto, to which angels had supposedly transported it from the Holy Land in the thirteenth century. Joseph II (1780-90), who opposed superstitions of this kind, tried to remove the Loreto Chapel, but vehement protests from the aristocracy compelled him to reinstate it, albeit in the former crypt of the *Totenbruderschaft* (The Brotherhood of the Dead). The latter happened to be available because Joseph had also dissolved the brotherhood, whose duties involved taking the corpses of those who had been executed to the cemeteries after nightfall. That, too, had been an opportunity for spectacle, as the masked Brothers with their flaming torches dragged the corpses on a meandering route through the town to their last resting place—this to the macabre enjoyment of the Viennese and the disgust of the enlightened emperor.

Although the heart of Ferdinand IV was the first actually to be placed in the Herzgrüftl (Crypt of the Hearts) of the Augustinerkirche, chronologically (in terms of rulers) his is the fourth, after those of Emperor Matthias and Empress Anna, and that of Ferdinand II, which was brought here from the mausoleum in Graz on the orders of Joseph II. The hearts have been placed in silver vessels and altogether the crypt contains those of nine emperors, eight empresses, one king, one queen, fourteen archdukes, fourteen archduchesses and two dukes (one them the Duc de Reichstadt, Napoleon's unlucky son by the daughter of Franz I.) The last Habsburg to be given the treatment was Emperor Franz Joseph's father, Archduke Franz Karl.

The mausolean ritual did not end in the Herzgrüftl however. The embalmed entrails of the dynasty's deceased were lodged in copper urns in the Herzogsgruft (Ducal Crypt) of the catacombs of St. Stephen's Cathedral and the rest of them lay in sometimes splendid tombs in the Kapuzinergruft (Capuchin Crypt) on the Neuer Markt, half way between the other two resting places. The first Habsburgs to be buried in the Capuchin Crypt were the Empress Anna and her husband Emperor Matthias (ruled 1612-19). The crypt was reserved exclusively for the dynasty (with the exception of Maria Theresia's governess) and even in the imperial obsequies strict precedence was preserved; coffins draped in black velvet and gold brocade signified that the occupants were rulers or their spouses, while red velvet and silver brocade were for the archdukes, archduchesses and their immediate families.

So exotic are these elaborate burial arrangements as spectacles that their symbolic purpose has tended to be overshadowed. Visitors with inquiring minds will usually ask in vain from those who ought to know (historians and the like) as to what was the point of them. The most coherent explanation posits the three resting places as a pilgrim's itinerary in the inner city that combined expressions of loyalty to the dynasty with devotional piety. In this way the traditional alliance between "throne and altar", between the Habsburgs and the Catholic Church, could be demonstrated and celebrated. This idea is given some support by the (possibly apocryphal) story that has grown up round the arrival of Franz Joseph's hearse at the Capuchin Church in 1916. In life, the monarch could expect the Church to defer to him, though it did so with a certain exertion of privilege. In death, the Church was supreme and the monarch was humbled, a mere petitioner for absolution and grace like any other soul. And so, following tradition, the doors of the church were closed to the cortège on its arrival. The High Chamberlain was obliged to rap on the door. In response, the voice of the Capuchin Prior could be heard from within inquiring "Who seeks entry?" The High Chamberlain replied: "His Majesty Franz Joseph I, by the grace of God, Emperor of Austria, Apostolic King of Hungary, King of Bohemia, Dalmatia, Croatia, Slavonia, Galicia, Lodomeria and Illyria; King of Jerusalem; Archduke of Austria; Grand Duke of Tuscany and Krakow; Duke of Lorraine, Salzburg, Styria, Carinthia, Carniola and the Bukovina; Grand Prince of Transylvania; Margrave of Moravia; Count of Habsburg and Tyrol." To this the Prior replied: "We don't know him. Who seeks entry?" The High Chamberlain responded: "Emperor Franz Joseph, Apostolic King of Hungary, King of Bohemia." The Prior: "We don't know him. Who seeks entry?" The High Chamberlain then knelt down to pronounce in humble tones: "A poor sinner, Franz Joseph, who begs God's mercy." At this the Prior commanded "Enter!" and the church doors were opened.

Whether this ritualistic *mise-en-scène* actually occurred has been doubted almost as often as it has been described, *ma se non è vero*, it is indubitably *ben trovato*. It well illustrates the Habsburgs' incorporation of religious orthodoxy into their claims of temporal power, which had been the basis of their success since the Counter-Reformation. The paradox of worldly pomp and spiritual humility certainly appealed to the Viennese who could play out a little cameo of the same at their own funerals. Indeed, no decree of Joseph II caused more outrage than his demand that coffins should become re-usable in order to save wood, and be replaced by the so-called *Klappsärge*, whereby the body fell out of the hinged bottom of the coffin into the grave. In the end he had to rescind this decree. By the nineteenth century, the Viennese passion for a *schöne Leich* (literally: "a lovely corpse", but meaning a lavish funeral) had become something of an obsession and citizens were being exploited by a quasi-cartel of two firms named Concordia and the Entreprise de Pompes Funèbres. The populist mayor, Karl Lueger, endeared himself to his constituents by municipalizing these two undertakers and creating fixed-price funerals at modest rates.

The Viennese were less enthusiastic about the mayor's other great project in this regard, the vast Zentralfriedhof (Central Cemetery.) This was a legacy of liberal urban planning, and indeed sorely needed, but it was impersonal and far away. Lueger did his best by planting trees and initiating the great church there that bears his name; and the liberal regime had already instituted graves of honour for eminent Austrians, which both celebrated *Wienertum* and was a potential draw for visitors. But the long trek out to Simmering could be something of a nightmare, especially in winter. Otto Friedländer has described how the ornate horse-drawn hearses could be observed almost cantering through the fog towards the distant cemetery, once the mourners who had accompanied it (like those who once accompanied Mozart's hearse from St. Stephen's) had turned back on the freezing road:

> It is the most ghostly of fast polkas that rounds off the impressive obsequies. Each afternoon one funeral procession after another trots smartly along the Simmeringer Hauptstraße; in and out of these cortèges weave huge lorries laden with the palely beautiful, massively-horned steppe-cattle from Hungary. The eyes of the cattle have been bound, since they are going to the slaughterhouse, and now and then one of them lets out a furious, frightened bellow in the midst of the funeral splendour hastening by. Then come the heavily loaded drays of the Schwechat brewery, lumbering towards the hearses; the beer barrels hang like bunches of grapes on their metal frames, and giant horses drag the merrily clattering and clunking waggons—for the largest Viennese brewery, where Mr. Dreher brews his world-renowned ale, lies right next door to the Central Cemetery. Between the slaughterhouse and the great Mr. Dreher a Viennese finds his last resting-place.

Over the centuries the Viennese authorities have given considerable thought to the practicalities of disposing of the dead, but they have had to contend with a population that was both pious (outwardly at least) and deeply attached to custom. Death was always, as it were, a live issue. This rather feeble pun may perhaps be justified by reference to a widespread obsession with the danger of being buried alive, something about which the great Nestroy was positively neurotic. "The only thing that I fear," he wrote in his will drawn up in 1861, "is the idea that I might possibly be buried alive." Such fears were not entirely groundless in times of relatively unsophisticated medicine, but they were given wide and angst-inducing currency by a lurid pulp literature retailing stories of miraculous resurrections, gruesome tales of cries of help from inside the grave, hideously scratched internal lids of coffins and the like, which would do well as material for Edgar Allen Poe's horror genre.

From the seventeenth century, at least the upper levels of society were able to specify safety measures, such as observation of corpses for twenty-four hours before burial, together with regular blows to be delivered to the soles of the feet of the deceased to establish whether there were signs of life. During the Enlightenment there was some quasi-scientific investigation of the phenomenon of *Scheintod* ("apparent death"), by the energetic Moravian Count Berchtold among others. Under Maria Theresia and Joseph II, sensible laws were introduced, such as obligatory inspections of corpses in newly built mortuaries. In 1826 an Imperial Decree states bluntly that the "purpose of the mortuary is solely to insure that living persons are not delivered for burial." The most prudent measure that could be taken was still available in 1900 for the price of 100 Crowns, namely the appointment of a suitably qualified person to drive a stiletto through the heart of the deceased before burial. One such stiletto may still be seen in Vienna's Bestattungsmuseum (Burial Museum) at Goldeggasse 19 in the 4th District.

Also in the Bestattungsmuseum is perhaps the most bizarre of the devices that it was hoped would obviate live burial, namely the *Rettungs-Wecker* ("Rescue Alert"), which was designed to enable the unfortunate person who had been buried alive to alarm rescuers in the vicinity. One of these gadgets was designed by Johann Nepomuk Peter for use in the Währinger Cemetery, but there is no record of it having actually been used, successfully or otherwise. This is not too surprising, as the accompanying "Instructions to the Gravedigger" were so complicated that they would have provided a hilarious theatrical set piece if incorporated into a Nestroy farce. This did not prevent knowledge of the existence of the Wecker from influencing many luminaries of Biedermeier Vienna to favour the Währinger Friedhof for their burial, including Johann Nestroy himself. In 1797 another Imperial Decree had ordered that each open coffin awaiting burial at the cemetery should have a cord laid in it attached to a bell in the sexton's office, although suicides were not to be offered this assistance as presumably they would not want it. This order was updated for coffins at the Central Cemetery in 1874, whereby the alarm mechanism was also modernized with an electrical device that recorded any promising sign of movement in the coffins.

The Zentralfriedhof, the first inter-confessional cemetery of Vienna, was also the object of even more visionary plans for modernization. It was anyway a break with the past, insofar as people of any or no religion could be buried there, something that led to such antagonism from conservatives that the Cardinal Archbishop of Vienna secretly consecrated it three days before the official opening with Mayor Cajetan Felder in 1872, and thus thwarted the protesters. Most startling, however, were the plans developed to avoid the problems of the long trek to the cemetery developed by two engineers, Franz von Felbiger and Josef Hudetz. Their idea was to blow the corpses along a pneumatic tunnel running from a reception mortuary in the city all the way to the Zentralfriedhof, the technique being similar to the way in which invoices were whizzed between floors in old-fashioned department stores. Despite the infectious enthusiasm of its inventors, this plan eventually failed to recommend itself, partly due to technical problems but chiefly, as Franz Hawla artlessly observes, "on the grounds of piety".

The liberals' idea of creating graves of honour for eminent Austrians in the Zentralfriedhof has a surreal counterpart in the Heldenberg, which is about thirty miles north-west of Vienna at Schloss Kleinwetzdorf in Lower Austria. This was the brainchild of an army contractor named Josef Pargfrieder, reputedly an illegitimate son of Joseph II, of which there were rumoured to be several. Obsessed with Field-Marshal Radetzky, the hero of the Italian wars in whose honour Johann Strauss Senior wrote his immortal march, the parvenu Pargfrieder had a large crypt built on his estate. This he intended should be shared between the great man, another Field Marshal (Wimpffen)—and Pargfrieder himself! Pargfrieder was able to stage this remarkable display of ardent patriotism (mingled with self-glorification) by the simple stratagem of paying off both marshals' enormous debts—on condition that they agreed to be laid to rest *chez* Pargfrieder.

Poor Franz Joseph, who had wanted Radetzky to be buried in the Kapuzinerkirche, not only had to attend the ceremonial interment of the marshal in this "Austrian Walhalla" (Pargfrieder had been inspired by the Wagnerian pantheon erected near Regensburg by Ludwig of Bavaria), but was subsequently dismayed to receive the war-profiteer's necropolis as a patriotic "gift". The bottom line was that Pargfrieder's selfless donation to the nation was underpinned by a modest demand for 500.000 Gulden in recognition of his noble enterprise. The court officials were furious, but it appears that Franz Joseph paid up, although the Franz-Joseph Order, which Pargfrieder had hoped to have included in the package, was indignantly refused. Nevertheless, he was buried below the crypt of the field-marshals, as he had wished to be. Steps lead down to an iron door, behind which Pargfrieder's embalmed body has been placed in a sitting position and wearing an ornate suit of armour, as befits a man who had never seen active service. The whole episode has stimulated the Austrian sense of self-irony, to the extent that a satirical ditty was written about it, which turns on the two meanings of *liefern* in German (to give battle and to deliver):

Es ruhen drei Helden in seliger Ruh,
zwei lieferten Schlachten, der dritte Schuh."
("Here lie three heroes in blessed peace;
two fought battles, the third supplied shoes.")

All this may seem a little frivolous, but Austrian culture in general, and Viennese culture in particular, supply constant verification of Hermann Bahr's poignant observation quoted above. The fascination with death in particular, and eschatology in general, goes back at least to the sermons of Abraham a Sancta Clara in the plague year of 1679, but they reach even into modern times. Was it not the Viennese Hugo von Hofmannsthal who revived an English medieval mystery play describing death's relentless pursuit of "Everyman", and turned it into a perennial hit with the rich and fragrant festival goers in Salzburg? The Baroque also aestheticizes death both in the visual arts (one thinks of the great Baroque tombs in several Viennese churches), in music with a steady flow of requiem masses, and in drama. Nestroy, the roots of whose literary art lay in the Baroque, turned his personal neurosis about death into a marvellously ambivalent dramatic vehicle, mocking and pessimistic, but ultimately embracing a blend of spiritual resignation and ironic stoicism.

The feuilletonist Anton Kuh dubbed Nestroy the "Schopenhauer of the Wurstelprater" (Vienna's plebeian amusement park), a witty characterization of his populist pessimism, although some of his *bons mots* might better be described as nihilistic. "What has posterity done for us?" he once demanded. "I will tell you: it has done nothing. So I will do nothing for posterity." The Wienerlied's coquetry with death, the almost paranoid fear of it that Nestroy personally felt, the living death bemoaned by an insufficiently appreciated Grillparzer (who pictured himself as one who, though still living, "followed his own corpse"), the melancholic interdependence of life and death experienced by the Expressionist painter Egon Schiele, one of whose poems ends with the lines "Everything is living dead," the extraordinary modern recreation (1923) of Sebastian Brant's fifteenth-century satirical sermon "The Ship of Fools" by the artist Oscar Laske, Gustav Mahler's *Kindertotenlieder*... one could list *ad nauseam* examples of the permeation of Viennese culture by the notion of death and the struggle to confront it. Death and dying have a formidable metalinguistic presence, surfacing again and again in aphorism, jest and allusion.

This ambivalent obsession is not only found in higher and lower art, from Korngold's expressionist opera *Die tote Stadt* to the Wienerlied that begins *Wann i amal stirb!* ("If I should die!"), but also in countless situations of everyday life. A typically Viennese notion is that of *totschweigen* (literally, "killing by silence"), the process by which the critical establishment, or simply one set of intellectuals, attempts to bury the artistic contributions of their enemies by denying them publicity and column inches. Karl Kraus turned this to his advantage by writing virtually all of his journal, *Die Fackel*, himself and holding readings of his work that were packed out. This underlined his independence from the puffers, factional scribblers and corrupt hacks who were ubiquitous on the Viennese scene and whose scourge he was. But killing others, or at least their reputations, was as nothing to the comprehensive manner in which the Viennese chose to kill themselves, literally through suicide or indirectly by over-indulgence, which the locals jocularly call *Selbstmord mit Gabel and Messer* ("suicide with a knife and fork"). Ultimately, however, the dead are seen as fortunate; the final one is not the bitterest (as Karl Heinrich Waggerl observes) of the many deaths we die during a lifetime. In this Catholic culture, death is a showman, but not an impostor, and ultimately he brings a longed for deliverance, not only from physical suffering, but especially from the ruination that others make of our lives and that we make of our own. As the feuilletonist Daniel Spitzer aptly remarked (and it is a very Viennese remark): "The grave separates friends and unites enemies."

Chapter Eleven

THE LIFE OF THE PHAEACIANS: FROM HEEDLESS HEDONISM TO HAPPINESS IN A QUIET CORNER

A culture so thoroughly washed through by the waters of the Styx unsurprisingly also sets great store by the transient pleasures of the senses. *Carpe diem* is the tune of the merry jig that counterpoints the Viennese dance of death. The preoccupation with the visual arts, music and drama is in part a legacy of the Counter-Reformation's Catholic revival, which aimed to entice the populace away from the potentially dangerous *Kultur des Wortes* (word culture) by means of opulent spectacle (*Kultur der Sinne*—the culture of the senses). Maria Theresia, by no means a cynic, but educated by Jesuits who understood the value of artistic happenings, herself said that "there must be spectacles [in Vienna], the people need that." Obsequies were one kind of spectacle, an aesthetisization of death, but there were many others.

Maria Theresia was anyway not urging anything new. Leopold I, the "Baroque Emperor", had given out vast sums for theatrical performances, *Gesamtkunstwerke* (total works of art) before their time, involving music, dance, drama, exotic scenery and technical ingenuity. His most famous act of extravagance was the staging in July 1667 of *Il pomo d'oro* ("The Golden Apple", on the theme of the Judgement of Paris), the first Italian opera to be performed in Vienna. A theatre had to be specially built on the site of today's National Library for its performance and it cost 110,000 Gulden to pay, among other things, for sixty-five different stage settings by Ludovico Burnacini. The music was by Marc Antonio Cesti, except for one scene composed by Leopold himself, who like Ferdinand III , Josef I and Joseph II, was a competent composer. This was to mark the birthday of the emperor's young Spanish bride, Margarita Teresa. The festivities in January 1667 to celebrate the marriage had lasted a whole week. They included an allegorical "Battle between Air and Water" for which the courtyard of the Hofburg was flooded so as to have real ships on real water, while not only mythological figures but even horses and carriages hovered in the air above them. From two artificial mountains representing Etna and Parnassus some 80,000 fireworks were set off. Most of the population of the city attended and the cost of the stolen crockery alone amounted to 9,000 Gulden.

Vienna's reputation as a city of luxury, merrymaking and indulgence actually lies much further in the past, in the time of the Babenbergs at whose courts the Minnesänger were prestigious guests, similar to publicity-seeking pop stars of today. The half-censorious, half-envious comments of foreigners often reflect the ambivalence that so many have felt about a city that was both seductive and dangerous. Such was indeed how Grillparzer described the city he loved and hated in his "Farewell to Vienna"(1843) though he had more in mind than simply the temptations of the flesh. But if Vienna was insidiously threatening under its hedonistic surface for a Grillparzer, others have simply regarded it as cheerfully, even shamelessly, immoral. The humanist scholar Enea Silvio Piccolomini, private secretary to Friedrich III and subsequently elected Pope Pius II, expressed his astonishment at the sexual freedom of the Viennese in a letter to a fellow humanist in Basel written in 1450: "The number of whores is very great, and wives seem disinclined to confine their affections to a single man; knights frequently visit the wives of burghers. The men put out some wine for them and leave the house. Many girls marry without the permission of their fathers and widows don't observe the year of mourning."

The local equivalent of the Roman *cicisbeo* is an enduring feature of Viennese society, and the present author remembers a respectable middle-class intellectual (now dead) who habitually went on holiday with both wife and mistress in tow. Irregular liaisons are celebrated in a Viennese joke about two men who meet for the first time at a party. By way of conversation one says to the other: "You see those two attractive ladies chatting to each other over there? Well, the brunette is my wife and the blonde is my mistress." "That's funny," says his new friend; "I was just about to say the same thing, only the other way round." In Biedermeier Vienna (1815-48), *ménages à trois* seem not to have been uncommon, since the gallant who became a friend of the family was officially known as the *Hausfreund*. The ambiguous status of such a Hausfreund features in a Wienerlied written in 1856 by the usually non-risqué Johann Baptist Moser. It concerns a certain Herr von Hecht, who is evidently a very good friend of the family of the narrator. The first six lines of the song innocently praise the latter's wife, who is so delightful and companionable that "his sky is always blue"; but the next six relate how she imported a "friend", Herr von Hecht, and did so "immediately after the wedding". This friend loves the children so much "they could be his own." And indeed, the younger one looks remarkably like Herr von Hecht, who has promised that the boy will inherit from him, "which can't be bad, eh?" The *faux-naïveté* with which this apparently commonplace situation is described seems to have delighted Moser's public—the song was immensely popular then and is still sung today.

PERILS OF THE VIENNESE SKIN TRADE

There was, of course, a darker and exploitative side to the city's climate of sexual licence. Perhaps because Vienna was a Residenzstadt (i.e. where the ruling dynasty held its court) with many opportunities for domestic employment, it was usually awash with young females who were prepared to supplement their meagre earnings with quasi-professional prostitution. Around 1500, as certainly appears to be the case from contemporary woodcuts, the public baths doubled as brothels, mostly situated in the so-called Stubenviertel, centred on the Wollzeile and Lugeck in the Inner City, a red light district by any other name. The *Stuben*, which had existed since Babenberg times, offered an attractive package of mixed sex bathing and banqueting, with fornication thrown in. This thriving sex trade was brought to an abrupt end by the advent of syphilis, which was probably imported into Central Europe by the Habsburgs' Spanish troops. University students soon had a tag alluding to the twin health hazards of city life: *Vienna ventosa vel venenosa*—"In Vienna either the wind or the pox is always raging." However, closure of the baths actually meant that people were less clean than previously, and therefore less hygienic, as disgusted Turkish commentators were wont to remark. Nor did it put an end to prostitution.

From the late fourteenth century, when brothels first appear in official records, and until the reign of Maximilian I (d.1519), the authorities had seemed to take an ambivalent, but generally pragmatic view of the skin trade. Indeed, the city fathers taxed the pleasure houses and reinvested the proceeds—in one case to build a convent for nuns! Medieval ordi-

A skeletal death-like figure grins foolishly at a prostitute. This is one of a series of bitter evocations of the human psyche by the Expressionist Austrian artist, Alfred Kubin. The etching is from the series entitled *A New Dance of Death* (1947).

nances fixed a fee for the services provided in an attempt to avoid exploitation by brothel owners, and even stipulated that "if a girl has a man by her for a night, she must give the house-owner one Kreuzer as 'sleeping money' and no more. What the man gives her for herself she may keep." Maximilian closed down the brothels inside the city walls, and we next hear of such only in the eighteenth century, when today's ultra-respectable Spittelberg quarter was populated with "Spittelberg nymphs". Emperor Joseph II was famously thrown out of a Spittelberg brothel, whose owner failed to recognize him and objected to the way he handled the goods. The city's medieval prostitutes were theoretically all "foreigners", since prostitution was officially forbidden to native Viennese girls, a prohibition which may indeed have given rise to the tradition of "enthusiastic amateurs" referred to by so many visitors.

The otherwise popular Maria Theresia aroused almost universal opposition when she attacked loose morals by instituting a "chastity commission" that sought to root out and punish sexual infidelity among the married. Apart from the general inconvenience it caused, it was perceived as an unwarranted intrusion in the natural order of things, almost as unwelcome as Joseph II's attempt to institute re-usable coffins. Casanova, who was visiting Vienna when the chastity commission was at its most zealous, records his indignation at having his style cramped in this way.

That the medieval prostitutes were guaranteed a semi-official status is also demonstrated by the fact that they had their own entry in the bi-annual running races (on Ascension Day and St. Catherine's Day) instituted by Albrecht III in 1382. The race route from St. Marx to the River Wien passed through several vineyards and along what is still known as the Rennweg in the 3rd District. The race for "the public whores" was known as the *Scharlachrennen*, as the prize was a piece of scarlet cloth (for a "scarlet" lady?). The odium attached to the whores therefore seems to have been limited, and indeed a burgher could take one of them to be his wife without loss of social status; the only conditon imposed was that he must not have been acquainted with her in her former profession (presumably to guard against entrapment, but surely a quite unenforceable rule). In the Middle Ages there was even a municipally funded home (also set up by Albrecht III) for ladies who had been persuaded to retire from the profession. It was on the site of what is now the Franciscan cloister on Franziskanerplatz, and burghers could, if they wished, select a willing bride from one of the inmates. This sensible practice spared the whores a raddled old age and many modestly well-to-do widowers a lonely one.

The tradition of tolerance and pragmatism in dealing with prostitution continues in the present, where a region of the city along the Gürtel (Ring Road) has been set aside for legal, or at any rate tolerated, prostitution in the evening hours. Health checks are obligatory for the sex workers, and the trade, while less blatant than that of the girls who sit in windows along the Amsterdam canals, is pursued with the same judicious mixture of discretion and openness that traditionally characterizes the dealings between authority and the individual in Austria.

The confining of sexual commerce to certain areas, and its disengagement from mainstream social life, represents a major change from the situation prevailing in the Vienna described by Stefan Zweig in his posthumous 1943 autobiography, *The World of Yesterday*. Just as Arthur Schnitzler's dramas revealed a pressure-cooker environment of stifling convention and a politically deadlocked society that found an outlet in illicit sex, so Zweig attributes the libertinism of Vienna in his youth to social pressures that made "prostitution... the foundation of the erotic life outside marriage".

This was often a sordid matter, notwithstanding the cult of the *süsses Mädel* ("sweet little girl") to be found in the impressionistic stories of Viennese life by Peter Altenberg, the unofficial bard of turn-of-the-century Vienna. More candid was Schnitzler's deconstruction of erotic relationships that only seemed to intensify the participants' sense of anomie, aporia and accidie. While Schnitzler concentrates on the self-disgust of the sex-exploiting classes, Zweig is blunt about the reality of these one-sided affairs for the underprivileged partners: "Before the emancipation of women and their active participation in public life, it was only the girls of the very poorest proletarian background who were sufficiently unresisting on the one hand, and had enough freedom on the other, for such passing relationships without serious thoughts of marriage. Badly dressed, tired after a twelve-hour day of poorly paid work, unkempt (a bathroom in those days was still only the privilege of the rich)... these poor creatures were so much below the standing of their lovers that these in turn were mostly ashamed of being seen openly with them. But convention, always cautious, had invented its own measures for this painful situation, the so-called *chambres séparées*, where one could dine unseen with a girl; the rest was accomplished in the dark side streets in the little hotels which were equipped for these purposes exclusively."

The supposed discoveries of Freud made libidinousness seem something of a Viennese speciality. He made his investigations in a period when Vienna was soaked in the unashamed eroticism of Klimt's pictures and Mahler's music; his theories counterpointed the bitter psycho-sexual dramas of Schnitzler (Freud's literary alter ego) or the perverse and perverted pseudo-philosophy of Otto Weininger's work on *Gender and Character*. Yet it could be argued that this eruption of the erotic was merely a time-specific spike in the pervasive sensuality that had always been a feature of the city. In the Middle Ages this sensuality represented the spontaneous lust for life—and the good things of life—that Everyman had a weakness for, and the only curb on which was Death itself. The Minnesänger at the Babenberg court were the conspicuous consumers of their time. Vienna was one of their favourite stamping grounds, and it was Tannhäuser who coined the phrase "Phaeaceanism" to characterize the city's sybaritism. He complained (but only rhetorically) that his money melted away in expenditure on beautiful women, good wine, *Leckerbissen* (culinary delicacies) and twice-weekly "baths".

The Phaeaceans alluded to by Tannhäuser were a notoriously gluttonous people who are featured in *The Odyssey* as living on the island of Scheria. Friedrich Schiller picked up the Tannhäuser reference for one of his epigrams (in *Xenie*, 1797). With characteristic German censoriousness in regard to the Austrians, he depicted them given over to sloth and feasting, the very picture of self- and over-indulgence:

The Danube in Austria...
Around me lives with gleaming eye the people of the Phaeacians;
Every day is Sunday, every day the spit turns on the hearth.

The truth, of course, is more complex. The Viennese have suffered enough in their history from invasion, persecution, plague and sundry other evils to know the value of enjoying life while you can, and whether or not you should. This was something Maria Theresia (notwithstanding her chastity commission) understood very well, and so have various populist mayors of the city from Karl Lueger to Helmut Zilk. It is one of the reasons why there are so many theatres in such a modest-sized city, so much music, so many other cultural events—and four thousand eateries in a place with only 1.7 million inhabitants. This was the basis of Karl Kraus' previously cited remark that the streets of Vienna are surfaced with culture, those of other cities with asphalt. Culture may take the form of grand spectacles, nowadays laid on by André Heller, the specialist for sensational artistic "happenings"; or it may take the form of the "happiness in a quiet corner" of Biedermeier times. In an age of political authoritarianism, the music culture of Vienna still thrived, as did the cautiously dissident theatre. A joke on the regime was a private one shared between Nestroy and his audience—indeed, the censor may sometimes have laughed at it too, not realizing it was aimed at him. And while Nestroy was genially undermining the pretensions of authority (and anybody else's pretensions), Schubert was playing his music to appreciative but private audiences at the Schubertiads.

The lust for life of a true Viennese is bound up with his sense of himself as a creative person, as an artist who has not quite fulfilled his potential. If he or she cannot be recognized as a "real" artist, maybe he or she can be recognized as a *Lebenskünstler-in* (someone who has mastered the art of living). Ex-Mayor Zilk himself presents a series of TV interviews with prominent personalities, which runs under the title: *Lebenskünstler*. "The Viennese, " wrote Jörg Mauthe in *Wiener Knigge*, "suffers from an ever-present discrepancy between obligation and desire... like everyone else he is compelled to do all sorts of things his entire life: he must exist, he must work, eat, drink, sleep and undertake a thousand concrete, mundane things—he who was specifically created for the approximate, the accidental, and whose consuming passion is not for the factual but for the imponderable, not for the completed whole, but for the subtle nuance. And that is why he is unhappy the whole of his life, an un-genial soul, a frustrated artist, when he is not one anyway by profession. Fortunately, even in these respects, he is unreliable..."

Hermann Bahr elaborated on the same point, quoting Grillparzer to the effect that the Viennese live "half in poetry", and cites waltzes by Lanner and Strauss to illustrate the point: "Life as a Dance", "Merrily Vivacious", "Cheerful in the Worst of Times". *Carpe diem* is for the Viennese half defiance, half a creative submission to the inevitable. In an age deluged in champagne and bad debts, Johann Strauss Junior wrote a memorable aria for *Die Fledermaus* (1874), which has virtually become an ironic motto for the Viennese: "Happy is he who forgets/What anyway cannot be altered." No less in tune with his public, a military bandmaster wrote a merry "Krachpolka" ("Crash Polka") when the Stock Market crashed in 1873, to the strains of which one could presumably dance on the graves of the ruined speculators.

In respect of fleshly desires, the Viennese hovered and still hover between diagnosis (Freud, Krafft-Ebing, Weininger) and abandonment (the eroticism of Mahler's music or Gustav Klimt's paintings). In a remarkable degree he combines empathy with analysis, clinical detachment with heedless indulgence. The Viennese Enlightenment subjected society to rational diagnosis and the doctors of the nineteenth-century Wiener Allgemeinen Krankenhaus pioneered techniques for diagnosing individuals (sometimes they were still busily taking notes as the patient expired before their eyes). The rich culture of the city, however, from Mozart's *Don Giovanni* to the contemporary artist Hermann Nitsch's "Orgiastic Mystery Theatre", tends to deal in the atavistic, the libidinous, the irrational. The *Wiener* himself wavers between the sagacity of Sarastro and the elemental needs of Papageno. In this he is no different from the rest of us, but his particular gift lies in the dramatization of his predicament, his agreeable aestheticization of a metaphysical struggle.

Part Three

THE AGES OF THE CITY

"No city ever became a metropolis more unwillingly than Vienna."
Ann Tizian Leitich (1891-1976), writer and historian of Vienna

Hieronymus Sperling, the Karlskirche (copper etching, 1720). The magnificent church built in the early eighteenth century by Fischer von Erlach, father and son, drew inspiration from Ancient Rome for the two gigantic columns that flank the portico.

Chapter Twelve

THE ROMANS ON THE DANUBE

"Vindobona, the jewel of Austria."

Heurigen song by Josef Schrammel

In his wry and moving *Book of Reflections for Austrians* (1975), the Viennese writer Jörg Mauthe pictures the North African legionaries of the second-century Roman garrison on the Danube, as they brood on their situation in a far-flung outpost of empire. Their unease anticipates that of the Viennese, the notion that their city represents an oasis of order and culture at a European nodal point between East and West, likewise between North and South. It was a location that promised wealth from commerce to build a civilization, but it also lay in the path of military campaigns and crushing waves of whole populations on the move from Asia. Such invasions were to produce a recurrent sense of precariousness among the local inhabitants, an acute awareness of their exposed borderland existence. That is the way it always was and had been.

As his eye sweeps the Danube shore, Mauthe empathizes with the vulnerability of those rough-hewn soldiers at Vindobona (Vienna) and neighbouring Carnuntum (today Petronell), gazing apprehensively across the river from their fortifications:

> About halfway between Petronell and Bad Deutsch-Altenburg the road passes by a long escarpment to the left, the skyline of which is broken by trees and shrubs. If one advances a few paces to the edge of this escarpment, one is suddenly confronted with a steep drop, the plunge, in fact, to the Danube. Cresting the rim, one is made almost dizzy by the precipitous view to the other side. Far below lie primeval wastes of water and trees, stretching north and north-west into the distance, until they dissolve in blurred outlines and are swallowed in the mists of infinity.
>
> The upper regions of the slope are dotted with the remains of the watchtowers and the fortifications of the Roman "Limes", on which

Syrian and Palestinian legionaries once stood. It is easy to imagine how those men must have shivered, with the east wind at their backs, as they contemplated the *terra incognita* that lay before them.

But if one comes at the right time of day, one can catch the enormous orange ball of the sun, as it sinks below the western horizon in a blaze of violet and blue colours.

Mauthe salutes a public-spirited incomer (or a war profiteer?) who built an amphitheatre at Carnuntum, then a military headquarters of considerable importance to which Vindobona was a mere pendant. In fact, there are two amphitheatres laid bare on the green braes above the Aulandschaft, the woodland swamp and water meadows that flourish here in symbiosis with the river. Were they to sit in one of these amphitheatres, perhaps on an evening in summer as the sun slips down behind the Alpine foothills and black swarms of river gnats advance in wavering columns from the wetlands, the historically minded—or romantically inclined— might well experience this as a landscape full of historical echoes. And of these echoes, one perhaps may seem to dominate: the raucous, decidedly threatening sound of the soldiers' full-throated roar on an April day in AD 193 when Septimius Severus, a local governor of partly Punic descent, was proclaimed emperor by fellow North Africans.

Here at the Pannonian outpost of Carnuntum began the dazzling career of this grim soldier, the hammer of enemies at home and abroad. He became the conqueror of Byzantium and the subduer of Caledonia, finding time in between these campaigns to reduce the Parthians and hold victory celebrations of stupendous magnificence in Rome. Not until the year 211 was the comet eclipsed, when the old campaigner died in the inhospitable northern climate of Britain at a place called Eburacum, better known to us as York.

The privileges offered to the Danubian legions for their loyalty, and the economic boom consequent upon the stability produced by Severus' military successes, seem to have increased the significance of the Pannonian border cities. However, unlike Carnuntum, Vindobona seems never to have been granted the status of *municipium*. By the third century, with a network of outlying civilian villas stretching across the Wienerwald and east along the Danube, it had nevertheless come a long way since Pliny the Elder (23-79 AD) had described it unencouragingly as being on the edge of the *deserta Boiorum*. That was a reference to the local Celtic tribe of the Boier, whose name comes down to us in the word "Bohemia."

The name Vindobona is itself Celtic in origin but Romanized, and refers to the personal estates (Latin: *bona*) belonging to a Celtic leader called Vindos. When the Boier were all but wiped out by Dacians around 50 BC, Vindobona fell under the sway of another Celtic civilization known as Noricum, which was centred on Carinthia. Rich and powerful from its iron ore and silver deposits, Noricum was a power to be reckoned with, and the Romans seem to have subdued it around 15 BC more by adroit diplomacy than by military aggression. It retained its name as a Roman province, and bordered Pannonia, to which Vindobona belonged. Soon Celtic Norican troops were sent to reinforce the Limes garrisons along the Danube.

In the early days of Roman hegemony Vindobona was a place of secondary significance. The Celtic population of the Leopoldsberg was resettled by the Romans on a plateau overlooking the flood plain of the Danube's largest arm, and the garrison quarters were built on the standard *urbs quadrata* principle, with a north-south and an east-west axis. Streams on the south-east and north-west sides, and a steep drop to what is now the Danube Canal in the north, provided natural protection. The south-western periphery had no such protection and was therefore dug out with three lines of ditches, from which comes the name of Vienna's most fashionable street in the *Innere Stadt*, the Graben. The Roman civil town was located a mile and a half away, mostly in what is now the 3rd District and around the Rennweg.

The jurisdiction of the town stretched as far as Schwechat in the east (for a while the boundary of the empire) and to the west across the Wienerwald as far as Greifenstein, the border with Noricum. It is unclear how far south it stretched, but probably as far as Baden bei Wien, whose thermal springs were certainly used by the Romans for curative and recreational purposes. Technically speaking, territory north of the Danube was in the hands of the barbarians, but archeological finds suggest that, at least in peaceful periods, there was a lively trade between the latter and the Romans at Leopoldau, where there also seems to have been a military outpost. Vindobona's garrison of 5,000 soldiers was supplied with water brought by an aqueduct from the Liesing area (southern Vienna), while the *canabae legionis*, or recreation area, was situated on what is now the

Michaelerplatz (recent excavations revealed that it included a brothel). A highly respectable district, however, was today's Hoher Markt, where one may visit the remains of officers' quarters provided with sophisticated hypocaust (under-floor and wall cavity) heating.

The emperors who were most influential in Vindobona's history were Domitian (81-96 AD), who beefed up the garrison for his Dacian war with a 1,000-strong unit of so-called "British cavalry", Trajan, who strengthened the camp walls to a width of six feet and a height of twenty feet, Marcus Aurelius and Probus. The last-named is traditionally credited with introducing viticulture to Vienna, but there is evidence that the Celts already knew how to make wine. The legend seems to be based on a more prosaic imperial intervention, but also a more decisive one for the Viennese economy. Until the reign of Probus (275-82 AD), the production of Italian wine and its export to the empire was privileged under a mercantilist economic system. Production of it was accordingly forbidden in the non-Italian areas of Roman rule. Probus, who had always taken an interest in agriculture, lifted this ban in order to stimulate the local economies of Britain, Spain, Gaul and Pannonia. He even put his troops to work laying out vineyards, and it is from this wholly beneficial stimulus to the local economy that he has gained his favourable reputation in Vienna. A grateful city has named a street after him, the Probusgasse in Heiligenstadt, one of Vienna's most favoured wine villages. The former general certainly earned this tribute, since it may have cost him his life: his application of his troops to agricultural or engineering projects made him increasingly unpopular and in 282 he was killed by his own soldiers at Sirmium on the River Sava (today Sremska Mitrovica in the Serbian Vojvodina). There may have been more to it than that, however, since the abolition of the wine monopoly must surely have created enemies, as did the emperor's acceleration of barbarian settlement within the borders of the empire.

More significant for the history of the city is Marcus Aurelius (emperor, AD 161-80), who may be claimed (perhaps a little extravagantly) as Vienna's first literary figure. When he wrote of life as "a battle and a sojourning in a strange land" he might plausibly be recalling his campaigns on the Pannonian frontier that brought him to Carnuntum and Vindobona. In 167 AD, Germanic Quadi and Marcomanni tribes took advantage of the weakening of the Danube frontier, due to legions having been withdrawn to fight campaigns against the Parthians in

Armenia and Mesopotamia. Their incursions became increasingly serious and eventually began to threaten Italy itself. These otherwise obscure tribes are of some significance to Viennese cultural history, insofar as they are often supposed to have been part of the root stock, mixed with Langobardi (Lombards), Alemanni and others, which thereafter settled Bavaria; and it is migrating Bavarians who are often regarded as the "*ur*-Austrians."

Marcus Aurelius rallied the Roman forces and began the fightback in 168 AD. Between 171 and 174 he was on the Danube frontier line, directing a desperate but ultimately successful campaign against the invaders. His reward was to be celebrated in perpetuity with a huge column that still stands on the Piazza Colonna in Rome. It is remarkable that the two rather similar Roman monuments dedicated to Marcus Aurelius and Trajan, defenders of Vindobona as of Rome, were one day to inspire a masterstroke of late Viennese Baroque. The two stunning columns in front of the Karlskirche (1739), commissioned by Emperor Karl VI and designed by Fischer von Erlach, father and son, are clearly inspired by their Roman originals, especially Trajan's column. On the Roman columns the friezes winding diagonally upwards like an unravelling roll of papyrus celebrate the military triumphs of Trajan over the Dacians or Marcus Aurelius over the German tribes; but the Fischer von Erlachs adapted the same idea to show the life and works of the Milanese plague saint, Carlo Borromeo, to whom the Karlskirche is dedicated. And to the plague, or rather its end, we owe the construction of the church, commissioned by the Habsburg emperor as thanksgiving for the removal (no doubt by the Archangel Gabriel) of the last epidemic to sweep over Vienna in 1713. In all this there is perhaps another less obvious allusion to Marcus Aurelius, whose own empire was almost brought to its knees, not only by invasions and rebellions, but also by the plague brought back from the Parthian campaign after 161 AD by the troops of his co-emperor, Lucius Aurelius Verus.

The Karlskirche's two columns are also intended to symbolize Karl VI's motto, *constantia et fortitudine*, a motto which cannot but recall also the character and career of the stoical Marcus Aurelius. The latter's celebrated *Meditations* (written in Greek) are clearly inspired by stoic philosophy, although they are eclectic enough to include elements of Platonism and Epicureanism. It is generally accepted that substantial parts of them were composed during his campaigns against the Marcomanni and Quadi; the work is, in fact, a private journal in which a man who senses he has not very long to live contemplates human life and the inscrutable ways of the gods. We can imagine him scratching it out by a guttering candle in the rather inhospitable environment of the garrison camps at Vindobona or Carnuntum. It remains a seminal work of philosophical and spiritual ambivalence, one moment filled with wonder at the grandeur and order of the universe, the next overflowing with disgust at the folly of mankind and the arbitrariness of fate.

Marcus Aurelius died on 17 March, 180 AD, probably in Vindobona (although Tertullian says in Sirmium). It was not until the 1880s that two Viennese streets were named after him, but only one of them (the Marc-Aurel-Straße in the Innere Stadt running between the Hoher Markt and Franz-Josefs-Kai) retains the august name today. For the Habsburg emperors of the Enlightenment, however, Marcus Aurelius was a potent symbol of good governance. The equestrian statue of Joseph II (emperor between 1780 and 1790) stands, appropriately enough, before the entrance to the National Library on Josefsplatz. Joseph is presented as a Roman emperor dressed in a toga and crowned with a laurel wreath. His right hand is extended in a gesture implying the protection he offers the city. The work is a deliberate allusion to the famous Marcus Aurelius statue, now magnificently restored and displayed in a special room of the Capitoline Museum in Rome. Franz Anton Zauner's sculptural eulogy of Joseph II as an enlightened ruler was commissioned by the Emperor Franz, whose further education at the Wiener Hof from the age of sixteen was delivered according to his uncle's Enlightenment principles (not that Franz stuck to them). The laurel wreath alludes both to military and literary prowess, while reliefs on the plinth illustrate Joseph's own preoccupation with the common good through the promotion of agriculture and trade.

In this way the first great literary figure to be associated with Vienna has been co-opted for Habsburg propaganda and myth. However sceptically the historians, or indeed the Viennese, may view this manipulation of the stoical campaigner's image, there can be no doubt that he was a worthy role model for an authoritarian dynasty that claimed to rule disinterestedly on behalf of its peoples. "Waste not the remnant of thy life," wrote Marcus Aurelius in Book III of his *Meditations*, "in those imaginations touching other folk, whereby thou contributest not to the common weal." And another injunction recalls the emphasis on reason and restraint so characteristic in the political philosophy of enlightened absolutism:

"Blot out vain pomp; check impulse; quench appetite; keep reason under its own control" (*Meditations*, Book IX). There is an echo of this in the high-flown desiderata for the statue planned for Joseph II, as they were expressed by the Emperor Franz's High Chamberlain: "A monument worthy of the great monarch, who ruled himself with iron will and frugal discipline, but ruled his people with benevolence and good deeds."

RELICS OF THE ROMAN ERA

Carnuntum (today Petronell): twenty-five miles east of Vienna, the Archäologischer Park Carnuntum is spread over almost four square miles comprising the settlements of Petronell-Carnuntum and Bad Deutsch-Altenburg. Part of the Limes and its drainage system is preserved. Remains include the Temple of Diana (reconstruction), Roman baths, an impressive triumphal arch known as the Heidentor ("Pagans' Gate") and two amphitheatres. The Archäologisches Museum Carnuntinum is in Bad Deutsch-Altenburg.

Vienna: Roman officers' quarters survive on the Hoher Markt. There are excavations of the *canabae* on the Michaelerplatz, and Roman gravestones and other artefacts in the Wien Museum (Karlsplatz).

Baroque Monuments inspired by Roman triumphalism include two Trajanesque columns fronting the Karlskirche (Karlsplatz) and an equestrian statue of Joseph II "as Marcus Aurelius" (1807) by Franz Anton Zauner on the Josefsplatz. Franz I, who commissioned this, was also sculpted as a Roman emperor by Pompeo Marchesi (1846), and his statue stands in the main courtyard of the Hofburg ("In der Burg"). As with the statue of Joseph II, the monument was designed to promote the image of the dynasty; the Latin inscription reads: *Amorem meum populis meis* ("My love is for my peoples"), and the four huge allegorical figures seated on the plinth are allegories of the princely virtues supposedly embodied by Franz (Faith, Strength, Comity and Justness). Two years after it was unveiled, however, the 1848 revolution broke out and the monument probably only escaped destruction because of its infrangible solidity. Originally cast in bronze in Milan, its transport to Vienna had required 16 oxen and 18 horses and it took 33 days to arrive.

Margrave Leopold III of Babenberg (1095-1136), accompanied by his wife, rides out to the hunt from his castle on the Leopoldsberg.

Chapter Thirteen

LIGHT AT THE END OF THE TUNNEL: FROM THE DARK AGES TO THE BABENBERGS

"The greatest city after Cologne…"

Anonymous thirteenth-century chronicler

From the late thirteenth century onwards, the authority and legitimacy of rulers in Austria would rest on an alliance between the Roman Catholic Church and the dynasty, between throne and altar. Not for nothing were the Habsburgs proud to be crowned Holy Roman Emperors, exercising symbolic authority over the German territories and actual control over their Central European empire. It is therefore ironic that Joseph II and his nephew, Franz, should have looked to the pagan Marcus Aurelius as a role model, especially as persecution of Christians, though not directly attributable to imperial policy, should have reached one of its high points during the reign of this emperor.

For most of the Roman period of Vindobona (the first four centuries AD) a ragbag of cults provided spiritual nourishment for the Romanized citizenry. Egyptian gods such as Isis and Horus were popular, the forests and wine vintages were under the protection of Silvanus, and the propinquity of the Danube gave Neptune an important role. The chief Roman god, Jupiter, had of course to be given due reverence and one could not afford to ignore such potentially influential figures as Apollo and Mercury, the bringer of wealth. Among the soldiers, the secretive eastern cult of Mithras was the fashion all over Pannonia.

This agreeable syncretism of Graeco-Roman and Egyptian deities did not survive the disintegration of Roman hegemony in the area. In two onslaughts of Goths, Vandals and Ostrogoths in 401 and 405 AD the Vindobona garrison seems to have been all but wiped out, and in 433 the Eastern Emperor Theodosius ceded the camp to the Huns by treaty.

Yet a beam of light pierces the smoke-filled glimmer of burning towns and ravaged crops that hangs like a pall over the ruins of empire at this time. The light emanated from a remarkable Romanized Christian, one Flavius Severinus, who had begun his Christian mission as a monk in the Orient. On the death of Attila the Hun in 453, he made his way to Noricum, where the civilian population had been abandoned to their fate by the withdrawing Roman troops. Severinus, on the other hand, is said to have been tireless in negotiation with the invaders to save what could be saved of human life, if not goods and chattels. In the annals of the Church he appears as St. Severin, who proclaimed the gospel along the Danube from Passau to Vindobona and established the first monasteries on sites that were to see much of the most spectacular monastic architecture of the Baroque many centuries later. In one of these precarious sanctuaries (probably a predecessor monastery to Göttweig, near Mautern, Lower Austria) he died on 8 January 482, equally mourned (or so it is claimed) by the insurgent German tribes and the Romanized population alike. The last Roman families to leave the Danube region in 488 carried Severin's remains with them over the Alps, so that his bones should rest in Latin soil.

The village of Heiligenstadt (originally *heilige Stätte* i.e. *sanctus locus*) in Vienna's 19th District is traditionally regarded as taking its name from the converts that Severin made here on what had been the site of a pagan cult. However, the authenticity of this version of events was later disputed by the great Renaissance historian of Vienna, Wolfgang Lazius, who was likewise sceptical of the claim that Severin's favoured retreat for spiritual recuperation, described by his biographer as "at the vineyards" (*ad vineas*), also referred to Heiligenstadt. The confusion seems to have arisen because another influential twelfth-century chronicler, Otto von Freising, mistakenly identified Favianis (Mautern) with Vindobona. Whatever the truth, Severin is eternally associated with the "first" conversion of the local population to Catholic Christianity. Neither bishop, nor even an anointed priest, he was a great ecclesiastical diplomat who was able to negotiate protection of the surviving Romanized communities with the formidable Germanic leader, Odoacer (it is thought that Severin himself may have been of high-born Germanic origin). At the same time, he shielded his Catholic flock from the Arian heresy (Odoacer's faith), which denied the full divinity of Christ, and which had taken root amongst the Germanic tribes converted by Ulphilas (Wulfila). Astonishingly, Severin's diplomacy achieved a level of mutual tolerance whereby Catholics and Arians lived peaceably among each other and even shared their churches. This example of restraint is in stark contrast to the later history of Vienna, where first antisemitism, then Christian intolerance (both Protestant and Catholic) was endemic until the reforms of the enlightened emperor Joseph II in 1781— and once again reverted to type in the Nazi period. *Feindbilder* ("foe images"—many admittedly grounded in a frightening reality) were to become a staple for local propagandists down the centuries: Magyars, Hussites, Turks, Protestants, Hungarian kuruc raiders—and Jews....

Christianity was the binding thread that ran through the civilization of what was to become Ostarrichi (a name first mentioned in 996 in an imperial land transfer). It survived as a sunken culture among the Romanized inhabitants and their descendants through the period known as the Dark Ages, whose chief feature was the *Völkerwanderung* ("migration of peoples"). We have seen that at least some of the German tribes involved in that great upheaval, which was both a cause and a consequence of the collapse of the Roman empire in the west, were already Christian, albeit of the Arian heresy.

But the legacy of Catholic Christians, those converted as a result of Roman hegemony, did not disappear after the Roman retreat at the end of the fifth century. Indeed, when the "second" conversion of the region took place in the seventh and eighth centuries, in which Celtic missionaries played a major role, the newcomers could count on the support of surviving Catholic communities. Arguably this was because the "Dark Ages" were not always as dark as the cliché suggests, and certainly incoming tribes frequently adopted elements of the infrastructure, agriculture and even beliefs established by the Romans. Even so, the impact of the Huns in the fifth century, the Germanic Rugii (who took over Noricum in 488), then the Alemanni, Langobardii (Lombards), Avars, Slavs and finally Magyars from the late ninth century, ensured that "Vindobona" was in a state of flux for four centuries.

The end of Völkerwanderung is marked by the gradual repulsion of the Avars by Charlemagne's Frankish and Bavarian armies and the establishment of a *Marchia orientalis* or Eastern March of the Frankish empire. Charlemagne's crowning by Pope Leo III as "Emperor of the Romans" on Christmas Day 800 is one of the great symbolic moments in European history. As the first "Holy Roman Emperor", Charlemagne became the protector of all Roman Catholic Christians and "therefore had the obligation to bring the many tribes, peoples, princes and rulers constantly feuding with one another under the umbrella of his empire, to realise the peace of Augustus and the peace of Christ as the peace of Charles." These aspirations, so elegantly formulated by the historian Friedrich Heer, were later to become the subtext of the Habsburg imperial mission. That mission theoretically depended on the Papacy for its legitimacy, but generally could not be subordinated to papal writ when the dynastic interest took precedence over that of God's vicars. On the other hand, the all-embracing nature of Habsburg pretensions, practically as the secular arm of a divine dispensation, involved a constant struggle to prevent a uniquely sanctioned authority from being undermined. A sense of spiritual and ideological superiority, coupled with intermittent military and financial weakness, became manifest in the mildly schizophrenic oscillation between superiority and inferiority complex that runs through Habsburg history—and indeed through Viennese culture.

The Carolingian Eastern March was based on Bavaria and included most of modern Austria. However, it was an indication of the Austrian region's borderland character that such security as the Carolingian dispensation had provided increasingly fell victim to the Magyar onslaught from the east after 896. Between the defeat of the Bavarians by a Magyar army at Pressburg (now Bratislava) in 907 and Otto I's great victory over the Magyars at the Lechfeld by Augsburg in 955, the Ostmark all but collapsed. The Lechfeld marked a turning point. Otto I, "the Great", who became Holy Roman Emperor seven years later in 962, established a new Mark east of the River Enns, a Danube tributary which was historically the outer border of the Bavarian dukedom, but hereafter the border between Upper Austria and Lower Austria. From 976 these areas became the Babenberg margravate, whose rulers owed allegiance to the German kings and emperors, but in practice became increasingly autonomous. The Babenbergs, described by the *fin-de-siècle* writer Hermann Bahr as "an austere, sly and cautious stock", were to rule for two hundred and seventy years. They increased their patrimony with the addition of Styria (a substantial part of ancient Noricum) in 1192 through inheritance, and were active founders of monasteries and churches. It is with them that the growth and development of Vienna begins.

BABENBERG RULE

Initially the Babenberg margraves consolidated their power cautiously, moving their headquarters slowly eastwards along the Danube Valley from Melk to Tulln, to Klosterneuburg, finally to the settlement that had already appeared in a document of 881 as *Wenia*. For Vienna, the most significant years of Babenberg rule were 1155 and 1156. In the latter year Heinrich II was granted the *Privilegium Minus* by the then Holy Roman Emperor, Friedrich II Barbarossa, which elevated his territory to a dukedom. This was Heinrich's compensation for giving up the Dukedom of Bavaria, for which Friedrich had another candidate who suited the needs of his imperial diplomacy better. Heinrich had already (1155) moved his headquarters from Regensburg to Vienna itself, setting up his court on the large square in the Inner City that is still called Am Hof ("At the Court"). As a result of this ducal decision, the core of Vienna finally reached the same size as the Roman legionaries' original camp. It had taken 800 years to do so!

In 1155 Heinrich also invited twenty Irish monks from Regensburg to found an abbey in Vienna. It was known as the Schottenstift, because the Latin name for Ireland was *Scotia maior*, so for Central Europeans the Irish were "Scots". For Vienna, this was the most significant of the Babenberg religious foundations, though the others included all the great monasteries of Lower Austria that were to be so impressively transformed and enhanced in the Gothic and Baroque periods: Melk (eleventh-century foundation, 1089 Benedictine), Göttweig (eleventh-century foundation, 1094 Benedictine), Lilienfeld (1206, Cistercian), Seckau (1142, Augustinian), Heiligenkreuz (1133, Cistercian) and Klosterneuburg (early twelfth-century foundation, 1136 Augustinian.) It was in Melk that the first known work of "Austrian" literature was produced at the beginning of the twelfth century, a cycle of poems on the *Life of Jesus*, the *Gifts of the Holy Ghost*, *Antichrist* and *The Last Judgement* written by reclusive nun called Ava (died 1127).

Heiligenkreuz and Klosterneuburg were founded by Leopold III (1073-1136) of Babenberg, the most devout of an extremely pious dynasty, who was later canonized (1485) and became the patron saint of Lower Austria. Klosterneuburg preserves a Babenberg genealogical tree with portraits and scenes from the lives of the margraves and dukes (made by Hans Part in 1492 to celebrate Leopold's canonization). In the same monastery is the greatest artefact surviving from the Babenberg era, the Verdun Altar (1181), named after its creator, Nicholas of Verdun. It consists of forty-five beautifully worked enamel panels, the narrative of which unfolds the divine plan of world history, beginning with the Creation and continuing through the Old and New Testaments.

Catholic piety, of course, does not rule out sensual joys and display—rather the reverse in fact. Under Dukes Leopold V (1177-94) and Friedrich I (1194-98), Vienna enjoyed economic growth that stimulated the first "golden age" of Viennese culture. Not all the causes of the boom were entirely respectable; in 1192, the same year that he gained Styria, Leopold V imprisoned and later ransomed Richard I (the "Lionheart") of England, who was attempting to return home from the crusades in disguise. The circumstances of this oft-told incident are perhaps not quite as discreditable to the Babenberg duke as has traditionally been asserted. The immediate cause of Leopold's animus against Richard was that the latter had torn down the Austrian flag from a tower during the crusader siege of Acre. However, the prime mover in subsequent events was Emperor Heinrich VI, who believed that Richard was behind the assassination of Konrad of Monferrat, Heinrich's relative and personal appointee as King of Jerusalem. The emperor ordered that Richard be arrested if he was found anywhere in his dominions, or those of his vassals—so Leopold could claim he was just carrying out orders that had some legal basis. The ransom for Richard (150,000 Cologne Marks, between two and three times the annual income of the English Exchequer) was so huge that it could only be raised in England by ruinous taxes and the confiscation of church treasures. Leopold had to halve the loot with Heinrich, but even so his share was enough to remodel much of the core of Vienna round the Graben and the Hoher Markt, to found the city of Wiener Neustadt and to expand the external defences of Hainburg, Enns and Vienna. Under pressure from the pope, Leopold promised on his deathbed to pay back the unexpended portion of his ill-gotten gains, about 4,000 silver marks, but his successor declined to make good on the promise.

This unedifying episode had one literary connotation, the legend of King Richard's favourite French troubadour, Blondel, who supposedly roamed Central Europe until he discovered his patron's place of imprisonment. Blondel, so-called for his flowing blond locks, did actually exist, a minstrel whose real name was Jean de Nesle, and with whom some twenty-five poetical works are associated. Legend has him wandering the castles of the empire, until one day the second verse of a song much loved by the monarch came floating from a window of Schloß Dürnstein, in response to the troubadour's rendition of the first verse. (In fact Richard's place of imprisonment was well-known.) The story is largely the product of the eighteenth century (when it formed the basis of an opera) and the nineteenth century (when a dreadful epic poem by Eleanor Anne Porden transformed Blondel into Richard's wife, Berengaria of Navarre, travelling Europe in disguise). By the twentieth century there were versions suggesting a homosexual relationship between Blondel and Richard, and the story has finally come to rest in the dithyrambic graveyard known as the rock musical. The creators of the last named effort, however, have missed a trick in not incorporating the ditty that Richard himself composed in Dürnstein, *Ja nus hons pris*, which expressed his feelings of abandonment by his people. This is a bit rich, considering that Richard was a disastrous king who had himself abandoned England and nearly bankrupted it in having his ransom paid. Mythology is stronger than reality however, and the "Lionheart" was made an icon of chivalry by the Victorians, who erected an equestrian statue to him in front of the Palace of Westminster.

Blondel had his German equivalents known as *Minnesänger* who practised the cult of "courtly love" like their Provençal counterparts. The Tyrolean Walther von der Vogelweide (circa 1170-1230), who has been described as "the greatest German lyric poet before Goethe", was for a while resident at the Babenberg court. He did not confine himself to elaborate ethereal compliments addressed to untouchable ladies, but also wrote of more earthly and earthy joys, as well as penning some sharply observed *Sprüche*, satirical comments on contemporary events. Some of these last were evidently more dictated by a patron's money than moral fervour, but after all a poet has to eat.

High art was nevertheless considered to be embodied by the courtly love genre, a curious form of platonically adulterous love poetry that celebrated a great lady's unspotted grace and virtue, while simultaneously implying that she might consider relaxing these virtues a little for the sake of the poet. Since the lady's husband was traditionally the poet's patron, it is tempting to see this as an elevated medieval adumbration of the Biedermeier *Hausfreund* already mentioned, though of course the sexual ambivalence of the latter's role is missing and we are dealing with an altogether higher social stratum. Orotund celebration and pursuit of the unattainable in the aristocratic culture of the Middle Ages has been explained partly as a stylization of feudal hierarchical relationships, and partly as a fusion of the eternal feminine ideal with worship of the Virgin Mary.

Walther von der Vogelweide's range was perhaps the widest of these courtly poets, far wider than that of his mentor, Reimar von Hagenau, with whom he later quarrelled and who was responsible for having him banned from the Babenberg court. Walther's famous lyric celebrating love and sex in a pastoral setting broke the stiff rules of courtly love lyrics, not least because it is the girl who narrates her sensual joy:

> Under the spreading
> Linden in heather
> Where for our love a bed we found,
> You may see us bedding
> Fair together
> Crushed flowers and grass upon the ground.

The more frank approach to love lyrics was continued by a later Minnesinger at the Babenberg court, Neidhart von Reuenthal (1180-1250), who was from the Bavarian minor nobility. Like many Minnesänger, he accompanied his patron, Leopold VI of Austria, on a crusade, and was thereafter a fixture at the Viennese court. The 114 ballads attributed to him, most of them comic and many indecent, mark a sharp break with the courtly love tradition. His rustic verse comedies typically describe rivalry for the affections of apple-cheeked country maidens between decidedly down-at-heel knights (like Neidhart himself) and village blockheads. The poet has been described as an Austrian Till Eulenspiegel, a prankster through whose agency conventions are undermined and the socially disadvantaged take a symbolic revenge on the socially pretentious. Such themes, of course, appealed to the Viennese and were to recur in reinterpreted form down the ages. Neidhart's posthumous popularity was such that a prosperous Viennese named Michel Menschein later had the ceremonial hall of his substantial house on Tuchlauben frescoed with scenes from Neidhart's droll stories, where indeed they can still be seen.

The most exotic of the Babenbergs' singing canaries was Ulrich von Liechtenstein (1200-76), no relation to the famous family of the same name. He announced his devotion to his chosen lady at the age of twelve and thereafter pursued a career of noble, if increasingly eccentric, self-sacrifice. At one stage he embarked on a great ride from Venice through Austria to Bohemia, posing as the goddess Venus and assisted by an entourage of male volunteers, all dressed in beguiling frocks. Along the way he made frequent stops in order to stage tournaments in honour of his loved one. As the personification of love, he used these events to challenge all comers who might care to dispute his supremacy in service to his ideal. Having lost a finger at a tournament in Brixen in 1230, he sent his idol the amputated and bloody digit, thoughtfully wrapped up in a poem. Apparently she remained unmoved by this, as she was also by his sojourn in a leper colony set up before her castle gate expressly to demonstrate the extremity of his self-abasement. In the end he gave up in disgust and transferred his affections elsewhere. Throughout all his travails, it is pleasant to learn that Ulrich was safely and happily married, although one imagines that his wife was as long-suffering in her own way as he was in his.

Ulrich recorded his exploits (which included another ride through Styria, this time impersonating King Arthur) in what has been called the first autobiographical work of Austrian literature, the *Frauendienst* ("In the Service of Ladies"). It might more accurately be described as a work of "autobiographical fiction" in verse, and some of the events it records are considered to be much embroidered. Nevertheless the rides are attested, and they may also have implied a political agenda behind the ostensible rituals of courtly love. Ulrich was of the party of Duke Friedrich II of Babenberg (known as "the Warlike"), and could have been using publicity stunts to propagandize for his patron, who had been temporarily deprived of his lands by Emperor Friedrich II. Certainly, like other Minnesänger who followed their lords on crusades or were valued sources of counsel at the court, Ulrich was a political animal who held office as steward to Friedrich and was the latter's governor in Styria. His defence of his patron emulated that of Walther von der Vogelweide, who wrote satirical verses on behalf of Emperor Friedrich II at the expense of the pope, after the latter's excommunication of the former. The integration of the Minnesänger into mainstream politics and administration presages another peculiarly Austrian phenomenon, namely the combining of a bureaucratic and a writing career.

Numerous examples of this dual role could be cited from the eighteenth century onwards—we have already noted Maria Theresia's irritation with her minister Sonnenfels for writing theatre reviews—but the most striking example was to be Franz Grillparzer in the nineteenth century. Such writers were not, of course, obliged to write patriotic platitudes like the official offerings of the English Poets Laureate; on the other hand, they were part of the establishment, which led to a degree of schizophrenia, or at least ambivalence, for example when a Grillparzer's liberal instincts clashed with his loyalties as an imperial bureaucrat. One could argue that the willingness of Hugo von Hofmannsthal and other writers to work for the Austrian government during the First World War marks a continuation of this recurrent tendency for writing and officialdom to coalesce in Vienna. Hofmannsthal's undoubted patriotism could even be exploited by the Ständestaat: the play chosen by the "clerico-fascist" authorities to represent Austria at the Paris World Exhibition of 1937 was Hofmannsthal's *Das Salzburger große Welttheater*, of which cultural historian John Warren remarks: "No play could more suitably have presented the ideals of the new Austrian government than this [one,] which through the use of Catholic baroque images preaches medieval hierarchy as the response to the threat of Bolshevism." Nowadays the Austrian state and the federal provinces no longer co-opt the artistic and intellectual community, but they do shower prizes on it with a generosity bordering on the reckless (more than eighty at the present time, twelve for Vienna alone).

The flowering of Viennese culture under the Babenbergs also threw up a great Austrian chronicler, Jans Enenkel (or Enikel, circa 1230-90), who nostalgically celebrated their achievements in retrospect. He came from a rich burgher family in Vienna and his *Fürstenbuch* (Book of the Princes) chronicles the history of Austria in 4,259 verses, with the emphasis on Vienna. For this he seems to have drawn on the archive of the Schottenstift, and it was he who identified the "Berghof" on the edge of the Hoher Markt as the oldest building in the city, where judgements were handed down by the rulers in the Dark Ages (a plaque on the current building recalls this). Although Enenkel's topographical details have long been questioned by scholars, modern research has the pendulum swinging back in favour of his reliability. However that may be, his picture of the glittering Babenberg court is memorable and vivid:

At court was ever joy and honour,
Ladies wooed in knightly manner;
Sorrow each man kept away,
Nought but pleasure, night and day.

As a significant chronicler, Enenkel is preceded by some hundred years by Bishop Otto von Freising (1114-58). Although Enenkel had attempted a "World Chronicle", Otto made an altogether weightier contribution to medieval historiography with his *Chronicle or History of the Two Empires*, a history of the world in seven volumes, and with his *Life of Friedrich Barbarossa*. The brother of Duke Heinrich II of Babenberg, Otto gave his clan a suitably glowing write-up, providing it with an illustrious lineage stretching back to antiquity. His account of the manoeuvrings at the Reichstag of Regensburg in 1156, at the end of which Austria was elevated to a dukedom, is considered especially valuable.

THE BABENBERGS' SELF-PROMOTION AND ECONOMIC SUCCESS

In the Middle Ages pseudo-history often had as much weight as ostensibly pragmatic historiography, and anyway the lines between fact and fiction were fluid whenever dynastic honour was involved. During the Babenberg period, the most famous of all the pseudo-historical sagas of Europe appeared, the *Nibelungenlied*. This appears to have been compiled in the early thirteenth century from oral narratives of long standing by a native Austrian in the employ of Wolfger von Erla, the Bishop of Passau. The latter's devotion to poetry is indicated by his famous gift of a fur coat to Walther von der Vogelweide, who had fallen out of favour with the Babenberg duke and was in danger of freezing to death in the winter of 1203. The *Nibelungenlied*'s 2,379 four-verse stanzas, divided into 39 "Adventures", recapitulates a folk memory of historical events and personages as far back as the fifth century, the time of Attila the Hun. Much of the action concerning Attila himself (here presented as "Etzel", a considerably milder figure than in supposedly historical accounts) takes place in Austria along the Danube Valley. At Tulln Etzel receives Kriemhild, one of his many brides, marries her in Vienna and stops over at Hainburg on his way downstream to the "Etzelburg" (today Óbuda, the oldest of Budapest's three cities amalgamated in 1873). From the thirteenth to the sixteenth centuries the Nibelung epic was widely read and survives in 35 fragmentary manuscripts. A version dating to 1480/90 was discovered in the library of Vienna's Piarist monastery in 1856 and is now in the Austrian National Library.

The profane nature of much of the Minnesänger's material and the decidedly pagan elements of the *Nibelungenlied* (albeit with political and Christian undertones that appear to have accreted in the tenth century) illustrate the many-sidedness of Babenberg culture. This richness was the counterpart of Babenberg piety and statecraft. The dynasty was skillful at steering a middle course in the great investiture controversy between the popes and the German emperors, and then in the Guelph-Ghibelline conflict, that proved the undoing even of such an august personage as Dante Alighieri. They were also adept at making strategic dynastic alliances through marriage, a skill that was later to become the hallmark of the Habsburgs. In this way they not only consolidated their position vis-à-vis the imperial house (admittedly with a few unfortunate interludes) but also established profitable diplomatic ties with the East (two Babenberg dukes, Heinrich II and Leopold VI, married Byzantine princesses.)

For Vienna, two of their political and economic moves were especially significant. The first was the signing of the exchange treaty of Mautern (1137), by the terms of which the Peterskirche was formally yielded to the Bishop of Passau, but as a quid pro quo, half of the lands pertaining thereto, together with other churches of the parish, were placed under the aegis of the Vienna clergy. In the document Vienna is mentioned for the first time as *civitas*, that is, having the rights of a city. The second economic coup was the institution of the staple right by Leopold VI in 1221. This, it must be admitted, was virtually daylight robbery. It compelled merchants from the west or the east to land their goods in Vienna and offer them for sale to their Viennese counterparts within two months, the Viennese having a monopoly on the resale. If the merchants found no takers, they had to re-export their goods on payment of a hefty duty. The consequence of this measure, as might be expected, was that the Viennese let the traders sweat until the deadline loomed, then forced a fire-sale at knockdown prices. However, Vienna was impossible to circumnavigate, due to its strategic position for east-west trade on the Danube, and the foreign merchants felt obliged to submit. Perhaps the success of this Babenberg measure bred the fondness for monopolies and cartels that have been a feature of Viennese life until quite recently—doctors controlling the number of new entrants to the profession, chemists with monopolies over their specified areas, and surreptitious price-fixing which comes periodically to light, or in the past even enjoyed legal status.

More positively, the Babenbergs were personally great benefactors of the city, just as they were great founders of religious houses. Under their rule, besides the monasteries further afield already mentioned and the Benedictine Monastery of the Scots, the Minorite cloister was founded in Vienna in 1225 and that of the Dominicans a year later. Ten years after the Treaty of Mautern, the parish church of St. Stephen was consecrated, the first church to be built on the site (then outside the city walls) where the great St. Stephen's Cathedral stands today.

In 1205 Duke Leopold VI allowed some of the Teutonic Knights (founded in 1198 as hospitallers at the siege of Acre during the third crusade) to settle close to St. Stephen's, where they built a residence and a Romanesque chapel. In 1244 the last Babenberg, Friedrich II, even issued a privilege for the Jews, who had become increasingly important to the ruling house for the supply of credit as the money economy developed. The privilege protected the latter's rights of seizure in the case of unpaid debts and also allowed them to charge high rates of interest (Christians being forbidden the practise of "usury"), all of which naturally soon led to trouble with the gentile population, although the privilege survived the demise of the Babenbergs.

The new religious foundations and grants of land to nobles attracted setttlers to Austria and primed the pump of the agricultural economy. The strategic position of Vienna made it a magnet for trade, and Leopold VI also encouraged the important textiles industry in 1208 by issuing a privilege for Flemish weavers and dyers. For two centuries the Babenberg court in Vienna attracted artistic talent and craftsmen. In 1246, however, all this came to an abrupt end when Friedrich II was killed fighting the Magyars at the River Leitha, leaving no heir. Austria—and especially Vienna—were swiftly reminded, if they had ever forgotten, that there were great insecurities attendant upon their geopolitical location between competing powers. The fight for survival resumed and another turbulent interregnum began.

PLACES AND MONUMENTS ASSOCIATED WITH THE BABENBERGS

On the large square known as Am Hof, the Babenberg Duke Heinrich II set up his court in 1156, probably on the site of the (formerly Jesuit) church Zu den neun Chören der Engel on the square's eastern flank. (The church is now used by the Croatian congregation in Vienna.) To the west of Am Hof is the area known as Freyung, bordered on the north side by the Schottenkirche and Schottenkloster founded in 1155 by Irish monks of the Benedictine Order at the invitation of Duke Heinrich II. Both buildings have been much altered over the centuries and largely rebuilt in the Baroque period. The name Freyung ("liberation", i.e. from hot pursuit by the ducal officers) is an allusion to the asylum that fugitives from justice enjoyed if they reached the area within the jurisdiction of the Schottenkloster, an anomaly that survived up to the time of Joseph II (1780-90). Duke Heinrich II of Babenberg is buried in the crypt of the Schottenkirche.

Adjacent to the Schottenkirche is the residential Schottenhof (1832), a fine example of the the neoclassical architecture of Josef Kornhäusel. The latter houses the Museum im Schottenstift, the greatest treasure of which is the original late-Gothic winged altar (1480), painted for the Schottenkirche by the anonymous "Schottenmeister". Apart from its high artistic quality, the painting is valuable as the first topographically accurate view of medieval Vienna. The museum's picture collection contains fine Netherlandish works of the seventeenth and eighteenth centuries and Biedermeier pictures, *inter alia* by Thomas Ender and Johann Peter Krafft.

The Neidhart frescoes, depicting droll interludes from the verse stories of the Minnesinger Neidhart von Reuenthal (circa 1180-1250) may be visited at Tuchlauben 19 (Innere Stadt). The basic themes of the fresco cycle are the games and festivities associated with the Four Seasons, and they were painted between 1389 and 1399. These oldest profane frescoes of Vienna were discovered under plaster during renovation of the house in 1979.

MONASTERIES AND ABBEYS AROUND VIENNA

Heiligenkreuz (22 miles from Vienna in the Southern Wienerwald): the Cistercian abbey was a foundation of St. Leopold III of Babenberg in 1133, but the oldest and impressive Romanesque parts of the church (façade and nave) date to the eleventh century. In the early eighteenth century, Baroque features were added by Giovanni Giuliani. The chapter house contains the tombs of four Babenberg dukes (Leopold IV, Leopold V, Friedrich I and Friedrich II).

Klosterneuburg (easily reached by public transport from Vienna): the Augustinian cloister was also originally founded by St. Leopold III. It was much altered and expanded under Charles VI by his court architect Donato Felice d'Allio, the intention being to recreate the Escorial of the Spanish Habsburgs. Highlights include the Babenberg genealogical tree and the altar (1181) made by Nicholas of Verdun, whose work illustrates the transition from Romanesque to Gothic style.

Melk (about 55 miles west of Vienna) is the noblest Baroque monastery of Austria (designed by Jakob Prandtauer), but originally a Babenberg foundation. There are also a magnificent monastery church, library and Habsburg Museum.

Göttweig (located on a hillside of the Wachau in the Danube Valley, about an hour's drive to the west of Vienna): another magnificently Baroque-modified cloister from the Babenberg era, on which the eighteenth-century master-architect, Lukas von Hildebrandt, has left his mark. The Kaiserstiege (Emperor's Stairway) with frescoes by Paul Troger is considered the finest of its kind in Austria.

The imposing Baroque monastery of Melk in the Danube Valley at the western end of the picturesque wine region of the Wachau was built by Jakob Prandtauer and completed in 1736. It is one of the richest Baroque abbeys in Central Europe with a superb chapel and important library.

Nineteenth-century patriotic propaganda on behalf of the ruling house idealized the piety and asceticism of Rudolf of Habsburg, the first of the line to rule in Austria (1276-82). The picture illustrates a well-known story of Rudolf humbly offering his horse to a priest, who needed to carry the ciborium across a swollen stream on his way to administer the sacrament to a sick man.

Chapter Fourteen

THE EARLY HABSBURGS: FROM GOTHIC TO RENAISSANCE

"Vienna is the most beautiful of the barbarian cities…"
                                        Antonio de Bonfini (1485)

The death of the last Babenberg without issue sparked a struggle for hegemony in what had become a valuable Central European territory, and initially it was the aggressive Bohemian king, Přemysl Otakar II, who prevailed. He took the precaution of marrying Friedrich of Babenberg's widow (at 47, she was an old lady by medieval standards, while he was 23) and garnered considerable support among the nobility in Vienna and prominent burghers. Many of his measures were popular (confirmation of merchants' privileges and staple rights that had been eroded and extensive reconstruction after fires that devastated parts of the city). Otakar also established a Bürgerspital (poorhouse) for the indigent and ailing, and a leper hospital on Alsergrund (the disease had been brought to Central Europe by returning crusaders). St. Stephen's was largely rebuilt under his aegis following a fire in 1238, likewise the Minoritenkirche, whose Franciscan order of Minorites were confessors to the Bohemian king.

After Otakar's death on the Marchfeld in 1278, his embalmed but still bloodstained corpse lay in state in the Minorite church for thirty days, an indication of the esteem in which he was held by the Viennese. It also implied a degree of tact and diplomatic magnanimity on the part of his victorious Habsburg opponent.

Rudolf of Habsburg was elected German king in 1273 largely because his family was not considered powerful enough to disrupt the machinations of the Electors in Germany, who were squabbling among themselves. The Habsburgs, for their part, embarked on a policy that steadily shifted the balance of power in Europe. Eventually they laid almost permanent claim to the symbolic but influential office of Holy Roman Emperor and built up an empire "on which the sun never set," including not only the Central European territories, but also Spain and her possessions in the New World.

All this, however, was far in the future as Rudolf prepared for a show-down with Otakar on the Marchfeld, about 45 miles north-east of Vienna. His army was smaller than that of his enemy and his support was dwindling among the local nobility, once it learned of his intention to parcel out the Austrian territories among his family. Nevertheless, helped by the last-minute intervention of the half-Cumanian (and half-mad) Hungarian King Ladislas, Rudolf won a great victory in 1278 at Dürnkrut by the River March, which is now Austria's border with the Slovak Republic. The victory marked a turning point in Austrian history and the beginning of a Habsburg hegemony that endured six hundred and forty years until defeat in the First World War swept the dynasty away in 1918.

Rudolf appointed his son Albrecht as regent in the Austrian territories (henceforth the "Crown Lands"). The latter turned the Viennese against him by limiting the city's staple right and holding an extravagant Fürstentag, or princes' summit, in 1298, designed to promote his claims to the German throne. The town was filled to bursting with the unruly entourages of the princely delegates, the worst being the Cumanians from the Great Hungarian Plain, who stabled their horses in Viennese dwellings and flung themselves on the local women.

By contrast, Rudolf himself has gone down in history as the epitome of the pious, shrewd and ascetic Habsburg. As he journeyed towards Vienna before the battle on the Marchfeld, he was asked who was responsible for his treasury, and replied: "Treasury have I none; nor money for that matter. Only five shillings in bad coin." A legend popularized in nineteenth-century history paintings relates how the king chanced upon a priest who was en route to administer the sacrament to a sick man. A stream swollen with rain stood in the way, and Rudolf sprang from his horse, which then safely conveyed priest and ciborium to the other side of the torrent. The horse should then have been returned to its owner, but Rudolf said he was unworthy to remount a steed that had just carried on its back the lord of all creation in the form of the Eucharist. Shortly afterwards, Rudolf was elected King of the Germans, we are invited to believe in recognition of the humility before God he had just demonstrated. This legend, propagandistically and romantically underlining the alliance of *imperium* and *sacerdotium* that legitimized Habsburg authority, first appeared in medieval chronicles, was embellished in the Baroque era and became a commonplace in the nineteenth century, when Schiller treated it in his poem *Der Graf von Habsburg* (1804).

The Habsburg assumption of power in 1278 was also honoured in Franz Grillparzer's great history drama, *The Rise and Fall of King Ottokar* (1825). The play's immediate inspiration was the restitution of Habsburg power after the trauma of the Napoleonic wars, which had forced Franz II to renounce the title of Holy Roman Emperor in 1806 and restyle himself more modestly as Emperor Franz I of Austria. The figure of Otakar is to some extent a symbolic portrayal of Napoleon, a charismatic adventurer and would-be despot brought low by fate. The idealization of Rudolf as protector of the weak, the protagonist of knightly virtues and symbol of courageous independence is less plausible as a salute to the somewhat petty-minded, middle-class monarch, Franz I; nevertheless it stands as a literary contribution to what Claudio Magris calls "the Habsburg myth" in Austrian literature.

The play's most famous speech celebrates the land of Austria (for which Lower Austria here stands proxy) in terms that recall the eulogy of England ("this scepter'd isle", "this other Eden, demi-paradise") that Shakespeare puts in the mouth of Richard II. The Habsburg loyalist, Ottokar von Horneck, mingles idyllic description of the Austrian landscape with a celebration of the qualities of the individual Austrian. Some of the phrases are taken almost verbatim from a eulogy delivered in in the fourteenth century by Thomas Ebendorfer, Rector of the Vienna University, in honour of Duke Albrecht VI:

> Behold a noble ruler—a noble land,
> Well deserving of a prince's care!
> Look round: to furthest limits of your gaze
> All's radiant as bride should be for bridegroom!

Horneck goes on to provide one of the most moving evocations of Austrian landscape ever written, his idyll being gradually transmuted into a celebration of the Austrians themselves:

Therefore is an Austrian joyful and free,
Hiding not his faults, wearing his joys openly,
Never envious, but rather to be envied…

…His is the vision, the open honest judgement
While others spend their powers in speeches!
O noble land! O fatherland! Betwixt
The Italian child and German man
You lie, a youth with rose-red cheeks.
God preserve your youthful ardour,
Making whole what others have debased.

Despite Grillparzer's apparently patriotic motivation, Franz I was suspicious of the playwright's deeper intentions, anticipating a famous moment when Franz Joseph replied to a eulogy of someone's patriotism: "Yes, yes. But is he a patriot for me?" The piece was a huge success with the public, which if anything alarmed the emperor even more. He summoned Grillparzer to an audience, effusively praised the play and slyly offered to buy up the rights to it himself. Grillparzer, who knew that this was a ploy to suppress his masterpiece, refused.

Two years into the Nazi occupation of Austria, the Volkstheater staged *König Ottokars Glück und Ende*. At the word "Austria"—forbidden since the Anschluss in 1938—a storm of applause broke out. At a later performance, the speech of Von Horneck was greeted with spontaneous outbursts of cheering and clapping. The outraged Nazis had the play taken out of the repertoire.

RUDOLF THE FOUNDER

The next Habsburg to make a really profound impression on Vienna was another Rudolf, known as "Der Stifter" (The Founder, 1339-65), whose zeal in founding institutions was only equalled by his diligence in forging documents to further his dynastic claims. The most notorious of these was the *Privilegium Maius*, a fraudulent expansion of the (genuine) *Privilegium Minus* granted by Frederick Barbarossa to the Babenbergs in 1156. Duke Rudolf IV also helped himself to a string of titles such as Palatine Archduke, Duke of Swabia and Alsace, Chief Hunter of the Empire (*sic*) and several others that might supply plausible grounds for claiming fat inheritances later. In one of those delightful turns of history that demonstrate a sense of humour in the most unlikely persons, Emperor Karl IV (who was Rudolf's father-in-law) commissioned the humanist poet and scholar Petrarch to determine the authenticity of the supporting documents for his son-in-law's claims. Petrarch's admirably incisive report ended with the observation that "he who has fabricated them is an arrant knave; and he who believes in them is an ass."

Rudolf's principal aim in all this was to achieve a status for his line that would oblige the Kurfürsten (the German electoral college) to include him among their number, since otherwise there was a real danger of the Habsburgs becoming marginalized. His father-in- law, the emperor, at first indulged him in this but later applied the brakes as Rudolf's demands and methods became ever more brazen. But the consequences of his ambition were generally benign for Vienna, as the duke set about the enhancement of St. Stephen's by laying the foundation stone for its great South Tower in 1359, and raised the city's academic profile with the founding of the Alma Mater Rudolphina in 1365. However, Vienna was not made a bishopric, as Rudolf had hoped, and the Rudolphina was barred from acquiring the all-important Theological Faculty on the intervention of Karl IV, who feared competiton for his prized Karolinum in Prague.

Nevertheless Rudolf, who was only twenty-six when he died on a trip to Milan, packed an enormous amount into his short reign. His achievements included his major coup of peacefully obtaining Tyrol on the death (in 1363) of Meinhard III without issue (Rudolf arrived flourishing another of his forgeries, an inheritance contract supposedly signed by the late count.) In Vienna he reformed jurisdiction, city governance, the guilds, taxes and property rights, none of them without strong opposition from interested parties. He largely succeeded in raising the prestige of his line and he appears to have impressed his contemporaries from an early age. When Rudolf was only nine, Konrad von Megenberg, the learned and famous rector of the Stephansschule in Vienna, dedicated to the future duke his *Monastica* (1348), a treatise on ethics and the individual, which perhaps did not deal much with the ethics of forgery.

Von Megenberg, who seems to have held his post in Vienna for six years between 1342 and 1348, was the author of the first natural history in the German language (*Das Buch der Natur*), besides works on such varied topics as economics, plague epidemics and earthquakes. The academic distinction of the Stephansschule under his rectorship made it a worthy forerunner of the Rudolphina. In the next century the latter nurtured scholars of European distinction, among them Thomas Ebendorfer, the compiler of the *Cronica Austriae*, as well as a *Cronica regum Romanorum* and a *Cronica pontificum Romanorum*. A rhetorician and theologian of distinction, he took part in the anti-papal Council of Basel (1431-49) that was concerned with ecclesiastical reform. He managed to keep the university out of political difficulties in times highly charged with controversy and was sufficiently appreciated by Friedrich III (of whom more below) to be invited to accompany him to Rome for his coronation as Holy Roman Emperor in 1452.

VIENNA AND THE JEWS IN THE MIDDLE AGES

According to legend, Abraham the Jew came to Austria 859 years after the Flood and founded a dynasty with branches in Tulln, Korneuburg and Vienna. This legend had a practical and defensive function in times of persecution of the Jews, namely to show that the Austrian Jews settled before the crucifixion; therefore the standard accusation against them, that they "murdered Christ," was without foundation. In fact, the first Jews almost certainly arrived from Palestine in the wake of the Roman armies, but are not documented until the tenth century.

In 1156, under Leopold V of Babenberg, the first signs of the sucessful business activities of Jews may be observed—and of the hatred these aroused. A certain Schlom (Solomon), who was in charge of the ducal mint, was granted the right to keep Christian servants and own property. However, in the same year he and thirteen other Jews were murdered by crusaders then in Vienna, possibly a religiously motivated killing. By 1204 there was a synagogue in the city and by 1214 a Jewish cemetery outside the Kärntnertor, around the Goethegasse that today flanks the Burggarten.

The security of the Jews lay almost entirely in the hands of the rulers, who gave or withdrew privileges, borrowed money or reneged on their debts to Jewish credit providers. They also levied (usually high) taxes on Jews and regulated the terms of business permitted to them. The favour of rulers being so important, it is no surprise that the ghetto backed onto the Babenberg court Am Hof, where the Judenplatz still is, stretching westwards to Tiefer Graben, northwards to the church of Maria am Gestade and eastwards to Tuchlauben. At its greatest extent it comprised some seventy houses, all opening inwards towards the ghetto, so that their rear elevations formed part of a solid defensive wall, which could only be entered by four gates.

The Hohenstauffen Emperor Friedrich II looked with favour on the Jewish communities in his realms and issued a statute in 1236 that required any serious accusations against Jews to be upheld by at least one Jewish witness. This illustrates the sort of protection that was needed (other clauses dealt with penalties for killing Jews or abducting Jewish children for baptism.) The emperor's Privilege for the Jews, which would have held for Vienna, was immediately superseded by that of the Babenberg Duke Friedrich II "the Warlike", who was in the process of being reinstated in his lands after imperial suspension. His statute for the Jews became the model for other Central European countries. Its main motivation was to create the conditions whereby they would become a useful source of credit and taxes, for which function they of course needed guarantees and protection. Twenty-two of the thirty articles of Friedrich's new privilege were therefore concerned with the legal rights of the Jews, including seizure of goods against unpaid debts and the permitted level of interest that could be charged. Since this latter effectively fixed a ceiling of an APR of 173 per cent, future conflict between Christian borrowers and Jewish lenders was a foregone conclusion.

The canonical prohibition on "usury", together with the theological claim that the Jews were responsible in perpetuity for Christ's death, provided Christians with the excuses they wanted to escape their obligations to Jewish moneylenders by renouncing debts. In times of crisis like plague epidemics, the Jews were also useful scapegoats for those who could not explain why their own god was as bloodthirsty and indifferent to the suffering of humanity as was evidently the case. Natural disasters and other setbacks necessarily had to be explained as divine punishment for collective sins (the orthodox teaching of the Church), but this was the "educated" view. It was far more satisfying to sidestep an oppressive sense of guilt by uncovering conspiracies among a defenceless minority. Jews could be accused with impunity of poisoning wells during plague epidemics, of abducting and sacrificing Christian children, of desecrating the Host, or simply of bleeding their victims financially. That this last accusation had more to do with racism than reality may be seen from the fact that Jews supplied only about 25 per cent of the credit made available in Vienna, although it is true that their interest rates were high. But a high interest rate was in turn a reflection of the fact that the business was high-risk—a ruler had the right to renege on debts per edict—and the lenders were highly taxed. And there was always a possibility of violence against their persons, often inspired by Christian preachers.

For the reasons outlined above the Babenberg dukes and initially also the Habsburg rulers protected the Jews, though their protection was often ineffective outside Vienna, as in 1338, when a pogrom in Lower Austria, following a claimed desecration of the Host, resulted in many Jews being burned alive. In 1349 the terrifying plague arrived from Italy, the same plague from which Boccaccio's patricians took refuge in a Settignano villa and whiled away the time telling the stories of the *Decameron*. This time the Jews were accused of well poisoning (even though they were, of course, themselves victims of the plague) and more pogroms followed. Duke Albrecht II punished the villages concerned, but was virtually powerless against the hysteria and dread engendered by the horror of the symptoms and the death rate hyperbolically reported by contemporary chronicles as up to 960 persons in a single day in Vienna.

In the early fifteenth century, the Habsburg duke himself (Albrecht V) turned against the Jews, first by crippling them with taxes to pay for his extensions to the Hofburg, and then, when they could no longer pay, by torturing them to discover their supposed reserves of hidden treasure. The poor Jews were herded onto rafts like cattle and sent down the Danube to Buda, where the Emperor Sigismund took them in. In Vienna, the pogrom culminated in the horrific "Wiener Geserah" of 1420-21. Jews imprisoned in their synagogue committed mass suicide on hearing of the duke's plans to abduct all Jewish children under the age of fifteen and have them baptized by force. In March 1421 the surviving 92 men and 120 women of the Jewish community, having refused to be baptized, were burned alive on Erdberg's "Goose Meadow". Contemporary reports describe them going to their deaths with manic joy, singing psalms and dancing before the pyres as they contemplated imminent release to a better life beyond this one.

All relics of Jewish life were destroyed and for thirty years there was no Jewish community in Austria, now referred to by the Jews themselves as *Erez Hadamin*, or "Land of Blood". A grisly "memorial" to this event may still be seen affixed to Great Jordan's House at Judenplatz 2. The punning relief shows the baptism of Christ in the River Jordan and the

Latin inscription reads: "The River Jordan washes the body clean from disease and evil. Even secret sins take flight. The flames rushing furiously through the city in 1421 purged the horrible crimes of the Hebrew dogs. The world was once cleansed by the Deucalion flood: but this time punishment came by means of the raging fire."

In a recently published biographical lexicon of the Habsburgs it is interesting to note the circumspection with which the writer treats the rule of the presiding Duke Albrecht (motto: *Amicus optima vitae possessio*—"a friend is the greatest treasure in life"). It is conceded that the qualities attributed to him of "steadiness, generosity of spirit and a sense for justice" [sic] belong too much to the ritualized categories of princely virtues for one to take them entirely seriously. On the other hand, Albrecht was "without doubt much loved and respected in Austria." In the entire entry, which is long and detailed, the writer has only this to say about the events of 1420-1: "Albrecht did not shrink from persecuting the Jews in order to use the money thus raised for the struggle against the Hussites." In this observation at least there is a hint of more rational, if not excusable, grounds for the persecution of the Jewish community: the Hussite menace was very real at this time, both in terms of armed incursions in Upper and Lower Austria, and in terms of theological infiltration (Albrecht was obliged to force all teachers at the university to swear an oath abjuring Hussite heresies). Hans Tietze, the respected historian of Viennese Jewry, points out that the Hussite attitude to the Bible showed "a certain Judaising tendency", and further cites "a defender of the Jews" as conceding that instances of arms trading between Jews and Hussites was quite plausible, "since the Jews traded in everything."

EMPEROR FRIEDRICH III

If the Hussite threat was serious, inter-Habsburg rivalry became even more so, the "Albertine" and "Leopldine" lines having been engaged for generations in a Habsburg equivalent of the English "Wars of the Roses". Indeed, when Friedrich was born in 1415, the dynasty's patrimony was split three ways between Upper and Lower Austria (*ob und unter der Enns*—"on and below the River Enns"), so-called Inner Austria (Styria, Carinthia, Carniola [today Slovenia]), and Tyrol with the "Vorlande" (possessions in Germany and Switzerland). Friedrich succeeded in outliving all his rivals, including the Hungarian king, Matthias Corvinus, who occupied Vienna between 1485 and his death in 1490. He consolidated the dynasty's power in Vienna by buying out his brothers' shares of the Hofburg, although he had to be rescued from the same by the Hussite Bohemian king, Georg von Podiebrad when his brother reneged on the agreement.

Friedrich's achievements for Vienna were considerable: he laid the foundation for the North Tower of the Stephansdom, work continuing on it until 1511. Only in 1556 was the unfinished tower capped with the Renaissance lantern which we see today. The magnificent Gothic winged altar (1447) in the cathedral's north aisle came from the imperial workshops in Wiener Neustadt, while the late Gothic marble tomb for the emperor himself, one of the most magnificent artefacts in the city, was commissioned from Niclaes Gerhaert van Leyden during Friedrich's lifetime, but not completed until 1513.

Friedrich was intensely disliked by many of his powerful subjects, not least when he took urgently needed measures to put the administrative finances in order. On one occasion he was jostled in the Augustinerkirche by knights and lords who mistrusted his renewal of financial dealings with the Jews, and who began shouting "King of the Jews! Crucify him!" No wonder Friedrich wrote in his private journal that the Viennese were "worse than the Bohemians and the Hungarians". Yet this "Styrian" outsider, despite constant humiliations and setbacks, eventually restored the finances of Austria and a measure of security to a land in the grip of Albrecht's unpaid mercenaries at his accession. He secured the symbolically important canonization of Leopold III of Babenberg and the even more important elevation of Vienna to a bishopric. He began to lay the foundation for the dynasty's expansion eastwards, firstly by selling the Hungarian crown back to its rightful owners for 80,000 Ducats, to which transaction was attached recognition of Habsburg succession rights in Hungary. He pushed the famous "marriage diplomacy" to a higher level by betrothing his son Maximilian to the daughter of Charles the Bold of Burgundy. And for the Viennese he curbed the rapacity of innkeepers by regulating prices and enforced quality control in the products of the guilds.

Friedrich got no thanks and less praise for his efforts. After he instituted another symbolically important title for all members of the ruling house, that of "Archduke" and "Archduchess", the Viennese rushed to dub the late-sleeping emperor the *Erzschlafmütze* (The Arch-Nightcap"—he probably suffered from low blood pressure). His motto, attached to documents and engraved on buildings, may have been a sign of the ambitions he harboured behind a phlegmatic façade. The enigmatic letters AEIOU have been interpreted as meaning *Austriae est imperare orbi universo*, in German: "Alles Erdreich ist Österreich untertan" ("The whole world is subject to Austria"), though we simply do not know what Friedrich really intended them to signify. The interpretation of the acronym as a "maxim signifying Austrian rule" (*Staatsdevise*) was heavily promoted by the court librarian Peter Lambeck (Petrus Lambeccius) in the seventeenth century, and since then over three hundred solutions have been proposed in Greek, Latin and German. Its mystical aura was evident as late as 1913, when the historian Richard von Kralik saw it as embodying "the most sober of political programmes", on the grounds that Austria was the only state that had fulfilled its role down the centuries of "bringing together lands with different traditions and languages in a common legal framework. And this Austrian role is a model for the future development of the entire world." (It is a pity that this was written on the eve of the First World War.) Of course, Vienna being Vienna, the satirists have not neglected to offer their own nihilistic interpretations, e.g. *Am End' is' ollas umasunst* (roughly: "When all's said and done, everything is in vain.")

To Friedrich we indirectly owe one of the more vivid descriptions of the Vienna of his day, since he employed a charismatic Italian humanist as his private secretary (and here it may be remarked in passing that Friedrich III was the last Holy Roman Emperor actually to be crowned by the pope in Rome in 1452). Enea Silvio Piccolomini (later Pope Pius II) had a sharp eye and a sharp pen (his views on Viennese morals have already been quoted). He complained bitterly of bad food and worse wine at Friedrich's court—something almost unbearable for an Italian, and no doubt due to the emperor's economy drives. He adds that officials had to sleep in dormitories, instead of separate rooms, and were only paid after long delays, or not at all. He gives quite a detailed account of the houses of evidently prosperous Viennese burghers with their "vaulted entrance passages, wide courtyards… heated living areas… glassed windows letting the light stream in from every side… the cages with singing birds that hang there… and generous stables." He notes that the buildings have "high gables and roofs that unfortunately lack glazed tiles, the majority being of wood… [the houses] are mostly built of stone and are decorated with wall paintings inside and out… when one walks into such a dwelling, one could be forgiven for thinking one had entered a prince's palace." And finally he remarks that the wine cellars are "so deep and extensive, one can say that a second Vienna exists beneath the one on the surface," and "the streets are laid to cobbles, so that the carriages do not easily make grooves in them." All this bespeaks the evident success of Friedrich's financial management in the later part of his reign.

A far less flattering picture emerges, however, from passages in Piccolomini's "History of Friedrich III". "Elderly merchants," he writes, "take young girls in marriage and soon leave them widowed. The widows then marry young men from their circle, with whom they often have already started a relationship.In this way, yesterday's pauper becomes tomorrow's rich man." He goes on to report on the high incidence of murder for inheritance, and of the killing of aristocratic wives by their husbands because of affairs at court:

> Day and night there are brawls in the streets of the city, craftsmen against students, court employees against craftsmen, one guild against another. Seldom does any festivity end except in a brawl, often with death as a result… Neither the city authorities nor the princes intervene to put an end to this wretched state of affairs… The common people think only of their stomachs and eating. Whoever earns during the week with his hands, spends all of his earnings on Sunday's merrymaking, down to the last Groschen.

Another Italian visitor, Antonio Bonfini (Antonius de Bonfinis) was Matthias Corvinus' historiographer and was commissioned by him to write a history of Hungary according to the new scientific methodology of humanism. He seems to have visited Vienna before Matthias occupied the city in 1485, since his text "In Praise of Wien" dates to 1480, and begins memorably with the words: "Wien is one of the most beautiful of the barbarian cities." He relates how the Danube flood plain builds islets or *Werder* as they were called, where the Viennese laid out their gardens, in much the same way, it seems, as the *Schrebergärten* (allotments) are nurtured all over Vienna today as weekend retreats. He describes the defensive walls of the city, the moat that is easily filled with water from the many springs in it, and (like Piccolomini) the splendid town houses of the burghers with their living rooms filled with songbirds in cages—so many that "you fancy you are walking through a sylvan glade." The whole area around Vienna is one huge garden, with lovely vine-clad hills and orchards. Beyond these are country villas with fishponds and hunting grounds. And the nearest mountains "are an indescribable delight for the wanderer's eye" with their many castles and noble residences, their villages and flourishing settlements. This was the patrimony that Friedrich left on his death in 1492, to be inherited by his ambitious and dazzling son, Maximilian the "last knight".

SOME SIGHTS ASSOCIATED WITH PŘEMYSL OTAKAR AND THE EARLY HABSBURGS

The Minoritenkirche Maria Schnee: situated in the Minoritenplatz, the present church dates to the mid-fourteenth century. The earlier one on this site was erected, together with a neigbouring cloister, by the Friars Minor of the Franciscan Order in 1250. In that church Přemysl Otakar II lay in state after his defeat by Rudolf of Habsburg at Dürnkrut on the Marchfeld in 1278. The later fourteenth-century church is thought to have been de-signed by the confessor of the Habsburg Duke Albrecht II, a certain Father James of Paris. It has had a stormy history, having been commandeered during the Reformation by Protestants, who ripped out the then existing internal ornaments. During the Turkish siege of 1683, a cannon ball de-capitated the steeple, which was not rebuilt. The Baroque fittings added after the church returned to Catholic ownership in the Counter-Reformation were substantially altered or removed in the "re-Gothicization" of the Minoritenkirche by Ferdinand von Hohenberg between 1784 and 1789, a curious doctrinally motivated refurbishment which he also under-took in the Augustinerkirche for another mendicant order.

The painting over the High Altar is an eighteenth-century copy of the miraculous ninth-century image of the Virgin in the Roman church of Santa Maria Maggiore, the predecessor of the latter church having been built (according to the legend) on the spot where snow fell in August during the papacy of Liberius (352-66). The hideous mosaic copy of Leonardo's *Last Supper* was made by Giacomo Raffaelli in the nineteenth century as a substitute for the original, which Napoleon had wanted to remove from the Monastery of Santa Maria delle Grazie in Milan, but was fortunately dissuaded from doing so.

Since 1784 the Minoritenkirche has served the Italian community in Vienna. In Vienna's churches the influence of immigrant communities from earliest times is apparent in history, architecture or functions. A number of them in the Inner City still serve as the "official" church for one or other such community (though not necessarily one for which it was built). Both the Babenbergs and Habsburgs invited religious orders to settle in Vienna, a process that was renewed in the Counter-Reformation.

Stephansdom: the Albertine Choir, the most elegant part of St. Stephen's, was begun under the Habsburg Albrecht I (1283-1308) in 1304 and completed under Albrecht II (1330-1358) in 1340. Construction of its great south tower, the city's landmark and focus of civic pride, was begun on 2 March 1359 in the presence of Rudolf IV of Habsburg, the Founder (1339-65). It took seventy-four years to build the 450-foot high tower, which was completed by Hans von Prachatitz in 1433. From the Sexton's Lodge at its base visitors (if they are fit enough) can climb the narrow spiral stairway of over 300 steps to the "Starhemberg Seat", from where the commander of Vienna's defence could survey the manoeuvrings of the invading Turks during the siege of 1683. A few steps more bring you to a circular concourse with views in every direction over the rooftops of the city.

In the portal of the southern Singertor nearby are tombstone sculptures of Rudolf IV and his consort, Katharina, the daughter of Emperor Karl IV of the Luxembourg line. Rudolf's tomb is inside the cathedral at the first pillar of the north choir. His portrait, the first royal portrait in the German-speaking world, is to be found in the Erzbischöfliches Dom- und Diözesanmuseum north of the cathedral at Stephansplatz 6. It was painted by a Bohemian master between 1360 and 1365.

Embellishment of St. Stephen's is also associated with the Emperor Friedrich III (1415-93). During his rule a start was made on the north tower (the so-called Adler or Eagle Tower) in 1450. Work on it was stopped in 1511 when the architect, Hans Puchsbaum, fell to his death from the scaffolding. According to legend, his demise came about because he broke a pact he had made with the devil, who promised to hasten the work, provided he avoided any mention of a name sacred to Christians until the tower was finished. As luck would have it, Puchsbaum was up on the scaffolding one day when he spotted his fiancée Maria below and rashly called out her name.

The two most important monuments associated with Friedrich III are the Wiener Neustadt Altar in the North Choir and the emperor's superb sepulchral monument of red marble in the South Choir. The former dates to 1447 and is an elaborate winged altar. The images of seventy-two saints are displayed on exterior panels, which close on groups of narrative sculpture showing the life of Christ and the Virgin. The emperor's cryptic device of AEIOU is engraved on the predella. The late Gothic sepulchral monument was commissioned by Friedrich from Niclaes Gerhaert van Leyden, to whom is attributed the figure of the recumbent ruler in his coronation robes sculpted on the lid. Other craftsmen completed the tomb in 1513. The balustrade-like structure round it was in fact a walkway for the canons of St. Stephen to progress round the tomb singing and praying *in memoriam* Friedrich III. Theirs was a ritualistic celebration of the Habsburg emperor most strongly associated with the preservation (against all the odds) of the Habsburg mission and the alliance between *imperium* and *sacerdotium*.

The Judenplatz is north of Am Hof and partly occupies the area of the medieval ghetto, which was devastated by fire in 1406 and finally destroyed after the "Wiener Geserah" of 1420-21. Its building blocks were used in part for building an extension to the university, in which lies an unpleasant irony: Vienna's students were notorious for leading the mobs against the Jews during pogroms and plundering Jewish homes. After the incineration of the unbaptized Jews in Erdberg, the students were also active (together with the *Pöbel* or rabble) in scrabbling through the ashes to find valuables such as rings, which the victims had supposedly swallowed before their death. Great Jordan's House at no.2 on the Judenplatz is named after its merchant owner, Jörg Jordan. The plaque on the wall dates to 1500 and gleefully celebrates the pogrom of 1421 against "the Hebrew dogs". In the 1930s a counterweight to this was erected on the square in the form of a statue of Gotthold Ephraim Lessing (1729-81) whose drama *Nathan the Wise* was written as a plea for racial and cultural tolerance during the Enlightenment. It is still performed from time to time in Vienna.

In the north-west corner of the square is the Misrachi House, one of Vienna's two Jewish museums. The remains of a medieval synagogue can be accessed from its basement. However, the square itself is now dominated by Rachel Whiteread's controversial Holocaust Memorial (*Mahnmal für die Opfer der Schoa*, unveiled in 2000), also called *The Nameless Library*. The outside walls of a large white cube feature books with the spines turned inwards. To complain that the monument is obtrusive and unaesthetic is perhaps to miss the point—it is meant to be both obtrusive and more didactic than aesthetically pleasing. Perhaps it is in this spirit that one must accept the ruination of the sight-lines of the Judenplatz and the somewhat obscure iconography of the monument. It is a commentary on the Jews as "the people of the book" and hints at the Nazi book burnings, referring therefore to cultural as well as physical genocide. With it, 65,000 Austrian Jews, victims of the Nazis, are commemorated.

Chapter Fifteen

Humanism, Reformation and Counter-Reformation

"...Walking the city with studious care,/I thought that paradise was there."

Wolfgang Schmeltzl (1548)

By the death of Friedrich III in 1493, the Habsburgs had consolidated their position in Central Europe and were ready to move from the defensive to the offensive. The dynasty's factional struggle was behind it and Friedrich had pulled off the first expansionist master stroke in securing the hand of the Bugundian heiress for his son Maximilian, though it took ten years of negotiation. On Maria of Burgundy's tragic death in a riding accident, her young husband hastened to make good his claim to her inheritance. Maximilian's own marriage-bed diplomacy was unrivalled: he married off his son Philip "the Handsome" to Juana of Aragon, the daughter of Ferdinand and Isabella of Spain, while his daughter married the Spanish *infante*. On the death of the latter (1497) Philip and Juana became heirs to the Spanish lands. In 1580 even Portugal was to fall to the Habsburgs, again through marriage. That would bring possessions in Africa and Brazil, but the Spanish line already enjoyed the material fruits of earlier and continuing conquests in the New World, not to mention extensive territories in Italy.

On the eastern front of his empire, Maximilian was just as successful in his strategy for future expansion. At a betrothal ceremony in the Stephansdom in 1515, his grandchildren, Maria and Ferdinand, were married by proxy to the children (Louis and Anna) of the Jagellon king, Wladislaw II. This made the Habsburgs the heirs to the united thrones of Bohemia and Hungary, which were under Jagellon rule. It may well have been the previously mentioned Bonfini who coined the Latin epigram: *Bella gerant alii; tu, felix Austria, nube! /Nam quae Mars aliis, dat tibi regna Venus!* ("Let others make war; you, fortunate Austria, marry. While Mars

A highly romantic nineteenth-century representation of Maximilian I (1493-1519), depicted as "the last knight" (the description of the emperor in a verse romance by Anastasius Grün, 1830).

bestows realms on others, Venus showers them on you.") This is no hyperbole: Emperor Karl V, Maximilian's other grandson, inherited realms in 1519 that were simply too large and far-flung for one person and one administration to manage. In Schiller's drama *Don Carlos* (1787) his empire is retrospectively described as one on which "the sun never set." Following an old (and often unfortunate) Habsburg tradition, he divided his patrimony so that his younger brother Ferdinand I acquired the Austrian hereditary lands in 1521 and 1522. The Hungarian and Bohemian thrones then also passed to Ferdinand in 1526, after the catastrophic defeat by the Turks of the young Jagellon King Louis at Mohács in southern Hungary.

This was Maximilian's legacy, a gigantic empire built up in only three generations. As far as Vienna was concerned, he was of less significance, having moved his court to Innsbruck, one of only two Habsburg rulers who abandoned the Residenzstadt. His constant military campaigns left him permanently short of cash—at the very end of his life even the gates of Innsbruck were locked against him and his retinue, the payback for his unwillingness or inability to meet the bills incurred during his previous stay. Cities never liked rulers with empty pockets, and with good reason, since they were likely to be called upon to fill them. So he was probably no more popular in Vienna. He is remembered here, however, for founding the predecessor choir of the famous *Sängerknaben* (Vienna Boys Choir). He extended thereby a medieval tradition of Sängerknaben that had grown up because females were not allowed active participation in the Catholic Mass. In 1498 Maximilian issued a decree providing for eight boys to be trained under the Slovenian Kapellmeister of the Hofkapelle, Georg Slatkonia (later Bishop of Vienna—he presided at the double "wedding" of Maximilian's grandchildren and the Jagellon heirs in 1515).

The main function of the Hofsängerknaben was to provide music for the Mass, and their number soon grew to fourteen, then twenty. Their extremely thorough musical education meant that many went on to become musicians, singers or composers, among the subsequent Sängerknaben graduates being Joseph and Michael Haydn, Franz Schubert and (in the twentieth century) the conductor Clemens Krauss. With the proclamation of the First Republic in 1918, the Hofsängerknaben, as they had been hitherto, were dissolved with the other imperial and royal institutions. However, the Rektor of the Burgkapelle, Monsignor Josef Schnitt, succeeded in having the choir refounded in 1924 as the Wiener Sängerknaben of today, the world's most successful choir with countless foreign tours, films and recordings to its credit.

Later, an adult choir for former Sängerknaben was formed, the Chorus Viennensis, which sometimes performs alongside the Sängerknaben themselves. There are four separate groups of the latter with various functions, one always being available for Sunday Mass in the Hofburg's Burgkapelle. Those who do not mind rising early on a Sunday can go along to hear them. The state patronage of the choir was traditionally as generous as it was for the pampered Lipizzaners (who could look forward to a life of pensioned tranquillity among the green pastures of Styria on retirement), and competition to join them was fierce. The prestige attached to membership was also considerable. These two factors, perks and prestige, have given rise to the witticism that the most cherubic Viennese boys dream of becoming Sängerknaben in their youth and Lipizzaner stallions thereafter.

HUMANIST LEARNING IN VIENNA

Maximilian did something else that was crucial for Vienna: he furthered humanist learning. His own mindset was still largely medieval. The two great works of self-glorification that he (supposedly) dictated to his secretary—the *Theuerdank* and *Weißkunig*—reflect a somewhat anachronistic view of the world that owes a good deal to the idealizing romances of the Middle Ages. This impression is even more strongly conveyed in the unfinished *Freydal*, which chronicles Maximilian's exploits as the hero of the lists, a ruler of Herculean prowess. In an obsession with genealogy that recalls Rudolf the Founder nearly two centuries earlier, the emperor encouraged his court historiographers to construct lineages that traced his ancestry to the noble houses of Rome (Colonna and Pierleoni), or alternatively to the Trojans via the Frankish kings (this was the version Maximilian preferred). Even Konrad Celtis, a formidable scholar whom the emperor had summoned to Vienna, came up with a genealogy that traced the Habsburg line back to the God "Tuisko", the Zeus or Jupiter of the *ur*-Germans (but also the lawgiver, like Moses for the Jews), from whom they took their name of Teutons, and after whom they named the second day of the week.

Yet it is precisely in his relationship with Celtis that we see a more modern side of Maximilian, less the "Last Knight" apostrophized by

Anastasius Grün in his verse romance (1830) of the same name, and more the "Renaissance man" of many parts and roles. Celtis even persuaded Maximilian to play himself as emperor in an antique drama the former had written, entitled *Ludus Dianae*. At the high point of this extravagant work, Celtis himself (dressed as Bacchus) recited a eulogy of Vienna and wine (*Wien* and *Wein*—a nice conceit) before dropping to his knees at the emperor's feet in order to receive the laurel crown from his master's hands.

Celtis was one of those outsiders who initially had a hard time of it in Vienna, notwithstanding imperial support. In fact, he stumbled into the nest of factionalism that traditionally plagues Viennese academe, where oleaginousness in public and back-stabbing in private are routine. The learning and *Weltanschauung* of Italian humanism had arrived in Vienna with the previously mentioned Äneas Silvius [Enea Silvio] Piccolomini, who had written a *History of Austria* during the reign of Friedrich III. However, Piccolomini made little headway in the university, which preferred philology and grammar to the rhetoric and literary virtuosity of the Italian. Celtis, a rhetorician and literary scholar par excellence, nevertheless did have his own body of supporters, despite strong resistance to him from the diehards. After a mediocrity, who had been appointed to keep him out, proved so incompetent that he had to be dismissed, Celtis was finally appointed Professor of Poetry and Rhetoric by the emperor in 1497.

His occupation of that position ("the Celtis epoch") is generally regarded as the high point of the Renaissance in Vienna. He revolutionized the dry humanities curriculum, in the embrace of which generations of moth-eaten professors had quietly been vegetating, founded a new academy for humanist scholarship and edited a stream of ancient texts. No wonder his acolyte Johannes Cuspinian, in his official address of welcome to the great man, likened him to the god Aesculapius, who once changed himself into a snake and swam up the Tiber to liberate Rome from the plague.

For all his great achievements, Celtis is a somewhat ambivalent figure. One of the first scholars of the early modern period to practise what has delightfully been dubbed "learned vagrancy", he lived entirely off his academic wits. While he was happy to graze among the rarified and dusty manuscripts of antiquity, he was also an earthy *Lebenskünstler* of the type the Viennese heartily appreciated. John Hale describes him spending ten precarious years in his youth (he had run away from home) "flitting from school to school and university to university and, indeed, mistress to mistress." The greatest ambivalence in regard to Celtis, however, was in his attitude to Italy, an ambivalence that mirrored a larger one, that of German scholarship in general. Learned Teutons hovered between feelings of superiority and inferiority in respect of an Italy perceived as cultural heritage, but now languishing in the shadow of past greatness. On the one hand it was the fount (with Greece) of the European civilization to which the German Empire was heir; on the other hand it was evidently in decline, especially Rome, where sloth and corruption made a poor impression on those German visitors, who, like Celtis, had idealized the city from afar. It did not help that the Italian scholars treated the prickly Celtis with open disdain, something he never forgave. Italian scholars, he complained, thought that humanists from north of the Alps were "mere mannikins, born in the midst of sloth and drunkenness."

At the same time, in his famous Ingolstadt Oration of 1492, Celtis lambasted the Germans themselves for their supposed backwardness. His incredible energy and application in the editing of texts like the *Cosmography* of Apuleius or Tacitus' *Germania* was applied with a twofold aim: firstly, to show that German scholarship could do what Italian scholarship did and do it better; and secondly, to appropriate the ancient works about Germany to German scholarship (not to mention early works by German authors). It was therefore no accident that he edited and published such works as the poems of the tenth-century nun, Roswitha von Gandersheim (who was instantly hailed as "a second Sappho") or Ligurinus' twelfth-century epos on the deeds of Friedrich Barbarossa in Italy.

The schizophrenic envy of Italy was on the whole fruitful, spurring Celtis and his followers to develop and parade their skills; at its worst, however, their attitude recalls that of Dr. Johnson's tailor, whom he describes as licking his boots while simultaneously shaking his fist at him. Something of the ambivalence towards Italy lingered into the twentieth century, the Prussians tending to complain that too much of the *dolce far niente* of the sunny south had infected Viennese attitudes to life and work. And what are we to make of those extraordinary lines in Grillparzer from Ottokar von Horneck's eulogy of Austria in *The Rise and Fall of King Ottokar*? Austria (does he mean Austria in 1278, when the drama is set, or in 1825, the year of its first performance?) is bizarrely described as a "rosy-cheeked youth lying between the child Italy and the man Germany." The closing lines of the eulogy make a rhetorical plea:

God preserve your youthfulness
And make what others have corrupted whole.

Rosy-cheeked or not, Vienna lies geographically and culturally between the Protestant north of Europe and the Catholic south, a glittering lode separating and joining two cultural monoliths. Sometimes it aspired to be "German" and disciplined, blackmailed with hellfire by fierce German preachers like Abraham a Sancta Clara or bullied by a Rhinelander like Metternich. More often it took its religiosity, its artistic or musical inspiration and culinary or other pleasures from the "child Italy", that is, the Italy that was old but forever young. "Vienna is the most un-German of all German cities," complained Hitler bitterly in *Mein Kampf*, his preference being for the "man Germany". His remark sounds like a perverse echo of Celtis' schizophrenia in regard to German aspiration and Italian heritage. But then again, just before the plebiscite on the Anschluss, Hitler sentimentally told the new Nazi mayor of Vienna that the city, in his eyes, was "a gem", and he intended to "entrust it to the care of the entire German Reich."

REFORMATION AND COUNTER-REFORMATION

Konrad Celtis died in 1508 aged forty-nine. The faithful Cuspinian delivered the necrology, and was himself to continue to work in the spirit of his mentor with his history of Austria. Nine years later, Martin Luther pinned his "Ninety-five Theses" to the door of the Schlosskirche in Wittenberg, lighting the taper from which the bushfire of the Reformation spread across Northern and Central Europe. Two years after that, Maximilian I died and Charles V inherited the empire, splitting the Habsburg lands with his brother Archduke Ferdinand in 1521.

Like so many Habsburgs, Ferdinand had to rebuild his power base virtually from scratch, not least because Maximilian had left huge debts which limited the military and administrative room for manoeuvre of his successors. Moreover, insurgent Protestantism delivered a powerful weapon of obstruction into the hands of the nobility, upon whom Ferdinand was largely dependent for funds. Like the Wycliffe-influenced Hussitism of the fifteenth century, Protestantism also assumed elements of "liberation theology" that focused on social and political grievances. It thus appealed to the lower orders as well as the nobility, especially the exploited peasants, and indeed all who were disgusted by the greed, hypocrisy and increasingly secular lifestyle of the Catholic prelates and clergy.

The internal dangers that Protestantism posed were matched by external dangers from the Turks. With the death of the Jagellon king at Mohács in 1526, Ferdinand inherited Bohemia without difficulty, but the other half the of the united kingdoms, Hungary, was substantially in the hands of the Ottomans, who went on to take Buda and Pest in 1540 and even Esztergom in 1542. Tranysylvania became a Turkish vassal state with considerable autonomy, but was just as keen to ward off the attentions of the Habsburgs as it was to strike a deal with the Sublime Porte. In addition, there was a rival claimant to the Hungarian throne, János Zápolya. In 1529 the first Turkish siege of Vienna had taken place, but was broken off due to bad weather. This was a shock to the dynasty, as it was to the Viennese; thereafter (1531-66) a completely new set of fortifications on the standard Renaissance plan had been constructed for the city, the so-called *tracé italien*.

If Ferdinand was frequently on the back foot militarily, his strategy against the Reformation was necessarily one of *reculer pour mieux sauter*. This was due not only to the extraordinarily rapid dispersal of Lutheran ideas among the nobility, but also to the cautious or equivocal attitude of some senior clerics. The afore-mentioned Bishop of Vienna, Georg Slatkonia, avoided proclamation of the papal excommunication of Luther for a whole year between 1520 and 1521, and allowed a married Lutheran preacher and humanist called Paulus Speratus to deliver a sermon in the Stephansdom directed against the life of the cloister. The nobility soon went over *en masse* to the new teaching and forced Ferdinand to concede religious tolerance, if he wanted them to stump up for the Turkish wars. In vain did the archduke issue an edict on censorship in 1527 that was designed to protect his peoples from the baleful influence of Protestant writings, and which, as the historian Walter Pollak observes, "initiated that chain of intellectual tutelage which, with brief relaxations… lasted until 1848." "The Austrian has a hidden soul," remarks Friedrich Heer in his classic work *Der Kampf um die österreichische Identität* (The Struggle for Austrian Identity, 1981); "he does not reveal himself or say what he 'really' thinks, or believes, or feels deep inside, over the things that touch him most deeply—religion and the state. This 'state of concealment' in which so many of the educated class existed—theologians, scholars, bureaucrats—in the 19th and 20th centuries, provokes feelings of acute unease, especially in German visitors ('one never really knows where one is with these Austrians'), and is to a large degree the legacy of underground Protestantism in the 17th and 18th centuries."

Ferdinand's strategies for dealing with the Lutherans, however disingenuous, were founded in sincere conviction. He knew the Church was in urgent need of reform, if only because the commission he himself appointed to report on the state of the Austrian Church in 1561 told him so. The report was not encouraging, citing *inter alia* the example of Klosterneuburg, where priests and monks were living a life of pleasure with their *Lebensgefährtinnen* (concubines), and indulging in feasting and dancing. The monastery housed thirteen monks, two nuns, six women and eight children living in convivial, but hardly monastic, harmony. It was evident that addressing the general decay in morals and the more specific abuse of simony, a principal target of Protestant reformers, would require a huge administrative effort and take a long time. Meanwhile, the Peace of Augsburg (1555) enunciated the principle of *cuius regio eius religio*, by which the aristocracy and rulers chose their faith and their subjects were obliged to follow the religious practice of their lords. Ferdinand accepted this in theory, but only because he regarded it as a temporary compromise to be reversed in due course.

By the 1560s it has been estimated that four-fifths of the population of Vienna were Protestants and ten of its thirteen parishes lacked priests. On Sundays the so-called *Auslaufen* took place, when the Protestants streamed out of the city (where Catholicism was still officially imposed) to attend services at the seats of the Protestant nobility. Fiery Lutheran preachers castigated the pope as anti-Christ and Protestant noblemen cantered their horses round the aisles of St. Stephen's, slashing religious images with their swords. Desecration of the relief on the right-hand portal of the Minoritenkirche goes back to the period (1559-1620), when the church was in Protestant hands. By 1576 even the mayor was Protestant and three years later the citizens assembled outside the Hofburg to deliver their *Sturmpetition* for religious freedom, chanting in unison: "We want the gospel" This was, however, the high point of Protestantism in the city.

The counter-attack was begun by Ferdinand as early as 1551, when he summoned the Jesuits to Vienna. They soon established themselves in a former Carmelite cloister Am Hof. Its church was now dedicated to "The Nine Choirs of Angels", a picturesque concept arising from the elaborate system of "Celestial Harmonies" worked out by the mystical theologian, Dionysius the Pseudo-Areopagite (c. 500), whose speculative theology underwent a revival in the Counter-Reformation. The notion of the nine orders of angels mediating between god and man added a mystical element to Jesuit teaching that further distanced it from, and contrasted it with, Protestant doctrines of the time. Mysticism was generally regarded with suspicion by Protestant theologians from Luther onwards, not least because of its association with neo-Platonism, which in turn was regarded as closer to pagan gnosis (the "revealed knowledge" claimed by the heretical Gnostics) than to the Gospel's offer of salvation.

Likewise angels, though they are allowed as a colourful adornment to Protestant hymns, were avoided as a topic for theological debate, their substance, nature and roles being left deliberately vague. Jesuit psychology was in this respect superior to that of the Lutherans; completely absurd notions, such as angels and the like, or pre-filleted catechistic dogmas, were often more attractive to the masses than the kind of lonely religion that was tainted with the discouraging doctrine of predestination and insisted on the total depravity of man.

From 1549, the Jesuit stronghold Am Hof is also associated with the first German Jesuit, St. Peter Canisius (1521-97), a theologian to whom Ferdinand offered the bishopric of Vienna, but which the Jesuit General ordered Canisius to refuse. More than any other figure of his time he engaged the Protestant preachers intellectually, his most effective weapon being the catechisms that he devised, clarifying and codifying Catholic belief, as well as making it easy to instil through rote-learning. His *Catechismus Major* of 1554, with its 211 questions and answers, became standard and has gone through no fewer than 130 editions. "To him more than any other, " claims an authoritative source, "was due the remarkable success of the Counter-Reformation in the South German lands."

This success was initially built up through the Jesuit schools, the first being a gymnasium in Vienna's Dominican cloister opened in 1552 and already boasting 120 pupils by 1554. The triumphant progress of Jesuit teaching culminated in the merging of the University with the Jesuit

College under Ferdinand II in 1623. Indeed, under this Ferdinand, the Jesuits acquired a complete monopoly of higher education in Austria, with the exception of the faculties of Jurisprudence and Medicine, a monopoly that lasted until reforms made under Maria Theresia—who was herself educated by Jesuits.

The other great figure associated with the Counter-Reformation in Vienna was Melchior Cardinal Khlesl (1533-1630), the son of a Lutheran baker in the city who was lured to Catholicism by the Jesuits and who became (as is the way with converts) a fanatical defender of the Catholic faith. In 1579 he became chancellor of the Vienna University, where he purged the professorial college and instituted a test of religious orthodoxy as a condition of the conferment of degrees. As vicar-general for the Passau bishops he purged the Lower Austrian Church of Protestantism and this "political" experience stood him in good stead when he virtually took over the administration of government under Emperor Matthias. His *Klosteroffensive* (or campaign to found monasteries, 1603-38) involved calling no fewer than eleven orders to Vienna, some new to the city, others returning after expropriation by Protestants. As the aphoristic pun of the time has it, due to his efforts *Österreich* (Austria) became *Klösterreich* ("rich in cloisters".) Indeed, many of the splendid Baroque churches for the Catholic orders that can be seen today in Vienna were the later embellishment of religious settlement in this period. The incomers included Servites, the Brothers of Mercy (Barmherzigen Brüder—who still run a hospital in the Leopoldstadt offering free medical treatment), Dominicans, Capuchins (who preside over the famous Imperial Crypt), Barnabites (who took over the ancient Michaelerkirche) and the austere Carmelites.

HABSBURGS BETWEEN REFORMATION AND COUNTER-REFORMATION

If Ferdinand I died in 1564 in the deepest commitment to the Catholic faith and having initiated the Counter-Reformation in his lands, the situation with his immediate successors was more equivocal. Maximilian II (1564-76) is regarded by many historians as a crypto-Protestant. This was due not least to the influence of an early tutor, who turned out to be a closet Lutheran, and to his later close association with Protestant German rulers. Catholic propaganda has tended to paint him as a "two-faced" trimmer, whose affirmation of Catholicism was tactical and not sincere. He is indeed reported as saying: "I am neither Papist nor Protestant; I am a Christian"—which was enough (allegedly) for the Cardinal of Trento to lace the emperor's food with poison when he visited that city. After his death, a Catholic doctor hastened to discover a black substance in his dissected heart, which he explained as being the precise spot where the devil had made his lodging.

Maximilian seems to have steered a discreet course between conflicting religious lobbies, a policy largely founded on the previously mentioned Peace of Augsburg. On the one hand he neeeded to keep the Protestant nobility on side, for the sake of their revenues; on the other, he tried to mitigate the impact of more militant Protestantism, notably the Calvinism that quickly eclipsed Lutheranism in Hungary. He was a Renaissance patron of culture, remembered for appointing as his court painter the Milanese Giuseppe Arcimboldo (1527-93). Examples of the latter's astonishingly surrealistic "portraits," composed entirely from still-life objects, may be seen in the Kunsthistorisches Museum. A typical work of Arcimboldo is *The Cook*, a representation constructed entirely out of frying pans, roast meats and sausages. His supposed portrait of Maximilian himself is an allegory of *Fire* (1566), and is pieced together from (literally) flaming hair, weapons and Habsburg insignia. The intention is to symbolize the dynasty's military might.

As his father, Ferdinand, became increasingly sclerotic (in mind as well as body), Maximilian champed at the bit as the emperor-in-waiting. Splendid Viennese lodgings were built for him (now the Stallburg adjoining the Hofburg) with gracefully tiered Renaissance arcades. (The Stallburg acquired its later name when its ground floor began to be used for the horses of the Spanish Riding School, as it still is today.) On his accession, Maximilian built his magnificent Neugebäude ("New Building" or "New Work") in the imperial pheasantry out at Simmering, a palatial villa which showed some affinities with Giulio Romano`s Palazzo del Tè in Mantua. The Neugebäude was later to be destroyed by an Hungarian *kuruc* army in 1704, but ruined bits and pieces were later transferred to the park at Schönbrunn where they serve as a Romantic folly of "Roman ruins". As befitted a Renaissance monarch, Maximilian collected anything and everything, in which he was imitated by many later Habsburgs. He even imported parrots from the East and new plants such as lilacs, hyacinths and tulips; also the horse-chestnut, so called according to Gerard's

Herball of 1597, because the people of the East cured their horses of coughs with its fruits.

The Viennese were at first astounded by these discoveries, but then recovered themselves, pointing out sagely that such things were most likely plants originally from the Wienerwald. Nothing had prepared them, however, for the elephant that arrived in the city in 1552 in the entourage of the (then) Archduke Maximilian's Spanish bride. Its first appearance at the Kärntnertor caused panic among onlookers; then it was led with great solemnity through the city and finally placed on permanent display in the area which is now the Stadtpark. After enduring the stares of the curious for some time, it was honourably retired to the emperor's menagerie at Schloss Ebersdorf, where it expired in 1553. A chair was made for the mayor from its bones, which has ended up for some reason in the museum of Kremsmünster in Upper Austria. A number of houses and inns in Vienna have or had signs featuring elephants endowed with colours certainly not found in nature. They recall the great excitement aroused by this celebrated, if probably rather bemused and lonely visitor. In the underworld, a half million-Krone banknote of the pre-1926 currency was known as an "Elephant", but this may have had more to do with post-World War One hyper-inflation than with Maximilian's elephant.

Less exotic, but of more lasting value was Maximilian's passion for collecting books and manuscripts. The Hofbibliothek, now the Nationalbibliothek and one of the world's great libraries, had been founded by Ferdinand I in 1526. This brought together the extensive collections made by the Habsburgs since the fourteenth century, and its first librarian (appointed by Maximilian) was the Dutch humanist, Hugo Blotius (1533-1608). Despite its location in the damp and cramped quarters of the Minoritenkloster, Blotius was able to boast after a few years that his library was larger than that of the French kings and approaching the size of the Vatican's!

Blotius had pursued a career similar to Celtis, with a lengthy period of "learned vagrancy" that took him through Spain, France and Italy. He was a friend of the English spy and later ambassador to Venice, Sir Henry Wotton, who stayed with him on his visit to Vienna in 1590. (They were two of a kind, for Wotton was at that time "a wandering scholar, a bee sipping at academic flowers," as his biographer puts it.) The Dutchman was also splendidly arrogant, lobbying for his elevation to the nobility on the grounds that a person of no lesser rank than a cardinal presided over the Vatican library. Officially, written permission was required from the emperor for book or manuscript loans, but Blotius loaned them on his own initiative, with the result that his successor found that 203 priceless manuscripts were missing. "A library that is not open to anyone," asserted Blotius, "is like a candle which, even if it burns, does so as if hidden under a pot and fails to give light for anyone."

The Hofbibliothek was greatly enriched by Greek and Latin codices sold or bequeathed to it by leading humanist scholars of the day. It contains a number of uniquely valuable items like the *Tabula Peutingeriana*, a Roman itinerary probably of the fourth century, or the *Wiener Dioscorides*, a Byzantine copy of a first-century herbal. In 1565 the library acquired the books of the great cartographer and historian of Vienna, Wolfgang Lazius (1514-65). His *Vienna Austriae* (Basel, 1546), the first comprehensive history of the city, provided a solid basis for the archaeology, geography and historiography of Vienna, on which others were to build. Local patriotism was fashionable among the humanists (the classic is Philipp von Zesen's famous work in praise of Amsterdam) and in 1547 a schoolmaster at the Schotten gymnasium produced his "Lobspruch" (Eulogy) of Vienna in doggerel verse. He reels off statistics to show how prosperous the city was (180 cartloads of river crayfish were sold in season!)—but as Ilsa Barea remarks, "the dark side of the picture comes out not in these songs of praise with their whiff of primitive 'hand-outs', but in the documents of the first Turkish siege (1529), which tell of the stampede of the court, the great and the rich, of muddle, hunger and demoralising despair."

Still, city eulogies were a literary fashion. Twenty years after the Schotten schoolmaster's effort, the German shoemaker-poet Hans Sachs (1494-1576) produced a more graceful and well-turned *Lobspruch auf die Stadt Wien*. Interestingly, Sachs was a great protagonist of Lutheranism, although that does not deter him from praising the ornamentation of Vienna's many churches. He is, of course, the Hans Sachs immortalized in Wagner's opera *Die Meistersinger von Nürnberg* (1868).

Maximilian's successor, Rudolf II, was the only other Habsburg emperor (apart from Maximilian I) not to rule from Vienna (he moved the court to Prague). In his case, although he initially appeared a convinced Catholic, his intellectual adventures with necromancy, cabbalism, alchemy and the Philosopher's Stone led to suspicions of something even worse than Protestantism, namely agnosticism or even atheism. "After 1600," writes Robert Evans, the senior scholar of Rudolf, "he appears to have lived in a veritable terror of the Roman sacraments, and he certainly refused the last rites of the Catholic Church. 'Not only did His Majesty not confess,' wrote Cardinal Borghese sorrowfully and secretively, 'he did not even display any sign of contrition.'" He is said to have dismissed the struggle between Catholics and Protestants as "a monkish quarrel" (theologically speaking, rather an apt description) and to have defended the introduction of the controversial Gregorian calendar "not because it is Catholic, but because it functions better." All this was deplorable. Well before his death, his lack of counter-reformatory zeal and suspect tastes prompted Cardinal Khlesl to persuade the Archduke Matthias to unseat his brother, as he did in 1609. Three years later the melancholy and syphillitic recluse of the Hradčany died with debts of thirty-two million Gulden.

Rudolf is thus only peripherally a Viennese figure (though he too employed important scholars and artists inherited from Maximilian such as Arcimboldo and Blotius), but it is again the Viennese Grillparzer who has brought him into the mainstream of Viennese and Austrian culture with his drama entitled *Fraternal Strife amongst the Habsburgs*, first performed in 1848. The play is sympathetic to Rudolf, and a famous couplet has been taken to apostrophize the Habsburg ability to strive for unity even in the most unpromising circumstances, as Grillparzer believed that Rudolf tried to do:

I am the cord that holds the sheaf together,
Itself unfruitful, but vital while it binds.

As usual, there is an ambivalence. Did Grillparzer know Arcimboldo's incredible portrait of Rudolf as *Vertumnus* (the "God of the Seasons", but in this case an allegory of autumn), composed from a veritable riot of fruit, vegetables and ears of corn, the incarnation of fruitfulness and plenty? Is Arcimboldo's picture hugely ironic under the guise of dynastic eulogy? Grillparzer, a reclusive, self-doubting and often agonized individual, probably had some fellow-feeling for this most spiritually ambivalent of emperors. Rudolf's policy of religious appeasement, like Maximilian's, may well have staved off something worse for the time being. Certainly it bought time for the Catholic constituency to regroup and prepare its comeback. Ultimately a showdown was unavoidable, and that was to come with the famous Defenestration of Prague, followed by the Battle of the White Mountain.

Renaissance Sights in Vienna

Basteien: one reason why Renaissance buildings are relatively few and far between in Vienna is that huge amounts of money were sucked into construction of the *tracé italien*, the new Italian system of fortifications built round the city after the Turkish siege of 1529. Archduke Ferdinand ordered the sale of church treasures in Upper and Lower Austria to help finance a duplicate system of fortifications with curtain walls, chiefly erected by Leonard Colonna von Völs between 1541 and 1560. These massive fortifications were decisive in holding off the Turks during the siege of 1683. By the nineteenth century, the bastions had become the fashionable promenade for the Viennese, until they were demolished on the orders of Franz-Joseph in 1857 to make way for the Ringstrasse and its monumental Historicist palaces and institutions. Little remains of the bastions today, but an idea of their size may be gleaned from the remnant known as the Augustinerbastei, into which is incorporated the entrance area for the Albertina graphic collection.

Hofburg: in 1550 the Hofburg was still relatively small, consisting of the area beyond the Schweizertor, a small Hof closed on four sides. Matthias Corvinus had resided in the Schweizerhof (1485-90), and had the gardens to the south of it transformed into "hanging gardens" (praised by Bonfini), such as he had laid out for his Buda castle. Emblazoned on the Schweizertor itself (so-called because of the Swiss guards later employed by Maria Theresia) you will see the Habsburg coat of arms and a Latin inscription to Ferdinand I. It lists his titles and kingships and is followed by the date of completion MDLII (1552). The rollers for a drawbridge chain can still be seen.

Between 1534 and 1566, Ferdinand made many alterations in Renaissance style to the medieval Burg. The most remarkable Renaissance building in the Hofburg complex is the Stallburg, now the stabling for the Lipizzaners on the ground floor, but originally built between 1558 and 1569 as the lodgings for the future Emperor Maximilian II. The beautiful arcades of the upper storeys were blocked up for many years, and reopened only in 1956. The Amalienburg, closing the northern side of the Hofburg's main courtyard (known as "In der Burg") was built between 1575 and 1611 and retains Renaissance features. It acquired its name only from 1711, when it became the quarters of the widow of the prematurely deceased Josef I, Amalie Wilhelmine of Brunswick-Luneburg. She came from a German Protestant line that converted to Catholicism during the Counter-Reformation. Later she founded the Salesian cloister on the Rennweg and lived in retirement there until her death in 1742.

Kirche zu den neun Chören der Engel (Kirche am Hof): the present structure is Baroque, but the picturesque name ("Church of the Nine Choirs of Angels") betrays the fact that it was for a while the first Jesuit church in Vienna. The order took it over from the Carmelites in 1568, together with the attached convent. The first Jesuit Provincial Superior was Petrus Canisius, the well-known theologian and writer of catechisms, who often preached here. The Kirche am Hof lies on the site of the early Babenberg court, established in 1156 (hence the name "Am Hof"). Its Baroque façade (1662) is by Carlo Antonio Carlone. From its "benediction loggia" (modelled on those of the patriarchal basilicas of Rome) a herald announced Franz II's abdication as Holy Roman Emperor in 1806, the end of nearly 900 years of tradition. Franz abdicated under pressure from Napoleon, who took the view that there was only room for one emperor in Europe; anyway the empire was largely symbolic by then, neither Holy, Roman nor Imperial, as Voltaire acidly observed.

Stephansdom: the additions to the Stephansdom that fall into the "Renaissance" period are still Late Gothic. The most celebrated of them is the superb "People's Pulpit", so-called because it was set back in the body of the church among the laity, and now doubtfully attributed to Anton Pilgram. It is an astoundingly vivid work whose four side-panels show the Fathers of the Church represented as the Four Humours. Definitely attributed to Pilgram is the vividly sculpted self-portrait (inscribed "1513") under the former organ loft on the north wall of the cathedral. Other Renaissance elements include the lantern capping the unfinished North Tower (Adlerturm), the latter housing the famous bell of St. Stephen's known as "Die Pummerin". On the west wall is an epitaph to Konrad Celtis, the humanist Professor of Rhetoric at Vienna University and nearby is the sarcophagus of his successor, Johannes Cuspinian.

Salvatorkapelle (Salvatorgasse 5): the wonderful Renaissance portal to this chapel adjoining the Altes Rathaus dates to circa 1520. Its magnificence for such a modest building may seem puzzling, but the reason is that the previous church had become a centre for passive resistance to the authorities through the cult of the Haimonen. In 1308 the brothers of this leading burgher family led an unsuccessful revolt against the Habsburg Duke Friedrich "the Handsome", who thereupon confiscated their properties around what became the Altes Rathaus from 1333, and which included a Marian Chapel founded in 1296. Unfortunately, the Viennese continued to revere the Haimonen family and the chapel became the focus of a cult that even honoured Haimonen Otto as a saint ("St. Ottenhaim"). This scandalous situation was ended by a Papal Bull in 1515 outlawing the Ottenhaim cult as heretical and the chapel was rededicated to the "The Saviour".

The importance of this break with an heretical tradition was underlined by the erection of the ornate Renaissance portal (thought to be by a Lombardy master) with its traditional Christian imagery of the Virgin and Christ. However, in modern times the chapel has reverted to its subversive tendencies, having been the place of worship for Vienna's "Old Catholics" since 1871. Old Catholics rejected the declaration of Papal Infallibility promulgated by "Pio Nono" (Pius IX) following the First Vatican Council of 1869-70. The resulting interdict placed on them by the Cardinal Archbishop of Vienna was only lifted by the ecumenically minded Cardinal König in 1969; in 1971, on the hundredth anniversary of the schism, he participated at Mass here as a gesture of reconciliation.

Fine Arts: some of the remarkable "surrealist" (actually mannerist) pictures of Giuseppe Arcimboldo, which create portraits from montages of still life objects, may be seen in the Kunsthistorisches Museum. A very remarkable portrait of Cardinal Khlesl (or Klesl, 1553-1630) by the mannerist painter of the Bolognese school, Annibale Carracci, may be seen in the Erzbischöfliches Dom-und Diözesanmuseum (Stephansplatz 6). It is a compelling portrait of a cunning and ruthless cleric, who devoted his life to manipulative politics and the extirpation of "heresy".

Chapter Sixteen

BAROQUE VIENNA

"The number of foreigners in the city is so great that one feels oneself simultaneously foreigner and native citizen..."

Baron de Montesquieu (1728)

On 23 May 1618, leading members of the Bohemian Protestant nobility met in the Prague Hradčin with the local representatives of the newly elected Habsburg king of their country, Ferdinand II. The representatives (described as "Statthalter" or governors) were accused of violating the Letter of Majesty that Rudolf II had issued in 1609, which guaranteed freedom of religion. The immediate dispute, however, concerned Ferdinand's attempts to stop Protestants building chapels on land claimed by Catholics. The meeting turned into a trial of the governors, who were found to be in breach of the Letter of Majesty, summarily condemned and finally thrown out of the Hradčin windows, together with their secretary.

This was the celebrated "defenestration of Prague", though it was not as dramatic as it was subsequently painted, since the victims were ejected from the windows on the side with a shorter drop (only fifty feet!), and anyway landed unharmed on a heap of manure. Catholic propagandists hastened to explain that angels had intervened to break their fall, and the secretary (Philip Fabricius) was knighted by Ferdinand with the absurd title "Philip von Hohenfall" (Philip of Highfall.) Still, the incident was an unheard of degradation of the king-emperor's personal representatives, and punitive military action followed.

The Battle of the White Mountain (Bilá Hora, just outside Prague) of 8 November 1620 resulted in the resounding defeat of the Protestant Bohemian army by the Catholic League. It was the first great clash in the religious and political struggle known as the Thirty Years War, which drew in virtually all the countries of Central Europe and Scandinavia, and was only brought to an end by the Peace of Westphalia in 1648. But the immediate effect of the battle was the consolidation of Catholic Habsburg

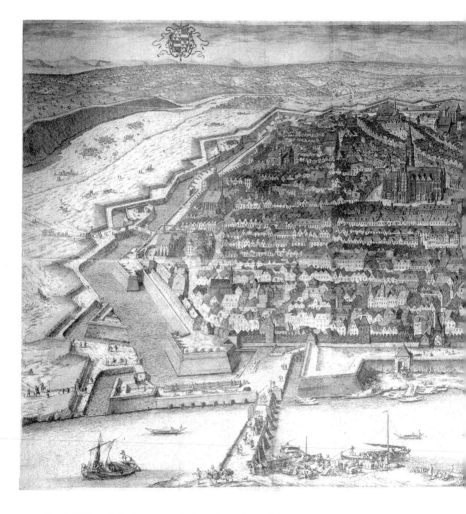

Jacob Hofnaegel: Birdseye view of Vienna from the north (copper etching, 1640). This is the last depiction of the Gothic city with its Renaissance fortifications on the Italian model. After the defeat of the second and final attempt by the Turks to take Vienna in 1683, a Baroque building boom ensued.

power in Central Europe and the expropriation of Protestant Bohemian nobles, to be replaced by German-Austrian appointees of the emperor. The war dragged on, however, and Swedish armies even threatened Vienna briefly in 1643 and again in 1645. Meanwhile, the Catholic zealot Ferdinand forced all Viennese citizens in 1625 to profess themselves Catholic or emigrate. As is the way with such draconian measures, the result was superficially effective but in the longer term disastrous, since those with strong principles left and those with elastic ones stayed. From the religious trimmers of the seventeenth century to the lickspittle opportunism of a twentieth-century Dr. Waldheim, the accusation of time-serving accommodation to their superiors has dogged the Viennese, though not always fairly. The cabaret artist Rudolf Weyr summed up this corrosive view of the city and its citizens in the 1930s:

> I'm two thousand years Viennese,
> And I always say "yes", you see,
> Ever loyal and anxious to please
> Whichever the powers that be.

Just as France's loss of Huguenots after the Revocation of the Edict of Nantes (1685) was another country's gain (notably England's), so the loss of Vienna's entrepreneurial Protestant burghers was Germany's gain and arguably a drag on the city's future development. As elsewhere, the Protestants tended to be the craftsmen, technicians and businessmen. Administratively, the centuries' long power struggle between the burghers on the city council and the dynasty was now decided in favour of the rulers. Vienna became the Residenzstadt of an imperial line whose supply needs and bureaucratic apparatus offered the bulk of available employment opportunities. The result, as historian Felix Czeike has observed, was that "the smallest job at court seemed more attractive than a high office in the city council."

By 1629 Ferdinand III was confident enough to issue his Edict of Restitution, restoring to the Catholic Church all properties removed from it by Protestants since 1552. In 1632, as already noted, the Jesuits finally gained complete control of both higher and lower education. Protestantism was all but vanquished in the Austrian and Bohemian (but not the Hungarian) part of the empire. On the other hand, another threat was growing by the day, namely the relentless advance of the Ottoman Turks. "For nearly three centuries," writes a French historian, "the Austrian identified himself as the enemy of the Protestants and the Turks; without those two foes, one is tempted to say he would not have existed." This, too, is an exaggeration, but it captures something of the spirit of the times.

LEOPOLD I: "THE BAROQUE EMPEROR"

If the three Ferdinands may be said to have laid the groundwork and built the infrastructure of the Counter-Reformation in Austria, Leopold I was its apotheosis. Educated by Jesuits, the emperor was a bizarre mixture of picayune obsessions and wasteful extravagance. Brought up in the claustrophobic mental and religious environment of the Spanish Habsburg court, Leopold imported an unpopular Spanish retinue to Vienna and insisted on the tiniest details of Spanish court ceremonial. Evliyâ Çelebi, the renowned Turkish traveller and spy, described the emperor's unprepossessing appearance in 1665 as follows:

> I doubt if the Lord God ever created a man less endowed with Allah's gifts; he has a bottle-shaped head pointed at the top like the glove of a dervish and thick black eyebrows which are too far apart. His ears are like baby potatoes and he has a red nose like an unripe berry which is the size of an aubergine from the Morea. In his broad nostrils, into which three fingers could be stuck with ease, hangs hair like a beard. His lips are like a camel, and when he talks, the spit flows from his mouth. When this happens dazzlingly beautiful pages rush to him with red handkerchiefs. He is always combing his hair and plays all the time with his comb. His fingers resemble cucumbers.

One does wonder if Çelebi had been looking at the Arcimboldos in the imperial collection, but in truth the portraits of Leopold show that the Turk was hardly exaggerating.

If Matthias had had his Khlesl, Leopold had his Kollonitsch, Bishop of Wiener Neustadt, sometime Primate of Hungary and latterly also a cardinal. While Kollonitsch displayed selfless heroism during the terrible plague of 1679 and the Turkish siege of Vienna four years later, he was implacably hostile to Jews and Protestants. In Hungary, under his aegis, the latter were imprisoned, tortured and in 1675 forty-two of their pastors were even sent to the Neapolitan galleys. His probably apocryphal remark in regard to the Hungarians is certainly not belied by his actions: "First I will make them beggars, then I will make them Catholic and finally I will make them Germans."

It was, however, against the Viennese Jews that Kollonitsch acted most notoriously. Jews had gradually returned to the city and were once again becoming a mainstay of imperial finance. Indeed, the imperial banker was Samuel Oppenheimer, who was also factor to the court and a military supplier for the army. However, he needed to become ever more ingenious to accommodate Leopold's mounting indebtedness, while at the same time his influence and apparent wealth aroused the usual hatred among Christians. In 1700 rioters (perhaps officially inspired) attacked his house on the Bauernmarkt and conveniently burned his lists of debtors. His death provoked the final collapse of his business empire and drove the state into temporary bankruptcy. His successor as Hoffaktor, Samson Wertheimer, was more successful and died extremely rich, having also been a great benefactor of the Jewish community.

That community had been (re)settled in the area known as the Unterer Werd on the Danube flood plain by Ferdinand II in 1625. Leopold himself does not appear to have been especially ill-disposed towards Jews, but his young Spanish wife (she was actually his niece and addressed him as "Uncle" throughout the marriage) was educated in the ferocious bigotry then perceived as Catholic piety. Kollonitsch, too, was determined to see the back of the Jews. Between them they persuaded Leopold to issue a decree in February 1670 requiring all Jews to leave their settlement by Corpus Christi (the second Thursday after Whitsun). The deadline was, of course, significant: the Corpus Christi procession through the city represented "the ecstatic finale of dramatised religiosity", as one writer puts it.

When all the Jews had gone, Kollonitsch preached a celebratory sermon in the Carmelite Church on what seemed to him the apt theme of Hagar's expulsion from the house of Abraham, demonstrating thereby that zealotry is heroically impervious to irony. The Vienna Council then auctioned off Jewish properties to pay outstanding debts and the taxes which there were no longer any Jews to pay. Even before the Jews had left, their synagogue was appropriated and the Leopoldskirche was subsequently built on its site. A year later the whole area of the Unterer Werd (not all of which had been settled by Jews) was renamed the "Leopoldstadt". In the nineteenth century this was the Jewish quarter (but no longer a ghetto like the medieval one on Judenplatz), and home to thousands of immigrant Orthodox Jews from the eastern reaches of the Empire and Russia. It remained so until the Nazi pogroms began in 1938, under which those Jews who did not succeed in fleeing to the West were deported to the concentration camps. The Nazis planned, but never built, a huge forum here for their mass rallies. The Leopoldstadt became quite fashionable after the 1670 expulsion, favoured by the nobility for their summer palaces. One such who built a pleasant residence here was Sigismund Count Kollonitsch, Archbishop of Vienna and the nephew of the man who had driven out the inconvenient Jewish neighbours...

The expulsion of the Jews, like the expulsion of the Protestants, proved to be a spectacular own goal. The auction of expropriated houses failed to bring the sums anticipated, and the 10,000 Gulden of annual residence tax levied on the Jewish community was sorely missed. These self-inflicted losses were bad enough, but without the Jews much of the economic activity of the city ceased and credit dried up. The situation became so critical that the Hofkammer (responsible for imperial finances) eventually had to force through the humiliating concession that certain specified Jews (meaning wealthy ones) should be allowed back to Vienna.

Although on a much smaller scale, what happened in the late seventeenth century was similar to what Hugo Bettauer prophesied would happen in the 1920s, if all those with Jewish blood were forced to leave Vienna. With prophetic insight, his satirical novel *The City without Jews: A Novel of the Day after Tomorrow* (1922) posits a situation where all the Jews have left Vienna. Economic stagnation sets in and the remaining professional, academic and artistic elite of gentiles also leaves, since business has ground to a halt and the city can no longer afford them. The remaining inhabitants wander around dressed in Loden and dirndls, greeting each other with *Heil*; cultural life slowly peters out. Eventually the situation is so dire—and the city so boring—that it is decided to call the Jews back.

Bettauer's book was the last straw for Nazi apologists, and also the Christian right wing, who further objected to the author/journalist's provocative espousal of causes such as feminism, abortion and more openness about sexual matters (for a while he published an erotic magazine). Following a hate campaign in the press, a Nazi assassinated the writer in the editorial offices of the *Neue Freie Presse*, where he worked. Most newspapers seemed to feel vindicated by this turn of events and the trial of his assassin reads more like a trial of Bettauer. His killer, defended by a Nazi lawyer, successfully pleaded that he had acted to defend young people from being corrupted by Bettauer's ideas and opinions. The defendant was let off with a light prison sentence and in 1938 released from prison by the Nazis. Perhaps Thomas Bernhard had this incident in mind when a character in his play *Heldenplatz* notoriously remarks: "In Austria you must either be Catholic or a Nazi. Nothing else is allowed, anything else will be destroyed."

ABRAHAM A SANCTA CLARA: PLAGUE, PROTESTANTS, JEWS AND TURKS

Hardly had the dust settled after the Jews were banished in 1670 than the menace of the insurgent Turkish armies became acute. At this point an apocalyptic Augustinian preacher appears on the scene, who is rightly regarded as one of Vienna's greatest literary figures, even if much of the content of his rhetorical *tours de force* could be taken as incitements to hatred. His sermons did nevertheless castigate the Viennese as mercilessly as they castigated the populist preacher's trinity of evil: Moslems, Protestants and Jews, particularly the last-named.

He was a German, born Johann Ulrich Megerle, but his *nom de guerre* was Abraham a Sancta Clara, and he has left us coruscating denunciations of the Viennese, whom he chastized for their laziness, libidinousness and general Phaeacianism in his famous diatribe *Take Heed, Vienna!* In 1679 he was able to exploit the climate of fear caused by the horrifying bubonic plague that was cutting down the population like ripened wheat. His message was simple and effective: "God has sent you the plague because of your sins; take heed, Vienna, and repent!"

Playing upon the street names of Vienna, Sancta Clara conjured a picture of a vengeful reckoning with the life of sin from which no citizen was safe: "In the street of the Lords, Death is the master; in Singer Street, Death has sung Requiems for many; on the Charcoal Market [Kohlmarkt], Death has ensured that only the black clothes of mourning are worn; and on the Graben, Death has done nothing but dig graves." One might think there would be a difficulty about blaming the Jews for the plague, since they were now almost entirely absent. It was not a difficulty for Sancta

Clara, however; it was common knowledge, he said, that the pestilence was caused by the "evil enemy, the Jews, the gravediggers and also by witches". Furthermore, Jews were "envious, depraved, dishonest and sinful", not to mention "godless, irredeemable and without conscience". Although its value as a generalization about Jews may be doubted, as a characterization of the Christian bigot this description could hardly be bettered.

Abraham was indeed merely the most gifted in a long line of anti-semitic Viennese preachers active in the city up to the Second World War. In the late nineteenth and early twentieth centuries, priests such as Father Abel S. J. and Josef Deckert sang an ecclesiastical descant to the political anti-semitism of Karl Lueger and the Christian Social Party with their theologically based racism. Deckert even ciculated a flyer promoting the ancient defamation of Jewish "blood sacrifice" of Christian babies (but was, however, convicted of forgery for his pains). Until quite recently there was still a Pfarrer-Deckert-Platz in front of his former church in Währing (renamed in the 1980s following a campaign by the liberal Catholic journal, *Kirche Intern*); also a Pater-Abel-Platz, that usurped the name of Friedrich-Engels-Platz in 1934, but was restored to Engels after the war. In such small details the marches and countermarches of Vienna's own *Kulturkampf* are manifest...

Savonarola-like, Abraham castigated the vices of the rich just as harshly as he lashed the sinfulness of the poor. He was not afraid to lecture the court on its luxury, or to attack the prevalent falsehood of the age—the way in which everything from dress, hair, make-up and language, to silverware, gold-plate and marble consisted all too often of mere façades concealing dross. All this was delivered in vivid Viennese and was accompanied by images and parables drawn from folk literature (including his reference to the bagpiper Augustin, later emblematic of the Viennese as survivor and *Lebenskünstler*—see p.61). His penitential rant to stir the Viennese against the Turkish menace, *Arise, arise, you Christians!* was heavily plagiarized by Schiller for the sermon of the Capuchin monk in his play *Wallenstein's Camp*. His major work (Abraham was, after all, a Benedictine-trained scholar), a four-volume life of Judas (*Judas the Arch-Rogue*), mingled lively anecdote, satire and moralistic observations.

Abraham is Vienna's outstanding literary protagonist of the Baroque, at least from the point of view of the richness and vitality of his language.

His content, however, might be said to be "anti-Baroque", an attack on its tendency to substitute appearance and spectacle for the unvarnished actuality. He was a realist who incorporated the rawness of Viennese life into his poetry and memorably apostrophized the teeming humanity of the plague-stricken city, or the idiosyncratic (and sometimes threatening) Viennese environment. His description of Vienna in the plague year played on the street names to dramatize the horror and fury of the epidemic:

> Many believed this was the general epilogue and end of the world. No street was spared death's visitation. In the Street of the Lords [*Herrengasse*], death was the lord of all.... In the *Singerstrasse* death sung many a requiem... in the *Naglergasse* [Nailmakers' Street] death sharpened his arrows, in the Himmelpfortgasse [Gate of Heaven Street] death despatched many through the gates into heaven...

It is scarcely possible to imagine the suffering of those trapped in Vienna during the plague year, and it is understandable that reactions to it were uncomprehending and irrational. Abraham may have provided a spiritual rationale for this terrible visitation, but some religious orders and Prince Eusebius Schwarzenberg, to their credit, provided much-needed practical support for the people when most of the well-to-do (and of course the emperor) had fled. The distinguished Walloon physician, Paul Sorbait, "General Inquisitor" of matters concerning plague, drew up a *Pestordnung* of sanitary measures. But the popular prophylactics against infection ranged from the eminently sensible, such as isolation of victims, to the bizarre and superstitious. The English traveller, Edward Brown, reported seeing a man drinking blood from a newly decapitated head in the hope of immunization, while wash and drink cures of human urine were also supposed to be worth a try. Since the movement of air was thought to disperse the infection, church bells were constantly rung and the many songbirds that had so impressed Bonfini were released from their cages and encouraged to fly around the rooms. Stinking billy-goats were also kept in dwellings in the belief that the smell would drive out the disease, although it more likely drove out the inhabitants. None of this was noticeably effective or prevented the death toll from rising eventually to around 75,000.

The plague generated its own iconology in the city. On the Graben a wooden *Pestsäule* (also known as a "Trinity Column") was erected as early as 1679, while the city was still in the grip of the epidemic, and inaugurated with a fire and brimstone sermon by Abraham a Sancta Clara. The magnificent stone column we see today was a later construction, completed in 1693 and designed by Ludovico Burnacini and Johann Bernhard Fischer von Erlach. Its doctrinal motifs are based on the concept of the Trinity, but also on the three pillars of Habsburg *Hausmacht* (dynastic power): Bohemia, Hungary and the Austrian Crown Lands are represented by their three coats of arms. In harmonization with the religious concept, Austria corresponds to the Father, Hungary to the son and Bohemia to the Holy Ghost. On the south side is a vivid relief by Paul Strudel showing Emperor Leopold kneeling in prayer for the deliverance of the city from the plague.

The whole ensemble repays closer scrutiny as a remarkable example of Baroque propagandist art, in this case worked out by the Leopold's Jesuit confessor, Franciscus Menegatti. Like other such monuments, it adroitly combines the traditional claims of *imperium* with *sacerdotium*, the notion of the dynasty's sacred mission to rule and the twin foundations of its power in constitutional legitimacy and religious sanction. The column was an intellectual construct, but for popular consumption the Baroque promoted the plague saints, especially St. Sebastian and St. Rochus. They were ubiquitous in the Habsburg territories as they were in Vienna—for example, both of them (sculpted by Johann Jakob Pock) are featured on the high altar of the Stephansdom. After the last plague epidemic of 1713, the new Karlskirche was dedicated to a man revered as the hero of the Milan plague, St. Charles Borromeo.

THE SIEGE OF VIENNA (1683)
The horrors of the plague had barely faded when Vienna faced the greatest test of its history with the Turkish siege of 1683. Vienna was vulnerable both geopolitically and because of the partial decay of its fortifications. The geopolitical element was due to the menace of Louis XIV, then at the height of his power, and requiring constant confrontation or negotiation in the west. This drained both men and money from the east and distracted the indecisive Leopold. On the other hand, the emperor's disastrous policy towards Hungary had weakened his hand on the eastern front, particularly his decision to concede to the Turks at the Peace of Vasvár almost all the Hungarian territory an imperial army under Montecuccoli

had just won from the Turks in a brilliant victory at Szentgotthárd in 1664. This led directly to the Zrínyi conspiracy of 1670 and contributed to the general alienation of the Hungarian elite, notwithstanding that a part of it, led by the Palatine Eszterházy, remained abidingly loyal to the Habsburgs.

But when the Turkish army approached Vienna on 14 July 1683, it consisted of a potentially formidable alliance between Ottoman commanders and the Crimean Khan, the Princes of Wallachia, Moldavia and Transylvania (as Turkish vassals) and the troops of Imre Thököly, the leader of the Magyar dissidents known as *kuruc*, a word possibly derived from Turkish *khurudsch*, meaning freebooter. As for the city's physical vulnerability, that had been detailed in a disturbing military report of 1674, which revealed the impressive-seeming defences of the *tracé italien* to be in urgent need of repair. No sooner was one part repaired than another fell apart, a situation complicated by the illegal erection of dwellings on the glacis.

The schoolboy version of the siege of Vienna paints it as the idealistic defence of Christendom against the forces of Allah, indeed of civilization against its destroyer. At least the first part of this is nonsense. Kara Mustafa embarked on his great adventure after listening to French agents at the Porte, among them Jesuits and Capuchin friars. There is a considerable irony in this, as Leopold's confessor and chief advisor was Marco d'Aviano, himself a Capuchin. Mustafa's strategy for the attack on Vienna itself is thought to have been planned by French and Italian experts in the pay of the sultan. Louis XIV, the "Sun King" of western civilization, calculated that the Turks would be useful in weakening his Habsburg rivals. Even the leaders of the Christian armies relieving Vienna—Charles of Lorraine, Herman Margrave of Baden and King John Sobieski of Poland—had differing agendas and were swift to revert to their own interests when the opportunity presented itself. Indeed, John Sobieski, who cost the alliance 500,000 Gulden, for which he undertook to attend with an army of 18,000 men, had hitherto been in the pay of the French, and one writer, Thomas Chorherr, suggests he might have been open to offers from the opposition if the price was right! He furthermore threatened to return to Poland in a huff unless he was made titular commander-in-chief over the imperial armies. Perhaps the most disinterested soldier among them, Prince Eugene of Savoy, was still in a subordinate position. Even he had only joined the Habsburg cause because Louis XIV had refused him a commission. Leopold himself was chiefly concerned with saving his own skin. On 7 July he travelled under cover of darkness to Linz, then on to Passau. En route he was jeered, and even spat at by the peasants, as his entourage rumbled through their villages.

On the other hand, Pope Innocent XI certainly took the Turkish threat seriously and financed the imperial army to the tune of one and half a million Gulden. Spain, Portugal, Tuscany and Genoa followed suit. Bavaria, Saxony, Brandenburg, Hanover and Württemberg supplied troops and there were Croats, Flemings, Walloons, Hungarians, Italians, Bohemians and even French exiles among the "Austrian" army. Altogether the Christians mustered around 74,000 men against a Turkish army of some 140,000.

The commander of the Viennese garrison, Count Ernst Rüdiger von Starhemberg, had only 11,500 regular troops at his disposal, together with citizen volunteers of uncertain reliability. But he was supported by the tough Bishop Kollonitsch, who had stayed to put backbone into the citizens, and a highly effective Czech military expert, Count Kaplíř. The Walloon Paul Sorbait, who had shown such conspicuous courage in the plague year, assisted in dealing with casualties. The mayor was the energetic Andreas von Liebenberg, who had distinguished himself during the plague epidemic, but whose earlier career in the city administration had been overshadowed by accusations that he had embezzled money raised for the city's orphans. Now he busied himself overseeing the civilian militia, and organizing the digging of trenches and the provisioning of the defenders. Like many others in the city, he eventually fell sick and died just as the rescue of the city was under way. His monument stands opposite the university on the Ringstrasse.

Vienna came close to falling. Every day Starhemberg mounted the spiral steps of the Stephansdom's south tower to survey (from the still existing "Starhemberg seat") the sea of white tents surrounding much of the city. On 4 September the Turks made a breach in the walls at the Burgbastei (near the Albertina today) and it seemed all was lost. But the defenders hung on and that very evening rockets soared into the night sky over the Kahlenberg announcing the arrival of the outriders of the imperial army. Mustafa's army was in any case on the verge of disintegration after two months with none of the promised booty for the soldiers. The Tatar irregulars had laid such waste to the surrounding countryside that it was becoming difficult to feed the rest of the army. Janissaries more than once refused orders to storm the seemingly well-manned ramparts. Thököly's troops began deserting to the imperial side. Senior officers were corrupt and more interested in collecting nubile girls to be traded as slaves than applying themselves to the siege.

On 12 September the imperial troops streamed down from the heights of the Wienerwald and put the Turkish army to flight. Sobieski appropriated Kara Mustafa's treasury (which the Turkish commander had rashly brought along, together with a harem and his personal musicians) while the Polish troops ran amok in the city. The citizens responded by stealing the horses of the Polish cavalry and even shooting at them, until Starhemberg managed to restore order. On the 14th, the emperor arrived for a *Te Deum* in the Stephansdom in a state of wounded pride, since Sobieski had entered the city in triumph before his paymaster arrived to share the glory. Then he rode out to Schwechat for a frosty meeting with the Polish king, which lasted just long enough for Leopold to deliver the lukewarmest speech of gratitude that could be managed without downright discourtesy. "I am, pleased, Sire, to have rendered you this small service," said Sobieski sardonically—and evidently forgetting the contribution of a great many others.

The Baroque Building Boom

The defeat of Kara Mustafa's besieging army turned the tide in Central Europe and over the next few years the Turkish armies were steadily pushed south and east. Buda was liberated in 1686. By 1697 armies under the command of Prince Eugene of Savoy had sealed their victories at the battle of Zenta in northern Serbia, though at one point even Belgrade had briefly been taken. Hungary and the Crown Lands were now finally free of the Ottoman threat and the work of reconstruction could begin.

The resulting economic and building boom marked Vienna as decisively and lastingly as that of the Ringstrassen era in the second half of the nineteenth century. The nobility, with increasing reserves of cash to spend as their estates returned to profitable management, built winter palaces in the city and summer palaces in the outskirts (Vorstadt). ("Building is a diabolical business," observed Prince Schönborn in one of his letters. "Once one has started, it's impossible to stop.") It has been suggested also that the nobility invested in real estate as a form of tax avoidance to evade imperial levies on their cash revenues. The Church, triumphant over both the Protestant heretics and the Turkish infidel, raised new temples with exuberant Jesuit-influenced decoration. Even before the siege, the dynasty itself had invested in a huge new wing of the Hofburg designed by an Italian (Philiberto Lucchese) and built by the Swiss Carlone dynasty of builder-architects. Its replacement (1680) was built by yet another Italian, Giovanni Pietro Tencala.

The omnipresence of Italian masters—in architecture, in sculpture, in the fine arts and of course in music—was the leitmotif of Viennese culture in the early and high Baroque era. Most of their great buildings are still standing. In the Rossau area of the 9th district may be found the Liechtensteins' grandiloquent summer palace designed by Domenico Martinelli. Martinelli also built the family's so-called "Primogenture House", a winter palace on the Minoritenplatz. The Viennese called the latter a "job creation scheme for artists and craftsmen", so many were involved in its construction. It was indeed "state of the art" when built, incorporating retractable floors, movable walls and even lifts to the four floors (presumably hauled by muscular servants). Not far away on the edge of the Freyung the huge Palais Harrach was another work by Martinelli, while the Palais Lobkowitz looking onto the northern Albertinaplatz was originally built by Tencala, altered later by Fischer von Erlach.

Native Austrian masters of Baroque architecture had all studied in Italy and came on stream in the middle and later period of the Baroque. The three greatest of these, Fischer von Erlach father and son and Hildebrandt, built the finest Baroque palaces of Vienna and one Baroque church (the Karlskirche) which is, by common consent, the most beautiful in Central Europe. These three architects have distinctive aesthetic profiles, the Fischer von Erlachs tending towards the monumental, while Hildebrandt's work is distinguished by its elegance and grace (notably the Palais Kinsky on the Freyung.) The rivalry between the two architects was intense, as indeed it was between their patrons. One fruitful result of such rivalry for grand "representation" is the juxtaposition in the 4th District of Schwarzenberg's palace, a work by Fischer von Erlach Junior, with Hildebrandt's stunning Belvedere palace, built for Prince Eugene of Savoy.

These great palaces were, of course, a statement of net worth, the Trump Towers of their day. Their representative function was deliberately emphasised with impressive façades, symbolic sculpture, and features such as ceremonial staircases (the "double-return" one in Palais Harrach and the ingeniously realized stairs in the Palais Kinsky are notable examples). Frescoes on internal ceilings glorified the life and deeds of the palace owner. The apotheosis of this could be seen in the Belvedere, where even the park displayed an elaborate symbolism through sculpture, Apollo (as patron of the arts) dominating the western area, Hercules (the victorious fighter) the eastern. The Belvedere garden as a whole offered a symbolic hierarchy in three divisions, with dramatic weather phenomena (or "nature") at the lower end, reflections of the owner as princely paragon in the middle, and the domain of the gods at the upper end.

The "rage for secular building" (*Bauwut*) continued into the eighteenth century; by the death of Charles VI in 1740, there were no fewer than 400 "summer palaces" of varying pretension around the old city, not to mention the numerous "winter palaces" within it. At the same time, there was money for the Catholic Church to celebrate its now unchallenged position as the custodian of the true faith. Symbolically important was the Peterskirche, just to the north of the Graben and supposedly standing on the site of the earliest (fourth-century) church of Vienna. (The nineteenth century romanticized this claim with a relief on the external eastern wall, which shows Charlemagne (re-)founding the church in 792, while the Baroque romanticized it with life-size statues of the Emperors Constantine and Charlemagne on the high altar. The figure of Constantine, the promulgator of Christianity as a state religion, is a metaphor for the Habsburg ruler as protector of the Church. An earlier Jesuit drama (1659) by Nikolaus Avancini, staged with amazing extravagance, had already made the identification of Leopold with Constantine.) The thirteenth-century Gothic Church of St. Peter had become so ruinous that the previously mentioned humanist historian of Vienna, Wolfgang Lazius, had borne the costs of restoration (1555-57) himself. Now it was again decaying and the emperor took a personal interest in the project of a new church to be built in memory of deliverance from the plague of 1679. He was present when the foundation stone was laid in 1702, although unfortunately a building trench collapsed, seriously injuring members of his retinue. Hildebrandt took over the project in 1703, and his elegant solution, whereby the building dovetails comfortably with the confined urban space allowed it, determines the remarkable aesthetic impact of the church.

Perhaps the most impressive and complex expression of imperial aspiration allied to Catholic orthodoxy may be seen in the Karlskirche,
begun by Johann Bernhard Fischer von Erlach in 1716, but not completed
by his son, Josef Emanuel, until 1739. Its name happily combines that of
St. Carlo Borromeo, the plague saint to whom it is dedicated, and that of
Charles VI, who commissioned it in thanksgiving for the end of the last
great plague epidemic in 1713. Its most striking features are the two
pseudo-antique columns at the front, based on those erected in Rome to
commemorate the victories of Trajan and Marcus Aurelius, two Roman
heroes specifically associated with Vienna (Vindobona, see p.95).

The friezes on the columns of the Karlskirche celebrate the life and
works of Carlo Borromeo, famous for relieving the plague victims in the
Milan epidemic of 1576. However, the columns embody a larger symbolism of imperial power, worked out in detail by the court historiographer,
Gustav Heraeus and the philosopher Leibniz. As emblems of the "Pillars
of Hercules" at the western end of the Mediterranean, they allude to
Charles VI's enduring but thwarted claim to Spain, lost to the dynasty
when the Spanish Habsburg line died out in 1700 (an event that sparked
the War of the Spanish Succession in which Prince Eugene of Savoy fought
alongside the English Duke of Marlborough). More complicatedly, the
columns are supposed to recall the bronze pillars that stood before
Solomon's temple in Jerusalem, known as "Jachin" (signifying permanence)
and "Boaz" (signifying strength), an allusion that dovetails with Karl VI's
motto of *constantia et fortitudine*. The exact interpretations of Jachin and
Boaz are disputed (some have suggested they symbolized "Peace" and
"War"), but it is clear that Fischer von Erlach's archaising symbolism is intended to stress the ancient roots of Habsburg legitimacy by means of bib-
lical reference (the solomonic columns have also been interpreted as
"David and Solomon")—even as the court historians and Baroque scholars continued to busy themselves with spectacular genealogies for the
dynasty that reached back into the mists of time.

The "Culture of the Senses" and the "Culture of the Word"

Although the Karlskirche is an extreme case of *saxa loquuntur* (symbolically
eloquent architecture) the Baroque style in general was concerned with
symbolic display and ideological or theological statements. It was the uni-

fying aesthetic of the Habsburg dynasty in its polyglot empire. As the historian Heinrich Benedikt has remarked, "the Baroque solved the problem of nationality before it even existed; it bestowed the unity of its mode of expression on a landscape that was geographically so very disparate, with its enormous variety of peoples." It serves therefore as the aesthetic component of Grillparzer's previously quoted image of the dynasty that binds the wheatsheaf together, "the band that holds." In most historical narratives, an English historian has observed, "dynasties are episodes in the history of the people; in the Habsburg empire, peoples are a complication in the history of the dynasty." The dynasty communicated its power and unifying presence through magnificent architecture and extravagant spectacle, while the Church engaged in a parallel display of didactic architecture, art, drama and music. The citizens of Baroque Vienna were given constant encouragement and opportunity for vicarious expressions of allegiance to the state and to the true faith, dynasty and Church being, as it were, joined at the hip.

The Baroque supplied vivid sensual experience for the eyes and ears through theatre, music, processions, passion plays, spectacles, orotund preaching, art and architecture. The distinction between this and Protestant culture made by the historian Friedrich Heer is that between the Catholic *Kultur der Sinne* and the Lutheran or especially Calvinist *Kultur des Wortes*, the latter an articulate defence of faith and works rooted in vernacular Bible-reading. By contrast, the Jesuits favoured community-oriented performance—the private Bible-reading of Protestants was after all a potential threat to orthodoxy. For this reason the literary production of the Austrian Counter-Reformation consists mostly of texts for the theatre and tracts which have attracted hostile criticism from German (Protestant) commentators. But also a nineteenth-century Viennese feuilletonist, Ferdinand Kürnberger, wrote contemptuously that "just as the immense literature of Germany was beginning to unfold, in Austria, under the tyranny of Spanish Jesuits, we were writing lists of sins (*Beichtzettel*), books of dreams and cookbooks from Linz." The strength of the Jesuits, from whose initiatives so much of public cultural activity stemmed, was certainly in the theatre and music. Although their dramatic texts were in Latin, they were accompanied by such splendid stage effects that all could and did enjoy them. As early as 1608 a *History of St. Leopold* staged Am Hof attracted a huge crowd to witness a "cast of thousands" as the

Hollywood producers say (actually 106 speaking roles), who performed for six hours. The audience stuck it out despite being periodically soaked by passing rainstorms.

As *Hofdichter* (court poet) the above-mentioned Avancini reflected an increasing trend to write specifically for the court, the greatest fount of patronage. Yet the humanist-educated Jesuits, as many of them were, adroitly mixed folk elements in their didactic and celebratory plays and operas, which went down well with the Viennese. Even the solemn passion play performed on the Neuer Markt at Easter, which ended with Mass in the Stephansdom, was followed by knockabout comedy like the medieval miracle plays in which undesirable characters were satisfactorily consigned to hell. And in fact the ordinary Viennese were developing a taste for satirical comedy, brought to them by the "Qualified Dentist and Surgeon" Anton Stranitzky from Salzburg (see p.59). Indeed, they managed to have the wandering Italian players expelled from the Kärntnertor Theatre (Hotel Sacher is now on the site) in 1711 so that Stranitzky and his company could occupy it exclusively. In his irreverent and subversive ad-libbing lie the roots of the great Viennese tradition of popular comedy and satire, a line that stretches from Stranitzky through Nestroy and Raimund in the nineteenth century to the coruscating political and social satire of the twentieth. This is certainly a remarkably "democratic" cultural tradition that has invariably attracted an audience from the highest to the lowest in the social pecking order, although its content is decidedly "popular".

BAROQUE PROFANE ARCHITECTURE: THE HOFBURG AND PALACES FOR THE NOBILITY

Extensive Baroque additions were made to the Hofburg by Leopold I and Charles VI. The Leopoldinischer Trakt, closing the south-western side of the Burg between the Amalienburg and the Schweizerhof, was originally built between 1660 and 1666 to plans by Philiberto Lucchese and almost immediately (1668) burned down. It was rebuilt (with a floor added) by Giovanni Pietro Tencala (completed 1680). The corresponding north-eastern side of the Hofburg, the Reichskanzleitrakt (to house *inter alia* officials of the Holy Roman Empire) was begun (1723) with a plain Baroque wing by Lukas von Hildebrandt. The main part was built between 1726 and 1730 by his great rival, Johann Bernhard Fischer von Erlach.

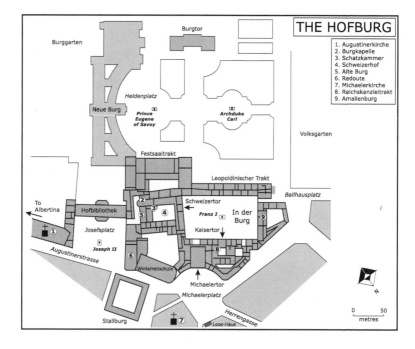

Burgtor

Burggarten

Heldenplatz

Neue Burg

Prince Eugene of Savoy

Archduke Carl

Festsaaltrakt

Leopoldinischer Trakt

Ballhausplatz

Volksgarten

THE HOFBURG

1. Augustinerkirche
2. Burgkapelle
3. Schatzkammer
4. Schweizerhof
5. Alte Burg
6. Redoute
7. Michaelerkirche
8. Reichskanzleitrakt
9. Amalienburg

To Albertina

Hofbibliothek

Schweizertor

Franz I

In der Burg

⑨

Josefsplatz

⑤ ③ ④

⑤

Kaisertor

Joseph II

Augustinerstrasse

⑥

Winterreitschule

⑧

Michaelertor

Michaelerplatz

N

Stallburg

⑦

Herrengasse

Loos-Haus

0   50
metres

Above: The magnificent Belvedere Palace (1714-22) built for the hero of the Turkish Wars, Prince Eugene of Savoy, by Johann Lukas von Hildebrandt. The Habsburg Residence of the Hofburg (*below*) was also extended considerably in the Baroque era with the building of the *Leopoldinischer Trakt* and *Reichskanzleitrakt*, the latter comprising the offices of the Holy Roman Empire.

The last part (including the elegant cupola over the exit to the Michaelerplatz) was completed only in 1893, using Fischer's plans. The Hofbibliothek (entrance on Josefsplatz) was commissioned under Charles VI and designed by Joseph Emanuel Fischer von Erlach (completed 1734).

The library is on the upper floor and is didactically decorated by Daniel Gran and others. Gran's astonishing cupola fresco (1730) is an elaborate representation of the "Triumph of the House of Austria through Knowledge and Learning" eulogizing the contributions to civilization of the dynasty and Charles himself; the ceilings of the adjacent wings are painted with allegories of "the knowledge of heavenly and earthly things". The library is also an ancestral gallery (genealogy being an obsession with the Baroque Habsburgs) featuring busts (superbly executed by Lorenzo Mattielli) of other members of the dynasty notable for their patronage of the arts or military prowess. Visitors should collect the crib on sale at the ground-floor reception to interpret the iconology of the frescoes and identify the Habsburg busts. Just as Prince Eugene is apotheosized in the Belvedere (see below), so the library counterpoints the religious didacticism of the Jesuits with a representation of the God-anointed ruler as quasi-godlike in his dispensation.

The Upper and Lower Belvedere are the greatest work of Lukas von Hildebrandt. The ensemble was built to glorify Prince Eugene of Savoy, the Habsburgs' impressively successful general in the Turkish wars, who was present as a junior commander at the siege of Vienna in 1683. The palace greatly impressed the visiting French philosopher Montesquieu, who remarked that "it is a delightful feeling to be in a land where the subjects live better than their ruler." The Lower Belvedere (completed 1716) was the prince's "office and living quarters", while the huge Upper Belvedere (completed 1722) was for "representation" and his collection of books and artefacts. The whole ensemble, from frescoes representing the prince as the Sun-God Apollo driving out the night to the iconology of the park alluding to his twin roles as military commander and patron of the arts, represents a typically Baroque form of lionization.

Three palaces built by Italian architects are of particular interest. The original palace on the site of Palais Harrach (Freyung 3) burned down during the Turkish siege of 1683, and Count Harrach commissioned Domenico Martinelli to build the replacement (completed 1702). It is now in commercial ownership and only the inner courtyard can be visited.

The Liechtenstein-Garten-Palais "in der Roßau" (Fürstengasse 2): the Roßau (now part of the 9th District) was originally an island between arms of the Danube, so-called because horses were watered here. Prince Hans Adam von und zu Liechtenstein engaged Domenico Martinelli to design a palace in this spot following the Turkish siege, and the building was completed in 1704. It now houses the Liechtenstein picture collection brought from Vaduz, which includes a substantial number of Baroque painting and artefacts. The gallery acquired the Badminton Cabinet at auction in 2004 for £17 million, which makes the latter the currently most valuable piece of furniture in the world. It was created in the eighteenth century in the Medici workshops of Florence for the Duke of Beaufort, who commissioned it while on the Grand Tour.

The Palais Lobkowitz (Lobkowitzplatz 2): between 1685 and 1687 Giovanni Pietro Tencala built this palace for Philipp Sigmund Count Dietrichstein. In 1710 the magnificent Baroque façade, perhaps the loveliest in Vienna, was added by Johann Bernhard Fischer von Erlach. Prince Lobkowitz acquired the palace in 1753. It was here that Beethoven conducted the premiere of his Eroica Symphony (1804) for his patron, Franz Josef Max von Lobkowitz. It now houses the Theatre Museum.

The Palais Kinsky (Freyung 4) was originally built (1713-16) by Hildebrandt for Field Marshal Daun. It is a good example of the former's graceful style, less monumental than Fisher von Erlach's (see, for example, the nearby Schönborn-Batthyány-Palais at Renngasse 4), and fits elegantly into a narrow plot. The fine stairway of the interior is richly decorated (*inter alia* with sculpture by the leading sculptor of the Viennese Baroque, Georg Rafael Donner). You can usually visit this part. The upper floor hosts events like wine-tasting, fashion shows and the like.

Prince Eugene of Savoy engaged Johann Bernhard Fischer von Erlach to convert the two houses he had acquired in this street into a Winter Palace (1696-8, Prinz-Eugen-Winterpalais, Himmelpfortgasse 8). Hildebrandt enlarged the palace (1708-9), but an embittered Fischer von Erlach claimed the entire plan as his own in his celebrated work on *Historical Architecture* (1721). The decoration of the interior, as in the Belvedere Park, plays on the iconology of Hercules and Apollo. The ceremonial staircase is arresting. The palace is now the Finance Ministry (public access on occasional "open days").

THREE BAROQUE CHURCHES

The Jesuitenkirche (Dr.-Ignaz-Seipel-Platz): the erection of the church (1627-31) was a consequence of the Jesuit takeover (1623) of the university, the building for which (Alte Universität) runs at right angles to the church on the south side of the square. The Italian Jesuit architect, Andrea Pozzo, redesigned the interior at the request of Leopold I and introduced the typically dramatic effects of Jesuit architecture (angled light, "barley sugar" columns recalling the baldacchino of St. Peter's in Rome, *trompe l'oeil* effects) seen also in his work for S. Ignazio and the seminal Baroque church of Il Gesù.

The Karlskirche "St. Karl Borromäus" (Karlsplatz): the ecclesiastical masterwork in Vienna of Fischer von Erlach, father and son. Like the Peterskirche, this is a "plague church" and was commissioned by Karl VI in 1713. However (see p.165), it also aimed to express the imperial aspirations and military success of the dynasty, notably through its two symbolic "triumphal columns". Except for the ceiling painting and the ambitious fresco in the cupola (*Apotheosis of Carlo Borromeo*) by Johann Michael Rottmayr, the interior decoration is almost entirely the work of Italian artists.

Peterskirche (Petersplatz): Lukas von Hildebrandt's ecclesiastical masterwork in Vienna. Built on the site of the city's first church (see above), the Peterskirche boasts Vienna's most lavish Baroque interior. Notable features are the elaborate pulpit by Matthias Steinl to the left of the triumphal arch, and Lorenzo Mattielli's superb gilded wooden relief of the martyrdom of St. John Nepomuk to the right of it. John of Nepomuk (thrown from the Charles Bridge in Prague in 1393 on the orders of Wenceslas IV for opposing the latter's use of royal prerogative) was a favourite iconic figure of the Counter-Reformation, emblematic of clerical immunity and the limits of secular power. The Jesuits succeeded in having him canonized in 1729 (notwithstanding that most of the background story to his martyrdom was legend). Fischer von Erlach designed the magnificent tomb for him in Prague's St. Vitus Cathedral. The Nepomuk cult in Bohemia was largely the product of Jesuit ideologues, who tried thereby to channel Czech patriotism onto safer ground than that occupied by Jan Hus. The co-opting of him here in Vienna as a spiritual, rather than a national, martyr is designed to appropriate his iconic charisma for the Church and the dynasty.

The graceful Peterskirche off the Graben, largely designed by Johann Lukas von Hildebrandt and completed in 1733. The earlier of two previous churches on this site is thought to have been the oldest in Vienna and legend has it that Charlemagne himself had founded it.

OTHER BAROQUE MONUMENTS

The Marian Column Am Hof was set up in thanksgiving for the city's deliverance from the Swedish army (1645) during the Thirty Years War. The Marian Cult was another effective weapon in the Jesuit armoury, enthusiastically endorsed by the ruling house. A wonderful jewelled facsimile of the column can be seen in the Schatzkammer of the Hofburg. On the Graben is the "Plague Column", or actually Holy Trinity Column (see above), commemorating deliverance from the 1679 plague. Its iconology elides the concept of the Holy Trinity with the three pillars of Habsburg *Hausmacht* (the Crown Lands, Bohemia and Hungary).

The Wien Museum contains vivid material on the Tukish Siege of 1683, including a portrait of Kara Mustafa, the Turkish commander. A statue of Abraham a Sancta Clara stands at the Albertina entrance to the Burggarten. A Baroque pulpit on the eastern external wall of St. Stephen's recalls Giovanni Capistrano, the fifteenth-century preacher who took part in an earlier campaign against the Turks and died at the siege of Belgrade (1456).

Chapter Seventeen

VIENNA IN THE ENLIGHTENMENT

"I am not a sacred relic…"
Emperor Joseph II to a subject who wished to kiss his hand

The Baroque world was one of extremes, of enormous wealth for the upper classes and grinding poverty for those at the bottom of the heap. Abraham a Sancta Clara had maintained that if one were to hang a bell round the neck of every thief in Vienna, the noise would be so great that no one could hear himself speak. However, *noblesse oblige* and self-promotion also required the lavish gesture, for which the spendthrift Leopold was notorious. Known as a soft touch, he was constantly besieged by "sturdy beggars" who arrived regularly at the Hofburg for their handouts, usually after a convivial hour or two drinking in the nearby Augustinerkeller. Hordes of them followed his carriage through the streets like flocks of herring gulls, on one occasion the press being so great that the windows of his coach actually caved in.

Karl VI, who inherited the throne in 1711 after the promising Josef I's brief tenure was cut short by death from smallpox, was less free with his cash for the poor, though he spent vast sums on the Hofbibliothek described in the previous chapter, and on his attempt to create an Austrian "Escorial"-style place at Klosterneuburg. By 1730 his court employed 2,050 persons in 302 different jobs, supporting around 10,000 people if the families are included. When Charles died (poisoned by mushrooms eaten on a hunting expedition), the impoverished Viennese rabble surged through the streets chanting: "The Emperor's dead/Now we'll have bread." Only when Maria Theresia succeeded (she was never "empress", though she was Queen of Hungary and Bohemia) was a serious attempt made to rectify the state finances, in the management of which her husband, the Emperor Franz I. Stephan from Lorraine, exhibited conspicuous talent.

In 1740 Maria Theresia inherited a desperate situation, financially and militarily, since neighbouring states refused to recognize Charles VI's "Pragmatic Sanction", which was intended to legitimize the Habsburg

*Premier projet que l'auteur a formé pour placer là...
d'un côté des terrasses & des cascades, aussi-bien que de...
fait ci-devant les délices de la Cour, découvrant à perte...*

J. B. Fischer D. Erlau...

Johann Bernhard Fischer von Erlach's original plan (1690) for the palace at *Schönbrunn* envisaged a hu...
complex rivalling Versailles and placed on the hill where the *Gloriette* now stands, overlooking the par...
The palace subsequently built was moved to the foreground, to the area where fountains are depicted
flowing from rocks.

Tab II

...mperiale sur la hauteur de Schönbrun, afin de profiter
...our l'avenüe de l'autre côté vers Hezendorf le Parc qui a
...Ville de Vienne avec les frontières de l'Hongrie

I. A. Delsenbach fecit.

inheritance in the female line. She was immediately faced with a Bavarian incursion and soon her great rival, Frederick the Great of Prussia, began his relentless aggression designed to detach Silesia from the Habsburgs and block the influence to which they aspired in Poland—and even eventually to dismember the empire altogether. By choosing excellent advisors and appointing competent generals (they were drawn from far and wide in the Habsburg realms, and even beyond) Maria Theresia saved her patrimony and bequeathed her son, Joseph II, a stable realm. After the death of Franz Stephan in 1765, she ruled jointly with Joseph until her death in 1780.

It was the age of "enlightened absolutism", beginning with important fiscal, educational, penal and administrative reforms under Maria Theresia, and continuing with much more radical ones under Joseph II. The latter curbed the influence of the Church and introduced his celebrated Tolerance Patent of 1781, which allowed freedom of religion and eased the burdens on the Jews. The sharp distinction between Maria Theresia's forceful maternalism and her son's enlightened paternalism can be seen in a characteristic letter she wrote him enunciating the three fundamental principles of government as she saw them. Firstly there should be no free exercise of religion ("which no Catholic prince can permit without heavy responsibility"); secondly there should be no "destruction of the nobility… for which I see neither the necessity nor the justice." And thirdly the nonsense about "liberty in everything" should be stopped ("I am too old to accommodate myself to such ideas").

THE ENLIGHTENMENT IN CENTRAL EUROPE

The "ideas" to which Maria Theresia referred, which are collectively subsumed under the name of "the Enlightenment", had their roots in the thinking of the "Philosophes" and the Encyclopaedists of France, who in turn drew substantially on the model of Britain. They believed that England had developed an impressive system of civil and political liberties based on Locke's theory of natural rights, and were impressed by the empirical thinkers of the Scottish Enlightenment like David Hume and Adam Smith. Indeed, the fashion for "English" ideas became so strong in France that it acquired the tag of *anglomanie*, and signs of the same could also be observed amongst reforming aristocrats in Central Europe. A preoccupation with empiricism and reason, indeed an attempt to reconcile the two, was the dominant feature of the work of the German philosopher Immanuel Kant, whose *Critique of Pure Reason* was published in 1781. Other ideas, such as the physiocratic belief (espoused by Turgot and Quesnay) that agricultural production was the basis of all national wealth, opposed the reactionary practice of mercantilism and the unproductive heaping up of wealth instead of investment. A favourite poster from the time of Joseph II actually shows the emperor behind a plough, though in truth the Habsburgs generally continued to pursue trade policies associated with mercantilism in their empire.

In Central Europe the ideas of the Enlightenment were generally circulated through freemasonry, which (in its modern form) had originated in London in 1717, from where it spread to the Austrian Netherlands. It was there that Franz Stephan, Maria Theresia's husband, entered a masonic lodge. Later he helped to promote freemasonry's ethos of philosophical, political, constitutional and economic speculation in Austria (the first Viennese lodge was founded in 1742). The Church was extremely hostile to freemasonry because of its fundamentally secular outlook and its challenge to traditional authority. Joseph II aligned the ideas of the Enlightenment with practical religion, treating the Church primarily as a source of education, charitable activity and social control, which meant that many religious foundations that did not meet these criteria were dissolved by imperial fiat.

Leading advisers of Maria Theresia and Joseph II, such as Van Swieten and Sonnenfels, were freemasons, as were many other intellectuals and creative artists like Haydn and Mozart. In a typical display of ambivalence, however, Joseph II put freemasonry under state control in 1785. Although he had embraced the basic tenets of the Enlightenment, above all an almost fanatical belief in the power of human reason, he did not think the people (whose servant he claimed to be) could necessarily be trusted to make the right choices. Censorship may have been somewhat more liberal under Joseph than under Maria Theresia, but censorship there was, including that of material likely to undermine the enlightened notions that the monarch himself proclaimed.

In general the Enlightenment, though modified by local circumstances, is regarded as constituting the foundation of our modern freedoms, upholding (as it does) the notion of fundamental human dignity and rights, as well as embracing social, political and scientific progress.

These ideas did take root in the Habsburg lands, even if political pressures militated against them from time to time, resulting in relapses into absolutism and neo-absolutism in the nineteenth century under Franz I and Franz Joseph. But even absolutism often pursued a course that was underpinned by basic Enlightenment ideas, and the later authoritarian servants of the Habsburgs, men like Metternich or Alexander Bach, were dedicated to rationality and good governance as they saw it.

Musical Culture under Maria Theresia and Joseph II

Despite the best efforts of her bigoted religious tutors, Maria Theresia retained a humane intelligence and a great deal of common sense. Her instinctive rejection of some Enlightenment ideas was tempered by a natural pragmatism and shrewd judgement of character. To the Jesuits may be attributed her anti-semitism, her long resistance to the abolition of torture urged upon her by enlightened counsellors and perhaps her chastity commission designed to regulate morals. Of her humanity there are many instances, including her observation that "the Viennese will do anything if talked to kindly and shown affection." There is also the impressive magnanimity with which she upstaged her husband's mistress (Countess Auersperg) after his death. "How much both of us have lost!" she remarked graciously when they met at the obsequies. (She even paid over the settlement that Franz-Stefan had promised to this remarkably disagreeable woman.)

Her pragmatism was evident in her adroit choice of advisors (also in the way she tactfully but firmly disposed of the living corpses she had inherited from her father's inner circle of administrators). It was typical of her to explain forcibly to the Hungarian nobility that the peasants would probably be able to pay more tax if they were not regularly beaten into the ground by irresponsible landlords. Her reforms of tax, education (1774/5), justice (1769) and the army all laid the foundations for a modern state. She tried to set an example of household thrift by reducing the over-crowded retinue of her father's household, but with limited success. It still proved impossible to do with fewer than 1,500 chamberlains, who were responsible for everything from arranging that snow should be brought into the city so the little archdukes and archduchesses could sledge on it, to ensuring that the imperial glass of milk arrived safely every day from the dairy at Schönbrunn.

The difficulty in making savings underlined the fact that the court itself in the Residenzstadt was even more the city's primary source of employment city than ever before. This situation was indeed intensified under Maria Theresia, who tried to solve the housing shortage at the cost of traders' premises. It was not until 1781 that Joseph II ended the mandatory quartering of court personnel in private houses. Stranitzky's *Volkstücke* aside, the story of Viennese culture under enlightened absolutism is therefore largely the story of Habsburg (and imitative aristocratic) patronage, though the Church played an important role in musical training and education generally. For example, the Piarist order, founded in the seventeenth century to promote good schooling, established itself in Vienna at the beginning of the eighteenth century, despite the hostility of the Jesuits, who felt that their jealously guarded control over higher education might be under threat. The Piarist gymnasium in the Josefstadt is still one of the best schools in Vienna: from its inception it provided a humanist, but religiously orthodox, education for its pupils, concentrating on skills in rhetoric and writing. Many of the most impressive intellectuals of today, like the philosopher Konrad Paul Liessmann or the political scientist, Peter Pelinka, were among its pupils.

Imperial and noble patronage remained substantial, particularly for music, in an age still dominated by workaday Italian masters (Bononcini, Caldara, Conti, Porsile, Predieri). Italian singers and musicians were imported at enormous salaries, their employers showing the same snobbish recklessness with engagement fees as the big city operas of today. By the same token, the best seats in the Burgtheater would be taken by loudly chattering aristocrats, the equivalent of today's snoozing rows of "corporate guests".

By the 1730s the court poet Pietro Metastasio had largely monopolized the market for opera librettos—significantly he never learned to speak German and did not need to. However, with the death in 1715 of Marc'Antonio Ziani, Director of the Court Music, the latter's position was taken by a native Austrian, the Styrian Johann Josef Fux (1660-1741), dubbed the "Austrian Palestrina". In truth, Fux's *Angelica vincitrice d'Alcina*, which Lady Mary Wortley Montague attended and claimed had cost £30,000 to stage, was still heavily influenced by the Neapolitan opera. It was given in the Favorita summer palace and the elaborate scenery was the work of the senior member of a renowned dynasty of illusionist architects, Ferdinando Galli-Bibiena. Although his five hundred scores are largely forgotten, Fux's instructional work on counterpoint entitled *Gradus ad Parnassum* (financed by Charles VI and published in 1725) held the field for half a century and influenced many of his successors.

Nowhere is the transition from a Baroque *Weltanschauung* to that of the Enlightenment more evident than in the Viennese music and drama scene. The Baroque mind conceptualized "life as theatre, the world as stage, God as the author and director of this world-theatre". Exemplary horrors were an important part of theatrical spectacles for "a sensation-hungry and novelty-seeking public", the equivalent of the blood-curdling sensationalism of the popular press today. The overall effect seems to have been tableau-like, bombastic and intellectually impoverished, but visually sensational ("entire 'dramas' consisted of nothing but ornamentally arranged, rhythmically moving components" with water and fireworks). And in all of this "man was a puppet, a pawn in the struggles of the powers above and the powers below." Arias, often ludicrous and interminable, were written primarily to show off the skills of a fashionable castrato, rather than to move the action forward (indeed, one often had the impression that the movement, if any, was backwards).

Upon this fustian scene burst the first "realistic" opera by Christoph Willibald Gluck on 5 October 1762. His magnificent *Orfeo ed Euridice* largely eschewed recitativo secco and Da-capo arias in favour of coherent plot, melodic singing and a foregrounding of the orchestra. In fact, most of Gluck's substantial output was still in the conventional mode of *opera seria* (and he continued to write operas in that mode after *Orfeo*), but this work, with its eclectic musical provenance, its attention to dramatic plausibility rather than abstract passions, and its melodic charm, pointed the way to a new type of opera. "[I have sought] a noble simplicity," he wrote to the Grand Duke of Tuscany about his opera *Alceste*, "and have avoided parading difficulties at the expense of clarity."

Gluck's real breakthrough, however, came with his *Iphigénie en Aulide*, based on Racine's drama, which was staged in Paris as part of the celebrations following the betrothal of Maria Theresia's daughter Marie Antoinette to the Dauphin. On his return to Vienna, he was made Court Composer and ended his days as a sort of public monument receiving illustrious guests from abroad, among them Dr. Charles Burney. The latter has left an interesting account of the city's musical life in the late eighteenth century and paid particular attention to the singing in churches. He remarked that these excellent performances, heard every day for free, refined and fixed the national taste for good music, a phenomenon Vienna shared with Italian cities.

Burney and the Irish singer Michael Kelly were in Vienna at the birth of the "Wiener Klassik", which flowered (roughly 1760-1827) with Haydn, Mozart and the early work of Beethoven, and which included some of the greatest music ever written. Its binding thread is provided by Haydn, hugely admired by Mozart, but also the teacher of Beethoven—who even quarrelled slightly less with Haydn than he quarrelled with everybody else. "Haydn was composing before Mozart was born," writes a musicologist, "yet it was not until after Mozart's death that virtually all his finest works were written. By the time he died Beethoven had written six of his symphonies and Schubert was a member of the Vienna Boys' Choir."

Joseph Haydn was born to a family in service to Count Harrach (the Harrachs still own the Schloss at Rohrau, Lower Austria) and was a choirboy at St. Stephen's until his voice broke. After working for various aristocrats as music teacher or Kapellmeister, he spent twenty-eight years as Kapellmeister for the Esterhazys at their palaces at Kismarton (Eisenstadt) and Esterháza. The bush telegraph and rivalry among aristocrats being what it was, Haydn's fame spread throughout Europe (in 1785 he was even commissioned to write a sonata sequence for the Good Friday service in Cádiz; and when he was asked if his ignorance of English would create problems on his trip to London, he replied magnificently: "My language is understood all over the world").

Haydn's contribution to Viennese music can hardly be overestimated: his eighteen string quartets written for the Fürnberg family in 1757 established that genre and he also laid down the template for the classical symphony. In addition, he has left us at least two truly magnificent choral works, the *Nelson Mass* and an oratorio, *The Creation*. His *Kaiserlied*, a dynastic anthem eulogizing Kaiser Franz during the Napoleonic War, greatly surpassed its supposed inspiration, "God Save the King". It has survived even its adoption by German imperialists and Nazis (as "Deutschland über alles" sung to words by Hoffmann von Fallersleben) to remain one of the best loved melodies of his oeuvre. It even pops up as the tune for an Anglican hymn, which goes to show that a good melody can be used to cel-

This kitsch illustration of the infant prodigy Mozart and his sister playing before Maria Theresia is a nineteenth-century romanticization of musical genius. The etching is from a picture by a German artist called August Borckmann and dates to about 1885.

ebrate any old ruler, or God himself, however incompatible these objects of veneration may be.

Mozart's sojourn in Vienna (1781-91, with excursions to Prague, where his music was better received) almost exactly dovetails with the rule of the enlightened monarch, Joseph II. The emperor was not ill-disposed towards Mozart (notwithstanding his celebrated complaint that *Die Entführung aus dem Serail* had "an awful lot of notes"), but the Italian clique, centred on Mozart's rival Salieri, hindered him at every turn. Gluck, on the other hand, admired *Die Entführung*, since it "observed the spirit of [his] reforms in calling for singers who could act and actors who could sing." Mozart was reckless, however, as he had been in his relations with his patron, the Salzburg Prince-Archbishop Colloredo, out of whose employ he was literally booted by a flunkey. His collaboration with Lorenzo da Ponte on the satirical *Le Nozze di Figaro* held up the more pompous type of aristocrat to ridicule; moreover, it sharply contrasted the moral standards of the Enlightenment (Mozart had become a freemason in 1784) with anachronistic feudal privilege (e.g. *ius primae noctis*). Not surprisingly, it caused huge offence among potential patrons. Its astonishing success elsewhere (Salieri succeeded in having it taken off after only nine performances in Vienna), together with the rapturous reception in Prague of the equally disrespectful *Don Giovanni*, only compounded Mozart's offence. In Prague, as Wolfgang Hildesheimer has pointed out, the "arrogant *arbitres spectaculorum...* who held expertise [in musical matters] to be a privilege of the nobility was weaker than in Vienna."

To his credit, Joseph II rose above the axe-grinding of the aristocracy, and ignored the very traditional Viennese envy of Mozart's talent among mediocre rivals, when he appointed him Court Composer in 1787. Unfortunately, the emperor simultaneously downgraded the salary to less than half that of the previous incumbent (Gluck), causing Mozart to remark ruefully that the pay was "too much for what I do, too little for what I can do."

Money was indeed important for Mozart, who was, after all, the first "freelance" composer in a world governed by patronage (in Colloredo's household, he had been seated for dinner "below the valets and above the cooks"). His personal finances were chaotic, as his many begging letters testify, while the housekeeping of his wife Costanze was, to say the least, erratic. While he was prepared to dash off an opera seria like *La Clemenza di Tito* for Leopold II's coronation in Prague (succeeding thereby in breathing life into an almost dead libretto by Metastasio), Mozart's genius lay in writing operas that appeal to a wide audience through their warm humanity and the skilful fusion of action with delightful, often wistful, music. All these elements combine in *Die Zauberflöte*, the quintessentially Viennese opera. It ingeniously combines elements of knockabout comedy familiar to the Viennese (Papageno recalls the previously mentioned Stranitzky's "Hanswurst" character) with some highfalutin' philosophical idealism derived from Freemasonry. Mozart collaborated on it with a bumptious actor-impresario called Emanuel Schikaneder, who was good at producing sensational theatrical effects and comic routines—he is said to have complained that he had written such a wonderful text, "but that Herr Mozart ruined it all with his music." Goethe complained magisterially that *Die Zauberflöte* was full of "improbabilities and jokes which not everyone is capable of understanding," and indeed some of Sarastro's more Delphic pronouncements are portentous drivel. The Viennese have always appreciated the joke, while learned musicological moles and earnest opera directors elsewhere often have not. Composed seven months before his death, *Die Zauberflöte* brought Mozart back into favour with the fickle Viennese and would probably have assured him fat commissions and a steady income, had he lived.

But Wolfgang Amadeus was as careless of his health as he was with money, and there is little doubt that his death was hastened by overwork and stress. *Così fan tutte* was premiered in January, 1790, *Don Giovanni* was repeated in Prague in September and the first performance of *La Clemenza di Tito* came only a week later, followed by *Die Zauberflöte* at the end of the month. As he lay dying Mozart was hard at work on the *Requiem* commissioned secretly by an aristocrat (but only because he wanted to pass it off as his own), which the composer soon realized was to be his own requiem. When he died aged only 35, he had written 626 works across all musical genres.

Retrospectively Mozart appears very much as a representative of the *Zeitgeist*, insofar as he broke musical, intellectual and social taboos, and opened the windows of the mind to let in much-needed light and fresh air. In this he had much in common with the Emperor Joseph II, who was as reckless with tradition and privilege as Mozart was with money. His treatment of the Church was a case in point; on his accession the Church owned three-eighths of the land in Austria and some 2,000 monasteries had income amounting to 300 million Gulden in total. In a crash programme of rationalization that thoroughly alarmed the pope, he reduced the monasteries by half and collected 60 million Gulden from taxes and expropriated assets. Much of the money was dedicated to building parish churches, the emperor believing that no one should be more than an hour's walk from his local church. He had no time for the sort of monastery memorably described by Gibbon as "wealthy and useless", and believed the clerisy should devote itself to good works and education. He would have agreed with Maria Theresia's advisor, Van Swieten, who combated her misgivings about the dissolution of the Jesuits in 1773 with the observation that the Society's aim had "always been one and the same, to enrich itself, and religion has only been a pretext for abusing the piety of your Majesty and her glorious ancestors."

The Enlightened Absolutism of Joseph II

The dissolution of the Jesuits marked the symbolic triumph of the Enlightenment in Austria. Joseph's Edict of Tolerance in 1781 was a logical consequence of the new way of thinking, allowing Protestant worship and ending the most severe restrictions on Jews. Lutherans and Calvinists took over two churches in the Dorotheergasse, though they were not permitted to build steeples—"one must take some account of the prejudices of others," as the emperor drily noted. Jews could now be admitted to schools, the university, the civil service (theoretically) and the professions, but the ban on synagogues remained (some limits, it seems, had to be observed) and a surrealistically named "tolerance tax" ensured that only wealthy Jews could live in the old city.

The emperor's practical reforms included founding a General Hospital complete with a cylindrical tower specially designed for the confinement of lunatics—its official name was the Narrenturm, but the Viennese soon dubbed it the *Guglhupf* due to its resemblance to a cylindrical cake of which the locals are fond. Nearby he also founded a school for military surgeons, the Josephinum. His reforms trampled on the great and the lower orders alike; "he always took the second step before the first," was Frederick the Great's comment on his rival's *modus operandi*. For example, erring members of the nobility were obliged to join street-cleaning gangs, while ordinary Viennese were outraged with Joseph's statute on reusable coffins (see p.73). Subjects who wanted to kiss the emperor's hand were met with the comment: "I am not a sacred relic." Although he was cultivated and musical, he lacked the Baroque taste for the sensual of his predecessors. He ordered Rudolf II's picture collection in the Hradčany to be sold off; the commissioners, perhaps taking their cue from their ruler's no nonsense approach, identified Titian's *Leda and the Swan* in the inventory as a "nude being bitten by an angry goose."

The spirit of the Theresian and Josephin age was scientific and philosophical, rather than literary. A Berlin writer complained in 1755 that "Austria has given us not a single writer that the rest of Germany need bother about." Instead, theses, manuals and other practical works of medical science, jurisprudence and education contrasted sharply with the excesses of Jesuit tracts and drama in the Baroque age.

Perhaps the most significant figure for Vienna was Maria Theresia's personal physician, a Jansenist Dutchman called Gerard van Swieten who combined this role with several others: court librarian, (liberal) censor and educational reformer; founder of the Viennese medical and veterinary schools; founder of orphanages and a midwives' school. He was a pupil of the great Dutch physician Boerhaave and published a commentary on the latter's book of medically instructive aphorisms. Maria Theresia sent him to report on rumours of vampires in Moravia, which resulted in a splendid report (1768) characterizing the stories as the "barbarism of ignorance" and explaining the likely natural origins of such superstitions. As censor he put a stop to Jesuit raids on bookshops and arbitrary book-burnings, and (to appease the fanatics) made a show of banning Fielding, Voltaire, etc. He did this in order to gain a space for Montesquieu's *De l'Esprit des Lois* (1748), the key Enlightenment text on liberal aristocratic government. It was a struggle, though, since clerics and conservatives on the censorship commission regarded Montesquieu's works with as much affection as communist regimes later regarded those of George Orwell. A century later, in *The Magic Flute: Part II*, Grillparzer satirized the general mistrust of literature in a *Beamtenstaat* (that is, a state in thrall to officialdom), attributing to Joseph II the command: "Give my officials more to do, because I hear they have been reading."

Yet Joseph II was personally interested in the theatre (and perhaps sensitive to the Berliner's sneer quoted above). In 1776 he founded the so-called National Theatre adjacent to the Hofburg with the remit to play serious drama, including translations, only in German (French comedies were popular, Stranitzky's Hanswurst farces in dialect even more so). Significantly, the players were appointed state officials (this is very Austrian) with attendant privileges. In theory, they decided the repertoire and the role allocations, but Joseph was always interfering. The censorship was so strict (nothing disrespectful and no *Sturm und Drang*) that after a period of deathly dull classical dramas by justly forgotten Austrian poets, the repertoire reverted to *Singspiel* (hence Mozart's premiere of the *Serail*). Nevertheless, Joseph had made a start, and the Burgtheater ultimately became the best theatre in the German-speaking world, a reputation that many believe it retains today.

SOME SIGHTS ASSOCIATED WITH MARIA THERESIA AND JOSEPH II

Schönbrunn (Schönbrunner Schloßstraße, Hietzing): the former hunting lodge of Maximilian II was burned down (1605) by Magyar *kuruc* fighters, rebuilt under Matthias and finally destroyed in the Turkish siege of 1683. The name Schönbrunn (first occurring in 1642) refers to the spring of exceptionally pure water discovered in the park. Emperor Leopold I commissioned Fischer von Erlach to build a new summer palace here, which was much altered (1744-49) by Maria Theresia's mediocre court architect, Nikolaus Pacassi. The *Gloriette* on the hill (originally Fischer's intended site for the palace itself) was added by Ferdinand von Hohenberg. It commemorates the great victory (1757) of Maria Theresia's army over Frederick the Great at Kolin (Bohemia) during the Seven Years' War. The interior of the palace is Rococo. Maria Theresia lived a *gemütliches* family life here with her sixteen children (a portrait by Martin van Meytens shows her at Schönbrunn surrounded by eleven little archdukes and archduchesses). The "Schönbrunn yellow" of the walls was used for official buildings all over the empire, while the imperial family's idiolect of *Schönbrunnerisch* (*hochdeutsch* and Viennese dialect sprinkled with French idioms) was adopted by the nobility and the city's café society.

Under Joseph II important institutions were founded, in particular the Allgemeines Krankenhaus (Mathias Gerl, 1784, Alser Strasse 4) with its famous Narrenturm ("Fool's Tower" for the confinement of the insane designed by Isidore Canevale). The latter is now a fascinating, if gruesome, museum of pathological anatomy. From Viennese reference to it as the

Guglhupf comes the expression: *er gehört im Guglhupf* ("he belongs in the Guglhupf"—applied to politicians and other persons deemed irredeemably stupid). Only a little less gruesome are the wax anatomical waxworks made in Florence by Felice Fontana for instruction of military surgeons. They can be seen in the Josephinum (also by Isidore Canevale, Währinger Strasse 25), the medical school founded by Joseph II in 1785.

The Mozarthaus (Figarohaus), where Mozart lived between 1784 and 1787 and composed his taboo-breaking *Le Nozze di Figaro* is at Domgasse 5. The display on three floors offers vivid insights into Mozart's life and works, and also into the Vienna of his day.

On the Neuer Markt is a copy of the Providentia Fountain (1739) by the greatest Baroque sculptor of Vienna, Georg Raphael Donner. The figure of Providentia presides over personifications of Austrian rivers, the Enns, the March, the Traun and the Ybbs. Maria Theresia's absurd chastity commission considered the putti and allegorical figures to be indecent and had the original removed (it may now be seen in the Lower Belvedere).

The greatest neoclassical monument in Vienna, Antonio Canova's cenotaph for Marie Christine (1805) is in the Augustinerkirche. She was Maria Theresia's favourite daughter and the wife of Albert of Saxe-Teschen, the founder of the Albertina graphic collection. Mourning allegorical figures (*virtus* and *caritas*) process into a monumental pyramidal tomb.

A romantic image of Beethoven performing for friends soon after he settled in Vienna in 1792. The chaos of manuscripts, sheet music and books reflects the disorder in which the great man lived, oblivious to tidiness and even hygiene. It is said he moved 25 times during his 36 years in Vienna, often to the relief of landlords and landladies who were fed up with piano practice at all hours and the composer's unemptied chamber pots.

Chapter Eighteen
BIEDERMEIER VIENNA

"An evening spent in the company of an intimate circle in Vienna is certainly the most delightful way possible of passing the time…"

Charles Sealsfield

Leopold II, a younger son of Franz I. Stephan of Lorraine and Maria Theresia, succeeded his brother Joseph on the latter's death in 1790, but proved (like Josef I eighty years earlier) to be another Habsburg "lost leader". Hitherto he had been Grand Duke of Tuscany, the territory with which the expropriated House of Lorraine was compensated in 1737 after the War of the Polish Succession. His record as Grand Duke of Tuscany had been remarkable for economic and fiscal reform, but also for social measures such as the abolition of torture and even (in 1786) the removal of the death penalty (Tuscany was the first sovereign power to do this). Unfortunately the Central European power base of the Habsburgs was again crumbling when he became emperor, and Leopold felt obliged to trim and tack to the prevailing winds. Joseph II had anyway repealed many of his most radical fiscal reforms on his deathbed. Then Leopold died suddenly in 1792 and was succeeded by his colourless and rather dull son, Franz II.

Even had Franz been spectacularly gifted, events were conspiring to render him powerless. Marie Antoinette, Maria Theresia's grotesquely extravagant daughter (known to the French, and not affectionately, as "Madame Déficit") was executed by revolutionaries on 16 October 1793. The Habsburgs were now threatened from within by the spread of revolutionary ideas and soon from without by French armies. In the subsequent Napoleonic War, Vienna was twice occupied by Napoleon, in 1805 and 1809. Humiliation was heaped on humiliation. Franz was obliged to give up his title of Holy Roman Emperor, styling himself more modestly "Emperor Franz I of Austria". And through the machinations of his wily chancellor, Metternich, he was manoeuvred into marrying off his favourite daughter to an upstart Corsican adventurer, who was unfortunately also

Emperor of the French. *Tu felix Austria nube!*—Maximilian I's boast of marriage bed diplomacy—was suddenly endowed with bitter irony: "what others achieve through Mars, the goddess Venus bestows on you."

Humiliation for the dynasty had its counterpart in the disillusion with Napoleon felt by the intellectuals. In 1804, Beethoven, now resident in Vienna, scratched out the dedication to Napoleon of his Third ("heroic") Symphony so violently that his pen-nib ripped through the page. However, he could not prevent officers of the French occupation force crowding into the premiere of *Fidelio* at the Theater an der Wien in 1805. Since the entire opera is a passionate celebration of liberation from tyranny, their presence hardly seems appropriate, but of course the French regarded themselves as liberators anyway. Whether or not the Viennese shared their view was immaterial…

The French bid to dominate Europe ended with the Congress of Vienna (1814-15), which attempted, with short-term success, to make Europe revolution-proof. The Prince de Ligne's famous comment that the "Congress does not get on [with its business]; it dances!" has summed up for generations its aristocratic mode of procedure, choreographed brilliantly by Metternich. It was not all frivolity; there was brilliant intellectual stimulation to be had at the salon of the Jewish banker's daughter Franziska (Fanny) von Arnstein, at whose home on the Hoher Markt scholars, diplomats, writers and artists foregathered.

Even so, a contemporary satirist characterized the Congress and the assembled monarchs less than flatteringly as follows: "Who skirt-chases for them all? Alexander of Russia. Who thinks for them all? Friedrich Wilhelm of Prussia. Who speaks for them all? Fredrik of Denmark. Who drinks for them all? Maximilian of Bavaria. Who eats for them all? Friedrich von Württemberg. Who pays for them all? Emperor Franz." The whole jamboree cost 80,000 Gulden daily, exacted from the Viennese in higher prices and taxes. Beethoven, at least, was happy. His marathon concert at the Redoutensaal of the Hofburg in November 1814 went on for several hours and featured a work called "Wellington's Victory at Vitoria" performed by an all-star cast; Beethoven himself conducted, with the indestructible Salieri priming the cannonades, Johann Nepomuk Hummel on drums and Giacomo Meyerbeer operating the thunder-machine.

When he first arrived in the city, Beethoven had lived from the irregular commissions supplied by his Viennese admirers. From 1808 he was promised a yearly stipend of 4,000 Gulden (the salary of a departmental head in the bureaucracy) by aristocratic patrons, trumping a seductive, but corrupting, offer from Napoleon's brother Jerome, the "King" of Westphalia. The reverence accorded to Beethoven was not confined to the nobility, however; his open-air concerts in the Augarten were major events and his performances at venues like the Theater an der Wien were packed out. He certainly gave value for money: a benefit concert in December 1808 included the Fifth Symphony and the Pastoral, the Piano Concerto in G Major, the Choral Fantasia and four other pieces. The audience stuck it out from 6.30 pm to late in the evening and almost froze to death in the unheated theatre.

Such musical stamina reflected the fact that the Viennese bourgeoisie were increasingly taking the initiative in the encouragement of music: the Society of the Friends of Music was founded in 1812, there was a Conservatory (later the Academy of Music) from 1817, the Wiener Philharmoniker were founded in 1842 and the Vienna Male Voice Choral Society in 1843. At the same time, there were still aristocrats who could afford to keep an orchestra, while others sponsored smaller ensembles and private concerts. For later generations of music lovers, says Henry-Louis de La Grange, the leading historian of music in Vienna, the last decade of the eighteenth century and the first of the nineteenth were "nothing less than paradisial".

Beethoven settled definitively in the city in 1792 and passed the remaining thirty-five years of his life here. Whatever his money problems (the payments gradually fell away as sponsors died) it says something for the Viennese elite's respect for genius that they appreciated this irascible and erratic oddball with alarmingly republican leanings. Yet the appreciation he received was overshadowed by the tragic elements of his existence—the obsessional legal battle to gain the wardship of his nephew, which exposed an ugly, unscrupulous side to his character; the tragic onset of deafness that provoked the *cri de coeur* of his Heiligenstadt Testament; the endless quarrels with landlords and neighbours that led to him move house twenty-five times in thirty-six years. Much of that personal suffering was channelled into his art, producing the emotional intensity of the late string quartets, or the Ninth Symphony's unbelievably exalted "Ode to Joy", a joy which Beethoven never seems to have experienced, only imagined.

It was remarkable that the Viennese public, by then accustomed to the elegance of the Wiener Klassik, so quickly embraced the dissonance and ardour of the revolutionary romantic style (not that Metternich approved). If Mozart had been the brilliant dissident whom they (eventually) took to their hearts, Beethoven was an heroic figure in a city that generally mistrusted heroics. From the house in the Schwarzspanierstrasse, where he died, to the Alser Church is only about 1,000 yards, but his funeral cortège took over an hour and half to cover the distance, so great was the throng. It was Grillparzer who gave the funeral oration ("we are left with the heritage of a mind that is still with us and always will be.")

One of the torch-bearers at Beethoven's funeral was the thirty-year-old Franz Schubert, who himself had only one year to live. Although he was Beethoven's contemporary, as a Viennese born and bred Schubert at first glance seems to provide a striking contrast with the brooding German. Where Beethoven creates grandeur and intensity, we are accustomed to associate Schubert's music with intimacy and restraint. The clichéd view of Schubert stresses quintessentially Viennese characteristics in his music of melodic charm and elegant harmonies tinged with melancholy; in reality, his works often feature audaciously innovative chromatics and outbursts of passion betraying an inner turmoil. Modern performances of his symphonies by the great Nikolaus Harnoncourt lay more emphasis on this "romantic" side of his genius. The travestied Schubert of Heinrich Berté's sentimental operetta *Das Dreimäderlhaus* (1916, given in New York as "Blossom Time", 1921, in London as "Lilac Time," 1922) with its "borrowed" music of Schubert is thankfully a thing of the past.

Far from the operetta depiction of him, Schubert was a man of ambivalent sexuality and often deep melancholy whose death was probably hastened by syphilis. The conventional picture is, however, correct insofar as his extreme modesty proved to be a handicap. Schubert showed no inclination to push himself and his work into the limelight, preferring the private performances for friends at the famous *Schubertiaden* (musical gatherings). On the other hand, the irrational Austrian inferiority complex in regard to the Germans is already becoming apparent in the efforts of Schubert's friends to promote him. They tried to interest Goethe in the composer's setting of a selection of his poems, but the great man did not even bother to reply. Then the *Erlkönig* was offered to a musical publisher in Leipzig, who erroneously returned it to a hack musician, also called Schubert, who lived in Dresden. The latter wrote the publisher an enraged letter vowing to seek out and exact retribution from the person trying to use his name to sell such "rubbish"…

Schubert's life-style might be described as one of restrained Bohemianism. His circle included singers like Johann Michael Vogl, painters like Moritz von Schwind or Leopold Kupelwieser and writers like Johann Mayrhofer or Eduard von Bauernfeld—the last two civil servants like Grillparzer. They enjoyed the camaraderie of eternal students, but it was nevertheless a select circle, entry to which depended on a recognizable artistic talent. They called Schubert "Canevas", because of his standard inquiry before any proposed introduction of a stranger: *Kann er was?* ("What's he good at?"). The sentimental image of Schubert playing the piano at a session of *Hausmusik* with his friends—painted by Moritz von Schwind and later by Gustav Klimt for his patron Nikolaus Dumba—came to be taken as the epitome of the "Biedermeier idyll".

THE WORLD OF BIEDERMEIER

"Biedermeier" is a concept that has undergone a curious transformation over the years. The original Herr Gottlieb Biedermeier (or Biedermaier) was a character featured from 1855 in satirical poems for *Fliegenden Blättern*, a Munich periodical. He was portrayed as a mildly philistine family man of modest ambitions and sober pleasures. He enjoyed his "happiness in a quiet corner", which was assumed to be adequate fulfilment of petit-bourgeois aspirations under a conservative and authoritarian regime. His type has been fixed by the painter Carl Spitzweg's gently humorous depiction of a Biedermeier family out for a *Sunday Walk*. Retrospectively, however, "Biedermeier" was adopted (from 1900) as a neutral description of the art and culture of the *Vormärz* ("Pre-March"). The thirty-three years of the Vormärz covered the period between the Congress of Vienna (1814-15) and the outbreak of revolution in March 1848. Thwarted in their political development for three decades, the Viennese turned inwards to "the good life", and channelled their traditional "Phaeacianism" into art, literature, music and superior craftsmanship. The ultra-respectable Karoline Pichler (1769-1843), who presided over a famous Biedermeier salon, wrote in her memoirs of the remarkable sensitivity to beauty of the contemporary Viennese, but also of their need for mildly sensual pleasures. She adds that even the ever-critical Germans, who "have dubbed us the land of the Phaeacians, … once they have tasted our roasts and Schnitzels, devote long passages to these matters in their travel accounts." This perhaps explains why the Biedermeier period was also known as the *Backhendlzeit* ("the era of fried chicken")—and to this day a large paunch is known in Viennese slang as a *Backhendlfriedhof* ("cemetery for fried chicken").

The once patronizing and contemptuous concept of "Biedermeier" has evolved over time to imply appreciation, even respect, for the culture it describes. Elegant and comfortable Biedermeier furniture built by Viennese craftsmen like Joseph Ulrich Danhauser (1780-1829) now fills the stands of dealers at the local antique fairs. Finely painted and idealized Biedermeier family portraiture and landscapes by artists like Ferdinand Georg Waldmüller (1793-1865) or Friedrich Amerling (1803-87) have an honoured place in the Austrian Gallery of the Belvedere, as do the moralistic works by Josef Danhauser (1805-45, the son of the furniture maker) or Peter Fendi (1796-1842).

Like Victorian painting in England, such works reflect bourgeois values with a certain degree of sententiousness, but also with a genuinely moral subtext. Typically they celebrate the family, dramatize the consequences of lack of respectability (as in a picture of bailiffs repossessing a house), or evoke personal sorrow in a patriotic context (for example, that of a mother receiving news that her soldier son has died for the fatherland). Dovetailing with this moralistic vision of the world is the contemporary art of topographical painting, which built on the tradition of Bellotto's *vedutas* popular in the previous century.

In Rudolf von Alt (1812-1905) Austria produced Europe's greatest master in this field, each work a consummate combination of precision and shimmering atmosphere. Much of his work features Vienna (he drew or painted the Stephansdom one hundred times), a declaration of love to the city grounded in topographical precision that forms the painterly counterpart (or correction) to the *Wienerlied* in music. The Alt school mingles scientific accuracy with idealizing ambience, a combination that exactly reflected its "Austrian solution" between Enlightenment and Romanticism.

The architecture of the Biedermeier period shows a similar purity and restraint. It developed from the austere neoclassicism that began under Joseph II in reaction to the sensuousness of the Baroque and the whimsical playfulness of Maria Theresian Rococo. Two leading architects domi-

The Bailiffs (1839) by Peter Fendi, one of the leading Biedermeier artists. Biedermeier taste generally favoured finely painted Alpine landscapes and glowing portraits of prosperous middle-class families. However Fendi specialized in pathos-ridden scenes of the poorer classes, as here.

nated the field, Josef Kornhäusel (1782-1860) and Alois Pichl (1782-1856). Kornhäusel's work can be seen substantively at Baden bei Wien, the spa made fashionable by imperial patronage and regarded as encapsulating the charm of the Biedermeier world in microcosm (it was known as "a little Vienna in watercolour"). One of his best-known works in Vienna is the synagogue in the Seitenstettengasse, this alone out of twenty-four Viennese synagogues escaping the conflagration of Jewish properties in 1938, because of the risk to neighbouring houses.

Two notable works by Pichl are the Erste österreichische Spar-Casse (now Erste Bank) on the Graben and the Schottenhof next to the Schottenkirche. After a brief period of *Zopfstil* under Joseph II (the word means pigtail-style, and refers to a recurrent motif of the external ornamentation that slightly resembled dangling pigtails), neoclassicism blossomed in Vienna, endowing both institutional and domestic buildings with simple elegance and graceful proportions. Ultimately, the inspiration for a rational architecture based on the laws of nature could be traced back to Winckelmann's rediscovery of the antique virtues of "noble simplicity and calm grandeur". Typically in Vienna this concept has been domesticated (and indeed most of Kornhäusel's projects were apartment blocks for the emergent bourgeoisie). The pompous stuff was left to architects like Peter Nobile, whose grandiose Burgtor sealing the Heldenplatz was built to celebrate the victory over Napoleon at the Battle of the Nations.

Kornhäusel grew rather cranky in later life and built himself a tower near his Stadttempel only accessible by a retractable ladder to the first floor. According to legend, this was to escape persecution by his nagging wife, though building an entire house seems quite an expensive way of achieving this end. From the roof of the building, the writer Adalbert Stifter (1805-68) observed the eclipse of the sun in 1842, of which he left a description in his collection of sketches "From Old Vienna". Stifter's classic Biedermeier novel *Der Nachsommer* (Indian Summer, 1857), and his "gentle law" of being reconciled to fate, have already been described in the chapter on Viennese topography (see pp.50-51).

Here it may be noted that the age of Metternich's police state, and therefore of rigid censorship, ironically produced the first major flowering of Austrian literature to rival that of the Germans, and thus to combat the dismissiveness shown by Christoph Friedrich Nicolai a century earlier. The irony of literature booming under censorship is reinforced by a further one, namely that the leading prose writers of the day tended to be officials in the service of the state, ambivalent pen-pushers so delightfully described by Waltraut Heindl as "obedient rebels". One of these, Eduard von Bauernfeld, was not untypical in his initial support (like most of his colleagues) for the revolution that broke out in 1848, which he hoped would bring an end to the nepotism, arbitrary power and exploitation that plagued the lower ranks of officials. Such hopes were swiftly dashed, however, and he could only vent his frustration in a subsequent poem (1854) entitled "Minor Officials", which contained the lines: "Children they rear, pallid and hollow-eyed/Condemned to office work./You should tremble, you mighty Austria/Before your minor officials."

The four leading "bureaucrat" writers were Bauernfeld, "Anastasius Grün" (actually Anton Alexander Graf Auersperg), Franz Grillparzer and Adalbert Stifter. Grün's bold, albeit generalized, criticism of the clerisy, censorship and the police state in his *Promenade of a Viennese Poet* (1831) may be contrasted with his personal life of blameless Biedermeier quietism—he spent much of his time on his Slovene estate cultivating roses, not unlike the "spiritual philosopher" whose *Weltanschauung* is idealized in Stifter's *Der Nachsommer*. His attitude is indeed not untypical of the spiritual dichotomy of such writers, for whom the imagined life was so much richer than the mundane reality of officialdom. More pointed than Grün's critique was the merciless description of a lethargic, oppressive and hypocritically religious state published (1828, in exile, and in English) by "Charles Sealsfield" (actually Carl Magnus Postl) under the title *Austria as it is or Sketches of Continental Courts by an Eye Witness*. Sealsfield believed in constitutional monarchy on the English model, and his work was hardly "revolutionary", but its reportage on the "absolutism mitigated by muddle" of the Metternichian system meant that his pamphlet was regarded as highly subversive by the authorities—and, of course, banned in Austria.

The domination of the theatre in Vienna is indicated by the almost desperate attempts of writers to succeed with dramas. Many of them failed (for example, Ferdinand von Saar and Marie von Ebner-Eschenbach, both of whom were successful as novelists of realism, tried repeatedly to gain a foothold in the theatre). Bauernfeld, on the other hand, wrote numerous social comedies of Viennese life for the Burgtheater, often with roles tailored to popular actors. The contemporary giants of the dramatic form were Ferdinand Raimund (1790-1836) and Johann Nestroy (1801-62) for comedy and satire, and the already much cited Franz Grillparzer (1791-1872), who explored the Habsburg myth in historicist dramas.

Grillparzer's historicism was often a cover for deeper preoccupations and has been replaced in modern productions with an emphasis on his abstract interest in the use and abuse of power. His play on the mythical founder of Prague, *Libussa* (1874), has even been treated as a feminist drama. Raimund was a self-educated lower-class Viennese whose passion for the theatre was fired as a young man, when he got a job selling refreshments in the intervals of Burgtheater performances. His works probably do not travel, but they re-energized the Viennese tradition of *Zauberposse*, a mixture of burlesque and fairy tale, which are recognizable elements in Schikaneder's *The Magic Flute*. With their gentle humour, sentimentality and "happy-ends", Raimund's works were a hit with the public; but they also contained a strongly moral subtext, for example in the *Peasant as Millionaire*, which describes how a peasant boy, unexpectedly enriched by wartime trading, is corrupted by the wealth he has accumulated. This piece could also be described as an early musical, containing two delightful songs which are still popular, "Brüderlein fein" and the "Aschenlied". Baroque elements survive in his work—the characters still play out the roles allotted to them on the great stage of the world, and the grace of God rather than the reason of the Enlightenment still drives the plot, but there is also realism in the form of close observation of human traits, gently ironic insights and even schizophrenia in one play. In this way Raimund's work straddles the old world and the new. As with Grillparzer, whose mother committed suicide, there is an undertow of surreal tragedy attached to Raimund; he took his own life after being bitten by a dog which he wrongly assumed was rabid.

The greatest master of comedy in Viennese theatrical tradition was Johann Nestroy, whom his contemporaries compared with Aristophanes and Shakespeare, but who has also been dubbed the "Schopenhauer of the Prater", a reference to his sardonic nihilism. He wrote over eighty plays, spiced with satire and poignant wit, and all provide us with rich insights into pre- and post-revolutionary Viennese society. Due to the deadly accuracy of his sallies against the regime and his dangerous improvisations on stage, he was constantly in trouble with the authorities, frequently being fined or even gaoled for brief periods. He was an all-round man of the theatre, combining the roles of actor-manager, playwright and director at the Theater an der Wien between 1854 and 1860.

Eschewing the whimsy and "magical" elements of Raimund, he moved Viennese popular comedy into a new era of social and political criticism, adroitly using parody, satire and mordant aphorism. He could also play all the moods from farcical merriment to resignation and nihilistic pessimism. Nestroy was the master of one-liners, many of which have passed into the language: "All right the Phoenicians invented money—but why so little?"; "The noblest nation of all nations is resignation"; "Everyone wants to live long; nobody wants to be old."

SOME SIGHTS ASSOCIATED WITH BIEDERMEIER CULTURE

The gallery in the Oberes Belvedere contains a generous selection of Biedermeier painting by Waldmüller, Danhauser, Amerling, Fendi and others. The bourgeois family portraits are aglow with colour and exude a life of prosperity, respectability—perhaps also a certain complacency. Danhauser's pictures are often moralistic and broadly allegorical, while Fendi is the master of closely (and sympathetically) observed everyday life. The topographical works of the Alt dynasty may also be seen in the Belvedere, but most are in the Wien Museum on Karlsplatz. Jakob Alt (1789-1872) from Frankfurt painted the Alps, the Salzkammergut and the Danube region in the *veduta* tradition. His sons Rudolf (1812-1905) and Franz (1821-1914) refined this into topographically exact urban scenes. By far the most distinguished was Rudolf, of whose 1,000 watercolours a large number are of Vienna. His exquisite rendering of light and atmosphere, together with his astonishing precision, make him the finest protagonist of fine naturalism that Europe has produced.

In the Beethovenhaus in Heiligenstadt (Probusgasse 6) the composer wrote his desperately sad *Heiligenstädter Testament* (1802), when he knew he was going deaf ("For me there can be no relaxation with my fellow men, no refined conversation, no mutual exchange of ideas." The full text, translated into English, can be read in Wikipedia). He also wrote the second version of *Fidelio* and possibly the 2nd Symphony here, although its joyous mood is in stark contradiction to the *Testament*. The house is now a museum with Beethoven memorabilia. The Pasqualatihaus (Mölkerbastei 8) is also worth a visit for Beethoven devotees.

Architecture: the work of Josef Kornhäusel can be seen extensively in the form of neoclassical *Miethäuser* (apartment blocks) around Vienna and buildings in Baden bei Wien (reached by the Badner Bahn from the Oper). Perhaps his greatest achievement is the Stadttempel (1826) for the Israelitische Kultusgemeinde (Seitenstettengasse 4) with its elegant oval interior flanked by ionic columns, its giant candelabra and blue, star-studded ceiling. Alois Pichl's fine Erste österreichische Spar-Casse (1838, now Erste Bank) is at Graben 21. Note the gilded bee in the pediment, symbol of the Biedermeier virtues of thrift and industry. Even more monumental is his Lower Austrian Diet (1839, Herrengasse 13). The grandiose Burgtor, leading from the Heldenplatz to the Ringstrasse, is an example of more bombastic neoclassicism by Luigi Cagnola and Peter Nobile. It was the Habsburgs' rather modest answer to the *arc de triomphe*, built by military veterans to commemorate the "Battle of the Nations" against Napoleon at Leipzig, and is today a cenotaph for the dead of two world wars.

The Theater an der Wien (Linke Wienzeile 6) has recently awakened to new life with a refreshed repertoire. Its predecessor, the Freihaustheater, which was situated nearby just across the Wienfluss, is associated with Mozart and Schikaneder's *Die Zauberflöte*. The present Empire style theatre was ready in 1801 and witnessed many important premieres, including that of Beethoven's *Fidelio* (1805). Although Johann Nestroy was actor-manager here, he had made his acting debut as Sarastro in a production of *The Magic Flute* at the Kärntnertortheater.

Nestroy is virtually untranslatable, but the musical *Hello Dolly!* has a distant ancestor in his comedy *Einen Jux will er sich machen* ("He Wants to Make a Fool of Himself", 1842). The playwright turned out for the civil guard in the 1848 revolution, but true to form spent as much time making fun of the revolutionaries as of the *ancien régime*; indeed, he wrote a satire on the events entitled *Freiheit in Krähwinkel* ("Freedom in Gotham", 1848). The original entrance to the Theater an der Wien in the Millöckergasse is now the "Papagenotor", with a sculpture of the disreputable bird-catcher playing his magic flute above the gateway.

Chapter Nineteen

FROM REVOLUTION TO RINGSTRAßE: THE GRÜNDERZEIT (FOUNDERS PERIOD) AND RINGSTRAßEN ERA

"When one walks out on the new Ringstrasse, one thinks of the future;
but walking in the old city, for anyone who has always lived there, brings
back memories of days gone by."

Feuilletonist Daniel Spitzer (1879)

Allegedly Franz-I once opened an address to educators at the Laibach
(Ljubljana) Lyceum with the words: "I do not need scholars, but well-
behaved citizens (*brave Bürger*)." Apocryphal or not, this observation sums
up the atmosphere of the Metternich era. To the emperor and his advisors,
banning political activity and censoring cultural expression seemed the
only way to prevent the revolutionary virus from spreading. (Franz also
remarked, prophetically as it happens, that his empire was like a "rotting
house. If one demolishes one part, one has no idea how much of the rest
may collapse.") For many years the emperor(s) and Metternich kept the lid
on discontent, until finally political frustration, coupled with economic
malaise, brought matters to a head in 1848.

Unlike in Hungary where the Habsburgs were temporarily dethroned,
the revolution in Vienna was, however, essentially bourgeois, with fairly
moderate aims, although students and workers had their own more radical
agendas and one minister was lynched. The main aim of the bourgeoisie was
the removal of absolutism and the institution of press freedom and representative assemblies. Karl Marx, who visited Vienna several times in 1848
as the first "revolution tourist", noted with disgust that this was not his
kind of revolution. Moreover, the simple-minded Emperor Ferdinand, who
had succeeded to the throne on the death of Franz in 1835, initially granted
almost all that was asked of him in a proclamation of 15 March. Metternich
had already fled to England on the first outbreak of violence on 13 March.

The early stages of the 1848 Revolution in Vienna were marked by spontaneous outbursts of violence against the regime. The picture shows the body of the Minister for War, Theodor Graf Baillet de Latour, hanged from a lamppost after he had been lynched in his ministry. Metternich, who might well have suffered a similar fate, was forced to flee the country and take refuge in England.

The ambivalent attitudes of intellectuals like Nestroy to the revolution have been noted in the previous chapter. Indeed, Nestroy's "Freedom in Gotham", premiered on 1 July, provoked at least one outburst in the (now liberated) press, accusing him of sacrilegiously parodying the very freedom for the sake of which so many were risking their lives. Grillparzer, for his part, was dismayed by any violence, and in January 1848 had already written the appropriately titled *Omen*:

This evil will its harvest reap,
A mighty crash if none resist.
Madness laughs, but I must weep
To see my country brought to this.

His patriotic instincts were later aroused by Field-Marshal Radetzky's remarkably rapid success in subduing the revolt in Austria's North Italian territories. This achievement the poet hailed with a poem to Radetzky, of which one line swiftly passed into the language: *In Deinem Lager ist Österreich* ("In your camp is Austria"). The words appear behind the imperial double-eagle on Caspar von Zumbusch's Radetzky Monument fronting the former War Ministry on Stubenring.

Grillparzer offered the same tribute to Radetzky in poetry that Johann Strauss Senior offered in music. The latter's celebrated *Radetzkymarsch*, which traditionally concludes the annual New Year's Concert in the "Golden Hall" of Vienna's Musikverein, may reasonably claim to be the best march ever written. Soaring above all others in a generally dismal genre, it was retrospectively regarded as combined signature tune and last post for the Austro-Hungarian monarchy. Indeed, Joseph Roth chose *Radetzky March* (1932) for the title of the first of his two elegiac (but also ambivalent) novels set in the days when bandmasters from Bregenz to Czernowitz could play this march on either civil or military occasions to equally warm acclamation.

The erstwhile socialist Roth was not alone in idealizing the monarchical Catholicism of Austria-Hungary, as he struggled in a world engulfed by the "brown plague" of Nazism. To a deracinated Jew, the empire with its philo-semitic emperor offered a spiritual homeland to replace the one that was both eternally lost to Jewry through history, and now again to modern Jews, for whom even assimilation had ended in disaster.

The Strauss Dynasty

Johann Strauss I (1804-49) was the founder of Europe's most famous musical dynasty, one which is rightly seen as having created and marketed a form of music that is quintessentially Viennese, but which also succeeded in eliding the borders between "popular" and "classical" music long before that elision was banalized into the "crossover" of today. The waltz, with which the Strauss family is eternally associated, had its roots in a popular dance of Upper Austria, Bohemia and Bavaria known as *Ländler*. The name was possibly derived from the dialect word *Landl* designating *das Land ob der Enns*, which was the medieval characterization of Oberösterreich (Upper Austria.) Although the waltz in 3/4 time was already infiltrating classical music in the late eighteenth century, the characteristic Viennese waltz begins with piano pieces by Schubert, which he played to his friends at *Schubertiades*. But it was the combos of Strauss and Joseph Lanner (1801-43) that made the waltz such a spectacular success. Its popularity for balls at the Congress of Vienna demonstrated that it had reached acceptance at the highest levels of society, a then rare example of an aesthetic genre filtering upwards through society, rather than from the elite downwards. The seal was put on its social desirability when Strauss was appointed Director of Music for the Court Balls in 1835.

Strauss and Lanner at first played in a quintet, travelling all over Europe, but eventually became rivals with competing orchestras. While Lanner continued to work in the idiom of popular folk music, Strauss began to build a more complex orchestral structure for the waltz, a process brought to perfection by his son, Johann Strauss the Younger (born in 1825). Strauss Senior also pioneered the professional management and marketing of music (he disposed over a pool of 200 musicians who could be called on at short notice when engagements were offered), a system that his son refined and streamlined. Indeed, Johann Strauss Junior, a handsome man with a mane of black hair, became Europe's first pop star, with a massive fan club to boot. He had so many requests for locks of his hair that he began sending clippings from his poodle to silly female admirers.

His career began with *éclat* with his wildly successful debut in the (still existing) Café Dommayer in Hietzing, but his choice of profession was in the teeth of opposition from his father, who wanted his son to go into business. That, of course, was ultimately what he did, but not as the father had envisaged. So long as Strauss Senior had a quasi-monopoly on performance rights in Vienna (he conducted the music for 76 balls during the Fasching of 1845) he could and did hinder Strauss Junior's career. Their rivalry was not only one of father against son and musician against musician; they were politically divided, too, the father supporting the authorities in 1848, the son supporting the revolutionaries. Painful though it may be for liberals to admit, the father's *Radetzky March* is musically, if not ideologically, far superior to the son's less than inspired *Freedom March* and *Songs of the Barricades*, which he composed in his capacity as Kapellmeister of the National Guard.

Strauss Junior's astonishingly rich and sophisticated later oeuvre shrewdly catered to the waltz craze that swept nineteenth-century Vienna, and thereafter enriched the genre of operetta towards the turn of the century. It has been estimated that mid-century up to a quarter of Vienna's three hundred thousand inhabitants might be found in establishments with music and dancing on any given night (*Wienerlieder* and *Heurigen* were also booming). With rapid industrialization sucking in immigrants and the incremental amalgamation of the suburbs and Vororte beyond the Gürtel (Outer Ring Road), the population had swelled to over 828,000 by 1869.

For both new and longer-standing inhabitants of the city, dancing and music were the natural form of entertainment and relaxation. Yet Strauss' music, greatly admired for its subtle orchestration by contemporary and near-contemporary composers like Brahms or Mahler, was not simply a vehicle for heedless Phaeacianism. The celebrated *Blue Danube Waltz* actually began life in 1867 as a piece for a male choir. The spectacularly inept words provided by Josef Weyl (one couplet was even anti-semitic), were meant to spread cheer in the general gloom caused by the disastrous defeat of Austria by Prussia the previous year at Sadowa (Königgrätz). Shorn of its vapid text, the waltz was later played at the Paris World exhibition in a purely orchestral version, and instantly made Strauss the "flavour of the month" in Europe—soon, indeed, the flavour of the decade.

It was not long before Strauss had conquered America as well. But it was in Central Europe that his work had a particular significance that is sometimes overlooked, namely that of providing a cultural artefact—

perhaps the only one—that bound the countries of the Habsburg monarchy together in a shared aesthetic experience. Even if the humourless modernist Hermann Broch later characterized the operetta as "sheer idiocy", for a time it was as popular in Brno, Budapest and Ljubljana as it was in Vienna. Moreover, it afforded a space for political persiflage and social commentary that was by no means as worthless and witless as Broch seemed to think. It enjoyed the advantage of being immediately accessible to all, which can hardly be said of Broch's own sprawling novels. Strauss' operetta *Der Zigeunerbaron* (1885), with a book based on a novella by the Hungarian Mór Jókai, was full of Hungarian musical references, a sort of homage to the *Ausgleich* ("Compromise") between Austria and Hungary concluded in 1867. There were to be many such "Austro-Hungarian" operettas, which were arguably even more "pluralistic" in the hands of composers like Franz Lehár.

THE RINGSTRASSEN ERA

Franz Joseph I had been installed as emperor aged eighteen, when the incapable Ferdinand had to be removed during the revolution of 1848. After a period of neo-absolutism, when the government was largely in the hands of Prince Schwarzenberg and Alexander Bach, he issued his famous decree in 1857 ordering the demolition of the bastions around Vienna's Innere Stadt. This marks the beginning of what historians call the *Gründerzeit* ("Founders Period"), and was partly inspired by Baron Haussmann's reconfiguration of Paris, begun in 1853. Over the next thirty years, the existing girdle of bastions and military exercise grounds was replaced by representative buildings of Historicism reflecting the aspirations of the emergent liberal bourgeoisie. The Parliament was built in antique Classical style, recalling the Grecian cradle of democracy, the university in neo-Renaissance style recalling the European-wide revival of learning in the fifteenth and sixteenth centuries, the Rathaus in neo-Gothic style recalling the free burgher cities of the Flanders in the Middle Ages, and neo-Baroque was adopted for the Burgtheater. Similarly appropriate styles were employed for the great museums (Natural History, Art History, the Museum of Applied Art), the Opera and the Stock Exchange. The distinguished architects of these projects—Gottfried Semper, Karl Hasenauer, Theophil von Hansen, Heinrich Ferstel, Friedrich Schmidt, Von Siccardsburg, Van der Null—produced a sort of *panopticum* of civil society.

The grand staircase of the Opera House (1869) designed by August von Siccardsburg and Eduard van der Nüll. Unfortunately the emperor ventured a mild criticism of the building at the opening ceremony which so upset van der Nüll that he committed suicide.

Reflecting political and social modernization, this new architecture encircled three-quarters of the old "Altstadt", the latter still steeped (like the Hofburg) in the medieval and the Baroque.

Not everyone was impressed by the grandiosity of the Ringstrassen style. At the turn of the century commentators like Adolf Loos and Karl Kraus frequently sneered at its pretentiousness (heavily ornamented "rent-palaces" for "His Majesty the Plebs" to live in), and above all its lack of functionality. That was precisely the criticism made of the Ringstrassen institutional buildings right from the start: the Parliament had terrible acoustics and its ceremonial ramp proved too steep for the horse carriages to negotiate; in the ill-lit Rathaus, funereal gloom prevailed in rooms that were either too big, or too small. The Rathaus heating was a forerunner of the system perfected by British Rail in the next century—some parts of the building were as hot as the Equator, others as cold as the North Pole. There were boxes in the Burgtheater facing away from the stage. Critics of the Opera complained that it "looked like an elephant lying down to digest its dinner." Even Franz Joseph unwisely commented at the opening that it appeared a bit sunken (the road level had been altered in the course of construction), prompting one of the architects to have a heart attack and the other to hang himself. Thereafter the emperor famously confined his post-inauguration comments to his formula: "It [the occasion] has been very pleasant. I enjoyed it very much," thereby avoiding direct reference to the objects inaugurated.

The most spectacular controversy questioning the whole ethos of Ringstrassen optimism came much later, towards the turn of the century. It involved Gustav Klimt's allegorical paintings for the faculties of Philosophy, Jurisprudence and Medicine commissioned for the university *aula*. He first delivered *Philosophy* (1900) and *Medicine* (1901), but their overt eroticism, combined with a pessimism bordering on nihilism, outraged the positivist professors. They preferred the unexceptionable *Triumph of Light* painted by Klimt's former colleague, Franz Matsch, for the central panel of the *aula*, where it may still be seen.

Of course, the world had moved on from the triumphal Historicism of Ringstrassen culture by the time the Klimt scandal erupted. The aesthetic star of that culture had been the artist Hans Makart (1840-84), described as a "monumental, historicising, society and portrait painter", and so much an expression of his time that it has been dubbed the *Makartzeit*.

Having been a pupil in Munich of the now risible-seeming *Schinken* painter, Karl Piloty, in 1869 Makart was invited to Vienna by the emperor personally and given a studio that he turned into an artistic lumber room, stuffed with Gobelins, Persian carpets, antique furniture, weapons, trophies, costumes, musical instruments, majolica, glass and much more. It looked like the wedding list for a *nouveau riche*. In 1879 he organized a huge pageant (modelled on Act III of Wagner's *Meistersinger*) to celebrate the silver wedding anniversary of Franz Joseph and Elisabeth, for which forty-three representatives of each level of society paraded along the Ring dressed in historical costumes. Makart himself headed the contingent of artists, carefully strapped to a white horse, lest he should fall off.

His largest history paintings, like *Karl V's Entry into Antwerp*, were acted out by Viennese society as tableaux and were also sent round Europe on money-making exhibition tours. His artistic inspiration was the Venetian Renaissance (Tintoretto, Veronese) and Rubens, so his work matched the historicizing Renaissance architecture of great Ringstrassen palaces like that of his patron, the financier Nikolaus Dumba, for whom he decorated the palace interiors. He is at his best in his female portraits that give back some of the overripe atmosphere of contemporary society, eschewing the cheap theatrical effects of his history pictures. Opinions of his painting were, of course, divided even in his lifetime; some were enchanted by his eroticizing use of colour, but others saw his work as merely vulgar. The (admittedly eccentric) German writer Karl Ferdinand Gutzkow said: "Makart's pictures are enlarged lamp shades for a brothel." Anselm Feuerbach, a less successful rival of Makart who had decorated the ceiling of the *aula* in the Akademie der bildenden Künste on the Ringstrasse, denounced his colleague's "diarrhoea-like production… churned out in his asiatic junkshop, which I detest, but which will go out of fashion in due course." This indeed proved to be the case, and seldom has an artistic reputation been eclipsed so rapidly as Makart's.

Musical Innovation and Rivalries in Ringstrassen Vienna

The building of the Ringstrasse was financed not by noble patronage, but commercially by selling the plots, an indication of the transformation that Viennese society had undergone since the Biedermeier era. The areas made vacant for building by the demolition of the walls and the military spaces in front of them were bought by developers and the proceeds placed in a building fund that was used by the state for public investment. Huge fortunes were made. All went well until 1873 when the first big financial crash of modern times hit Vienna hard and also coincided with an outbreak of cholera. It was the year in which Vienna held its only World Exhibition (a project inspired by the exhibitions held by France and Britain to celebrate their industrial achievements and to stimulate trade).

Unfortunately the Vienna Exhibition (held in the Prater) unleashed a frenzy of greed among hoteliers. There was wild stock market speculation and soaring inflation. All the investment swindles came home to roost eight days after the opening, when the Stock Exchange went into meltdown. The feuilletonist Ferdinand Kürnberger remarked sardonically in a letter written the day after the crash: "Since yesterday a thief is once again called a thief, and not a baron. Never has a more beautiful storm cleansed a more foul air." As for the Exhibition, it closed with a deficit of 15 million Gulden.

To mark the closure of the World Exhibition Prince Liechtenstein organized a concert in the main hall of the Musikverein on 26 October at which the Second Symphony of Anton Bruckner was premiered. It is hard to think of a figure more out of place among the materialistic excesses of the Ringstrassen era than Bruckner, a simple and modest being who had the misfortune to be taken up by the Wagner lobby as their musical protagonist in opposition to the late Wiener Klassik of Johannes Brahms. The famously cantankerous Brahms reacted with vitriol, referring to Bruckner's deep religious faith as "priest-ridden bigotry" and to his symphonies as "symphonic boa-constrictors, the amateurish, confused and illogical abortions of a rustic school-master". At Bruckner's funeral in the Karlskirche, he refused to enter the church, but was heard to mutter as he stamped up and down outside: "It will be my turn soon enough." (This was characteristic, as a contemporary joke about Brahms' taste for the morbid indicated: "When Brahms is feeling really cheerful, he sings to himself "The Grave is my Joy.")

Apart from simple rivalry, which has always sharpened the verbal stilettos of intellectuals and artists in Vienna to an extraordinary degree, the rift between Brahms and Bruckner represented a real "cultural turn" that was replicated in the arts generally. Late romantics like Hugo Wolf and Gustav Mahler respected the expansive architecture of Bruckner's music;

even though their own music was very different, they shared Bruckner's admiration for Wagner's stupendous iconoclasm and his distaste for Brahms' "not too hot and not too cold" productions.

The decisive role in this dispute was played by the musical pope of Vienna, Eduard Hanslick (1825-1904), skewered for posterity by Wagner in the petty figure of Beckmesser in the *Meistersinger von Nürnberg*. As with all caricatures, the representation of Beckmesser/Hanslick as a mediocre and envious talent taking revenge on genius is not entirely fair. Like the leading writers of the Biedermeier era, Hanslick was a bureaucrat (a senior one with the rank of *Hofrat*), but also a Professor of Aesthetics and History of Music, and the leading musical journalist in Vienna. Moreover, his treatise on "On the Musically Beautiful" (1854) was widely praised and translated. Lightweight he was certainly not, but his uncompromising belief (based on Hegel) that true music could only be an expression of form excluded any extra-musical inspiration or associations. This was the foundation of his objection to Wagner, Liszt and Hugo Wolf, for whom music had associative power and was an expression, *inter alia*, of political aspiration or historical identity. His objections to Bruckner were more to do with the latter's apparently arbitrary handling of form. The sub-text in all this was that Hanslick was partly Jewish, a fact to which his enemies in the music world made frequent and hostile reference, while Wagner's violent anti-semitism can only have spurred the critic's distaste for his music. Poor Bruckner, however, was not equipped for such battles. When he received the Franz-Joseph Order in 1886 from the emperor, the latter kindly inquired if there was anything he could do for him. In reply, Bruckner merely asked dolefully "if Your Majesty could perhaps stop Hanslick from writing such nasty things about me...?"

As the turn of the century approached, Vienna continued to nurture romantic music, not least as a consequence of Gustav Mahler's tenure as Court Opera Director (1897-1907). While a student in Vienna he had briefly shared lodgings with Hugo Wolf, whose *Lieder* are remembered, but whose opera *Der Corregidor* even his friend Mahler could not be persuaded to stage (Wolf eventually died in a lunatic asylum, partly as a result of his lack of recognition). Mahler was a Wagnerian, so it is no surprise that Hanslick and Brahms saw to it that his youthful submission for the Beethoven Prize (*Das klagende Lied*) was rejected out of hand. More importantly, he was a Wagnerian through his commitment to a plausibly acted and staged "music drama," a *Gesamtkunstwerk*, to replace the tableau-like singing costumes that his reforms did away with. In this he was assisted by a brilliant *Jugendstil* artist turned set designer, Alfred Roller. When the performers and orchestra protested that his style was against all tradition, Mahler famously replied that "tradition is *Schlamperei* (sloppiness)." An even greater affront to the *amour propre* of singers was his attempted abolition of the claque who had hitherto been given free gallery tickets (but of course the claque survived). He was equally strict with the audience, preventing late arrivals from taking their seats until the interval. He initiated the tradition of playing in darkness and had the orchestra pit lowered to conceal the reading lights of the players from the audience. His treatment of both orchestra and singers bordered on terrorism (he once pursued an erring tenor across the stage until the man finally took refuge in the lavatory). Since the Court Opera was for Mahler "no longer a glorified Viennese coffee house with music, but an artistic shrine", those whose attachment to it was more social than artistic soon began intriguing against him and the intrigues continued (with anti-semitic undertones) until Mahler eventually turned his back on the whole miserable *canaille* and went off to America.

Mahler's music was received reluctantly in Vienna, though retrospectively he is thought of as the founder of the New Viennese School (Arnold Schoenberg, Anton von Webern, Alban Berg). His quasi-expressionistic chromatics tied in with the work of the young Expressionist painters like Egon Schiele and Oskar Kokoschka, who were just beginning to make their mark. His symphonies were mostly written in the summer breaks in the Salzkammergut on the Attersee, or on the Carinthian Wörthersee; for four years one symphony was written each summer, but none of them was premiered in Vienna, though a few were given performances. Mahler being a Jew, the Nazis suppressed his works, but since the Second World War they have acquired an almost fanatical following. In particular, the Fourth Symphony ranks among the loveliest ever written, while the Fifth Symphony has acquired iconic status through its brilliant exploitation in Luchino Visconti's film of Thomas Mann's novella, *Death in Venice*. The marvellous song cycles are today staples of the concert hall. Mahler has triumphed over the earth-creeping minds, the bureaucrats and mediocrities who hounded him in his lifetime. Despite them all, however, he seems to have loved Vienna. When he knew he was on his last legs, he insisted on being taken back there to die. Now a vast and impressive portrait of him (by R. J. Kitaj) hangs in the main upstairs lobby of the Staatsoper.

HISTORICIST BUILDINGS ALONG THE RINGSTRASSE

Trams 1 and 2 run respectively clockwise and anticlockwise on the Ringstrasse. Simply sitting in the tram for a round trip enables you to see all the major edifices of the Ringstrassen era (1858-1900), as well as some other important buildings. Travelling from Schwedenplatz clockwise (Tram 1), you leave Max Fabiani's Urania (1910, a public education institute) on your left, as the tram turns south into Stubenring. Shortly on your left is the neo-Baroque former War Ministry (1913, Ludwig Baumann) with Field-Marshal Radetzky's statue (Caspar von Zumbusch, 1892) in front of it. Directly opposite, across the Ring, is Otto Wagner's Secessionist Post-Office Savings Bank (1903), set back from the square named after the anti-semitic founder of the savings movement in Austria, Georg Coch. There follow on your left the neo-Renaissance University of Applied Arts and the Museum of Applied Arts (MAK, 1871, Heinrich Ferstel), the museum having been inspired by the South Kensington (later Victorian and Albert) Museum in London.

Adjoining these, and still on your left, is the Stadtpark (1862/3), laid out on the initiative of Mayor Andreas Zelinka. It contains numerous monuments to nineteenth-century artists and composers, most notably that to Johann Strauß the Younger (Edmund Hellmer, 1921) at the southern end. The composer is depicted as the "waltz king" against a sugary white aureola featuring enraptured Danube nymphs. Just beyond it in the park is the neo-Renaissance Kursalon (Johann Garben, 1867), originally a spa and teahouse for park promenaders. Turning west, the Ringstrasse changes from Schubertring to Kärntner Ring. On your left you pass Schwarzenbergplatz, at its southern end the Hochstrahlbrunnen and Russian War Memorial. Next on your left is the Hotel Imperial (1865), originally the palace of Duke Philipp von Württemberg, which was turned into a hotel for the World Exhibition of 1873, and is now the Staatshotel for state visitors to Austria. Hitler lodged here in 1938. Behind it (but not visible) lie other Historicist buildings (the magnificent Hellenistic Musikverein by Theophil Hansen (1869), the Künstlerhaus (1868) and the Handelsakademie (1862)).

Continuing on the Ringstrasse, you pass the Staatsoper (August von Siccardsburg and Eduard van der Nüll, 1869) on your right, followed by the Akademie der bildenden Künste (Theophil Hansen, 1877) set back on Schillerplatz. The Burggarten, then Cagnola and Nobile's Classical Burgtor (1824), follow on your right. To the left is what remained of Gottfried Semper's ambitious "Kaiserforum" project, the Kunsthistorisches Museum (Semper and Karl von Hasenauer, 1891) and the Naturhistorisches Museum (likewise Semper and Hasenauer, 1889), with Caspar von Zumbusch's great monument to Maria Theresia (1888) situated between them. The Ringstrasse then turns north (Dr.-Karl-Renner-Ring), passing the Volksgarten on the right, and on the left, Theophil Hansen's Greek Parlament (1883). The latter is fronted by Carl Kundmann's huge Pallas Athene Fountain (1902—changed from a planned allegorical representation of "Austria" to avoid offending the various other nationalities represented in the Reichsrat). This is followed (Dr.-Karl-Lueger-Ring) on the left by Friedrich Schmidt's huge neo-Gothic Rathaus (1883), standing opposite Semper and Hasenauer's Burgtheater (1888) across the Ring.

As the Ringstrasse turns north-east, becoming Schottenring, you pass on your left Ferstel's neo-Renaissance University (1884) and further back the same architect's neo-Gothic Votivkirche (1879—but actually the first Ringstrassen building to be initiated, as thanksgiving for Emperor Franz-Joseph's escape from an assassination attempt in 1853). Finally, Theophil Hansen's extremely graceful Börse (1877) is passed on your right. The tram shortly turns back towards Schwedenplatz along Franz-Josefs-Kai.

Chapter Twenty

FIN-DE-SIÈCLE VIENNA

"The wonderful, inexhaustible, magical city with its mysterious, soft, light-drenched air!"

Hugo von Hofmannsthal (1894)

While 1873 was a year of huge economic and social crisis, it did not stop the liberal project in its tracks. Instead, the cholera outbreak spurred the city fathers to renewed efforts to improve infrastructure in respect of sewage, provision of unpolluted water and public services generally. As it happened, the long-planned supply of fresh Alpine water was realized with the inauguration of the Hochstrahlbrunnen on Schwarzenbergplatz in October 1873. This was a typical example of liberal entrepreneurial commitment combined with imperial patronage (the emperor "gifted" one of the water sources to the city). Mayor Cajetan Felder was justly proud of it, remarking in his inaugural address that the "huts of the poor and the palaces of the rich would equally benefit from this miraculous feat of engineering." The Central Cemetery opened in 1874. In 1875 a major regulation of the Danube was completed, making the annual flooding in the Leopoldstadt a thing of the past, although problems still occurred elsewhere. The first scientifically organised census was carried out in 1880. Due to the ingenious inventions of Carl Auer-Welsbach, most of Vienna's streets were efficiently gas-lit by 1900, by which time electrification was advancing rapidly. By 1905 a Berlin entrepreneur had even built 59 public conveniences containing 434 toilets and 314 *pissoirs*. Building on the Ringstrasse proceeded apace throughout these years, and trees were planted all along the boulevard. In short Vienna was well on the way to becoming an elegant, modern and efficiently administered metropolis. On the other hand, it was politically unbalanced: the liberals held power in the City Hall uninterruptedly from 1861 to 1895 on a narrow, tax-based franchise of about 3.3 per cent of the population. As soon as the franchise was broadened in the 1880s, their hegemony began to erode.

The young Gustav Klimt, later the leading light of the Vienna Secession, worked on the sumptuous stairway of the Kunsthistorisches Museum in collaboration with his brother Ernst and Franz Matsch ("The Artists' Company", as they styled themselves.) This openly erotic figure of an Egyptian dancing girl (or possibly priestess), with its mosaic-like background, hints at the techniques of Klimt's celebrated later work as a Secessionist.

Parallel to these developments came stunning population growth (from 726,000 in 1880 to 2,030,000 in 1910) and a financial boom. More money was therefore available for artistic and scientific activity, and a golden age of Viennese culture dawned. It ripened and flourished over two generations (firstly with the Secessionists, then the Expressionists). Two literary lobbies dominated the scene between 1890 and 1914: Hermann Bahr's "Jung-Wien" group (which included Arthur Schnitzler) and their arch-rivals, the circle of the coruscating satirist and social critic, Karl Kraus.

While diametrically opposed on the literary and coffeehouse battle-fields, both lobbies inhabited a mental world dominated by Eros and Thanatos, although the way they handled these themes were very different. The collapse of liberal political power, but preservation of bourgeois liberal wealth and urban comforts, encouraged the ivory tower introspection, extreme sensuality and wistful (sometimes nihilistic) symbolism that are the hallmarks of the art produced at the turn of the century. The process at work—"modern culture as political surrogate for a marginalised liberal bourgeoisie"—has been analysed in Carl Schorske's seminal work, *Fin-de-siècle Vienna*, which has guided the understanding of an entire generation (though revisionists are now at work). Denied the direct political influence to which (so they believed) both their wealth and their abilities entitled them, the scions of the liberal bourgeoisie turned to the free professions, the arts, medicine and science.

A very large number of them were assimilated Jews, as a roll-call of influential minds of the period will indicate: Arthur Schnitzler, Karl Kraus, Sigmund Freud, Arnold Schoenberg, Theodor Herzl, Peter Altenberg, Alfred Polgar, Egon Friedell, Otto Weininger. In the visual arts, perhaps because of the distrust of images anciently embedded in Jewry, non-Jews predominated (e.g. Gustav Klimt and most of the other members of the Vienna Secession). Hermann Bahr, the leader of the Secessionist literary movement known as Jung-Wien was not Jewish, though most of the Jung-Wien writers were; likewise the presiding architect of the Vienna Secession, Otto Wagner, was a gentile, and a very influential one as head of Vienna's urban planning department. His support for the Secessionists was pivotal in establishing their presence on the Vienna cityscape. Perhaps the most interesting aspect of all these figures is that each one of them was a strongly individual creative personality. Only in the Secession and its offshoot for applied art, the Wiener Werkstätte, was a limited degree of homogeneity observable in the product; but the Secession itself soon split into a Klimt faction and anti-Klimt faction.

Schorske revisionists however prefer to emphasize the specific "Jewishness" of turn-of-the-century culture, summed up in Stefan Zweig's claim: "Whoever wanted to promote something new in Vienna, or came to Vienna as a guest from abroad and sought appreciation as well as an audience, was dependent on the Jewish bourgeoisie." Inversely related to this as a factor stimulating culture at the turn of the century was the rise of nationalism. On the one hand, nationalist energy produced an upsurge in artistic activity in the lands of the empire which the Habsburg authorities felt it politic to placate. But the case of Austria, especially "melting pot" Vienna, was different; here the authorities believed that "high culture" could act as a "binding counterforce to nationalist divisiveness". This view explains why the Secession, despite its rebellion against the conservative artistic establishment, nevertheless gained state backing in 1897 because it was deemed to represent an integral "Austrian" art that stood "above and beyond national divisions".

Such an analysis may appear paradoxical, but then the Austro-Hungarian Empire was a somewhat paradoxical entity. Indeed, in the eyes of a writer like Robert Musil it retrospectively appears as not only paradoxical but absurd in the pages of his lengthy unfinished novel *The Man Without Qualities* (first two volumes published 1930 and 1933, an unfinished third volume published posthumously in 1943). Musil's massive work (and achievement) dealt with the modernist dilemma of the individual in a disintegrating society, described in psycho-sexual terms "an unfirm self in an unfirm world". The mandarin identity of heretofore, rooted in the values of liberalism and the Enlightenment, but still part of an archaic hierarchical political and social structure, was inexorably becoming marginalized; the new self, born of nationalism and mass politics, had yet to achieve political and cultural hegemony. This is Musil's large theme, which he presents in terms of the microcosmic world of a Viennese bureaucracy wondering how to celebrate the emperor's Jubilee after seventy years on the throne.

The irony was that this spiritual helplessness stood against a background of healthy economic growth: in that sense the Monarchy was not dying at all, though its institutions seemed to be. Artistic dynamism coexisted with socio-political paralysis. The intellectual haute bourgeoisie frequently behaved as if all they could do was rearrange deckchairs on the *Titanic*. Karl Kraus turned even that into an aphorism, referring to Vienna as "an experimental laboratory for world endings", a phrase which sounds like a modern version of Abraham a Sancta Clara's apocalyptic doom-mongering in the seventeenth century.

THE VIENNA SECESSION

In 1893 the first Central European "Secession" took place in Munich of artists dissatisfied with the prevalent fine naturalism of painting, and its total (aesthetic and commercial) subjection to the Academicians. Similar breakaway movements followed in Cracow, Berlin, Prague, Hungary (Nagybánya)—and, in 1897, in Vienna. Gustav Klimt (1862-1918) led the Secessionists, whose declared aim was to open up the somewhat provincial Viennese art world to progressive foreign influences. To this end, they held important international exhibitions in their revolutionary exhibition hall designed by Joseph Maria Olbrich, which was built cheekily right under the windows of the Academy of Fine Arts.

There were a number of fine artists among the Secessionists, but Klimt towers above them for his striking decorative style, his challenging perspectives, his virtuosity and his rich symbolism. Klimt had begun his career in the academic manner. Working with his brother and a friend, he received typical Ringstrassen commissions such as decorating the Empress Elisabeth's bedroom in the Hermes Villa or painting ceilings and lunettes in the new Burgtheater. It was success in this line that secured him the commission for the University *aula*, and the shock of the commissioners (as described in the previous chapter, see p.210) can well be imagined in 1900 when Klimt delivered work in a completely different, taboo-breaking style. His pessimistic allegories of Philosophy, Medicine and Jurisprudence introduced a leitmotif of turn of the century Vienna, the indissolubility of Eros and Thanatos. This was a Viennese *Liebestod* (*The Beethoven Frieze*, *The Kiss*, *Death and Life*), but is also pervasive in a writer like Schnitzler, or in Otto Weininger's *Sex and Character*, or in Freud's work as a psychoanalyst. It could even be argued that operetta, with its frenetic rhythms and insinuating eroticism, exudes a spurious vitality that constantly threatens to turn into a dance of death.

Actually much of turn-of-the-century art was a reaction against the self-indulgent excess that had been the hallmark of the *Gründerzeit* and the attitude of *Glücklich ist, wer vergisst* already cited from Johann Strauss's *Die Fledermaus*. The empty hedonism of that time (even the news of the crushing defeat by the Prussians at Sadowa, which finally extinguished the moral authority of the Habsburgs in Germany, had been received with indifference by the heedlessly waltzing Viennese) has been described as a *fröhliche Apokalypse* ("gay apocalypse"). Now there was a pessimistic (even nihilistic) backlash to this apocalypse in the painting of Klimt and later Egon Schiele; and a moralistic one among the writers like Bahr and Freud, or controversialists like the critic Karl Kraus and the modernist architect Adolf Loos. An outburst by an aggressive modernizer like Hermann Bahr (he was known as "the man of the day after tomorrow") claimed that "Viennese would forgive anything but greatness... the very name Vienna... appears inseparable from charm, merriment and nonentity."

Karl Kraus was less affected but characteristically more devastating: "What I demand of a city in which I am going to live is asphalt, street-washing, a key to the apartment block, heating, hot water. The conviviality is me (*Gemütlich bin ich selbst*"—Kraus was, of course, anything but *gemütlich*). Generalizations like that of Bahr, who actually adored Vienna as much as he claimed to hate it, show that the tirades against their homeland of Austrian writers today (a Thomas Bernhard or an Elfriede Jelinek) are not especially original.

The battle lines between literary factions indicated earlier were seldom, if at all, those between Jew and non-Jew. This was warfare over the direction that Vienna's culture should take, and to some extent therefore a conflict between protagonists of "art for art's sake" and "modernists" like Loos and Kraus. The last named was equally contemptuous of the artistic pretensions of the Secession (Klimt & Co.) and of the literary pretensions of Bahr's "Young Vienna". He excoriated the latter in a famous diatribe entitled *The Demolished Literature*, which attacked his fellow coffeehouse literati in such withering terms that Felix Salten gave Kraus a beating, much to the delight of others who had suffered at his hands.

In his quest to purify the language, Kraus attacked the sloppy, but more especially the deliberately misleading, language used in newspapers in a way that recalls George Orwell's attacks on disingenuous and mendacious journalism of the left and the right in the 1930s and 1940s. Kraus' denunciation of the *feuilleton* is applicable to many of the disingenuous columns written by "opinion formers" today. He blamed Heinrich Heine for having introduced the French feuilleton to the German literary scene in the first place, aphoristically accusing the German-Jewish writer of having "so loosened the corset of the German language that today every salesman can fondle her breasts." His response was to edit and mostly write a much more cerebral version of today's *Private Eye* or *Le canard enchaîné* entitled *Die Fackel* ("The Torch"). Within the first two weeks of publication in 1899 *Die Fackel* reached the astonishing circulation for such a magazine of 30,000 copies. By his death 37 volumes had appeared, mostly financed by Kraus himself, who was independently wealthy and therefore not beholden to commercial or political interests, as were the journals he attacked.

Orwell's prose has been compared to a pane of glass, its apparent clarity often concealing great subtlety of thought. Kraus, on the other hand, writes a highly sophisticated and complex German that has defeated most translators, and hence prevented him from being better known outside the German-speaking world. Another problem is the extreme topicality of his themes.

But what has made defenders and opponents of Kraus alike most uneasy is the strong vein of supposed anti-semitism in his works. The glib explanation of this is that Kraus was a "self-hating Jew" trying to discard his identity (between 1911 and 1923 he was formally a Catholic). A biographer of Kraus, Edward Timms, describes him as "a Jewish author helping to propagate the Germanic vision of a civilization threatened by Jewish influences." The trouble is that Kraus' attempt to distance himself from a Jewish identity that was "becoming contaminated by mercantile and opportunistic values" inherently concedes anti-semitic generalizations, even if Kraus saw himself as rising above racial categories "in favour of the humanistic ideal".

There is no doubt that he reserved his greatest venom for men like Salten, Theodor Herzl (then writing feuilletons), Freud and the Jewish editors and journalists of an admittedly extremely corrupt press. In many ways his confusion about his Jewish identity, his ambivalent attitude to women (conventionally chauvinist on the surface, yet also capable of writing "Female desire to male desire is as an epic to an epigram") and finally his political quandary (he ended up supporting the Dollfuss authoritarian regime against the greater evil of the Nazis) are all factors that mirror the confusion and indeed desperation of intellectuals at the turn of the century and between the wars. The only person who seemed to develop a clear vision of the way forward for Jewry was Theodore Herzl, former journalist and operetta librettist, who went on to be a founding father of Zionism. The Jewish Kraus' "anti-semitism" went so far that he published articles in his magazine *Die Fackel* by Houston Stewart Chamberlain, an English racial supremacist who had announced the coming struggle between "German" and "Jewish" culture, and had married one of Richard Wagner's daughters.

Chamberlain lived in Vienna between 1889 and 1908 and it was here that he wrote his astonishingly successful *Die Grundlagen des neunzehnten Jahrhunderts* (1899) in German (English edition, 1910), which impressed such diverse figures as D. H. Lawrence, Winston Churchill and even Albert Schweitzer. A *pot-pourri* of Social Darwinism, race theory influenced by Gobineau and Chamberlain's wide-ranging dilettante researches in other disciplines, it appealed to Viennese contemporaries for three reasons: firstly it appeared to offer a scientific view of man and society that short-circuited the painstaking and often inconclusive endeavours of positivist empirical research (everyone loves a short cut); secondly its eulogies of "the German spirit" in art and culture dovetailed with the cult of aestheticism and "art for art's sake" that dominated *fin-de-siècle* Vienna; and thirdly its creed of Germanic racial superiority offered reassurance to a generation of gentiles (and even some assimilated Jews) that was morally, politically and psychologically disoriented.

In Volume II of the *Grundlagen*, Chamberlain wrote: "Not only the Jew, but also all that is derived from the Jewish mind corrodes and disintegrates what is best in us." Yet the "Jewish mind" itself, when its owner was a Karl Kraus or an Otto Weininger, sometimes seemed anxious to corroborate this view. In particular, Weininger's extraordinary treatise on *Sex and Character* (1903) managed to elide sexual and racial anxiety in his identification of womankind's contemptible roles of adaptation and subservience with the same characteristics in Jews. The works of both Chamberlain and Weininger are best taken as revealing symptoms of widespread psychological and social malaise, rather than serious contributions to scholarship, but that did not restrict their influence (Chamberlain's book had sold 20,000 copies by 1904 and a cheaper version in 1906 sold 10,000 copies in a week).

EROTIC VIENNA

Fin-de-siècle Vienna was notable for its ambivalent eroticism, the sexual adventure that begins as *memento vivere* and ends as *memento mori*. In this atmosphere it is hardly surprising that two classic works of pornography were written close to this time, Leopold Ritter von Sacher-Masoch's *Venus in Furs* (1870) and the anonymous *Josefine Mutzenbacher, Memoirs of a Viennese Prostitute* (1906). (The latter amusingly turned out to be the *sub rosa* production of Felix Salten, the creator of *Bambi*.) Sacher-Masoch's book was based on the author's own experiences with Fanny Pistor, with whom he signed a six-month contract in 1869, stipulating that she should treat him as her (sexual) slave and always wear furs for their sexual encounters. Rather appropriately, the cover of the Penguin Classics edition of this notorious work features Klimt's depiction of an orgasmic Judith holding the head of Holofernes (1901).

The author of *Venus in Furs* has lent his name to "masochism", identified as a sexual perversion by his Viennese contemporary, Richard von Krafft-Ebing in his study *Psychopathia sexualis* (1886). The latter work was originally more influential than those of Freud, given a reassuringly learned title by its cautious author and partly written in Latin in the hope of discouraging voyeuristic readers (to no avail, of course). Krafft-Ebing betrayed his conservative Catholic upbringing in his assumption that sexual desire not directed towards procreation was a "perversion", but then got into trouble with the Church for associating the desire for martyrdom of the saints with hysteria and masochism. As to Salten's *Josefine Mutzenbacher*, the original book (there have been bogus sequels) actually deals with the sexual experiences of a girl between the ages of five and fourteen, and has therefore been considered a work of paedophilia. This, too, was characteristic of the age; both the writer Peter Altenberg and the architect Adolf Loos had equivocal relationships with young girls, a taste that disturbed the coffeehouse côterie of intellectuals not one bit. Certainly in Altenberg's case he idealized the feminine principle, while at the same time befriending young women vulnerable to exploitation (waitresses, seamstresses, prostitutes and the like).

The most celebrated figure to emerge from the sexual hothouse of *fin-de-siècle* Vienna is of course Sigmund Freud (1856-1939), the "father of psychoanalysis". Many commentators have taken the line that Freud was a typical, even an inevitable, product of his time and location, that he was

"Viennese to his fingertips" and to call him "un-Viennese shows a confusion between the stereotype of a Viennese operetta and the historical reality" (Henri Ellenberger). Of course in some sense Freud, as an assimilated Jew in one of the professions where Jews could get ahead most easily, was quite a typical Viennese of his time. He even played Tarock and took a constitutional along the entire length of the Ringstrasse each day, come rain or come shine!

Yet the idea that psychoanalysis could only be born in Vienna and nowhere else is hotly disputed by Peter Gay in his essay *Freud, Jews and Other Germans* (1978). He sees Freud as a lonely genius embarking on a voyage of pioneer discovery into the workings of the human mind, a figure somewhat marginalized from the salon and coffeehouse society of the Viennese chattering classes. At the same time, he "lived like the very kind of respectable professional man whose style of thinking he was to undermine beyond repair."

Gay draws an analogy between Freud's fascination with archaeology and the practice of psychoanalysis. Freud had a passion for collecting small antiquities on his Mediterranean journeys (as it happens, collecting is also a very Viennese passion—I once had a neighbour who filled an entire room of his flat up, right up to the ceiling, with his collection of coffee-makers). Just as the archaeologist reconstructs objects and buildings from fragments, the psychoanalyst "reconstructs the origins of a neurosis from distorted memories and involuntary slips." This analogy, apparently favoured by Freud himself, is interesting because it reflects his continuing anxiety that he be accorded his due as a *scientist*, working with scientific discipline.

In moments of (ostensible) candour, however, he confessed, as in a letter to Wilhelm Fliess in 1900: "I am actually not a man of science at all, not an observer, not an experimenter, not a thinker. I am nothing but a conquistador, by temperament, an adventurer, if you want to translate this term, with all the inquisitiveness, daring and tenacity of such a man" (quoted in Max Schur, *Freud: Living and Dying*, 1972). This, of course, may be an instance of the disingenuousness which is a recurrent feature of Freud's letters. Then again, according to Hanif Kureishi, he also worried that his famous case studies were more "like short stories than scientific papers." While Freud's basic theories regarding the unconscious and sexual repression, together with their ponderous pseudo-scientific jargon of

"Oedipus complex", "ego", "id", "penis envy" and so forth, have become common currency, this is increasingly seen as more of a literary achievement, than a scientific one. As H. J. Eysenck (among others) has pointed out, Freud misdiagnosed his patients and misrepresented the cases he "treated" (or in fact failed to treat). Sigmund Fraud seems to have been as active as Sigmund Freud.

Karl Kraus spotted Freud's addiction to power early on and was outraged by the psycho-analysis of persons *in absentia* that took place in the latter's "Wednesday circle". "Psychoanalysis," he remarked contemptuously, "is the disease it purports to cure." It surely did not help in Kraus' eyes that Freud was a Jew. However, the nastiest side to Freud, identified by Karl Kraus, was his totalitarian cast of mind, which determined the manner in which those who dared to question his theories were cast out from his circle and systematically slandered. Readmission was only possible (as temporarily for Otto Rank) through grovelling submission and self-criticism reminiscent of Stalinist show trials. Béla Menczer has summed up the difference between the two men as follows: "Freud had his dogma and his movement; Kraus was the servant not of any dogma, but of a living spiritual power... and himself carefully prevented the appearance of any kind of organised 'Krausianism'."

Inevitably, the master had his own risible hagiographer in Ernest Jones and for years the keepers of the flame managed to obscure the more dubious aspects of Freud's behaviour by keeping the lid on potentially damaging information. More weightily, Sir Karl Popper, like Freud an assimilated Viennese Jew, has identified the self-referential nature of Freud's system, the Kafkaesque way in which a refusal to agree with a diagnosis was itself treated as verification of the diagnosis. Freud's thought indeed precludes the principle of "falsifiability" on which Popper based his philosophy of (genuine as opposed to pseudo-) science. Others, citing Freud's own letters and *obiter dicta*, have criticized his arrogance, disingenuousness and Messiah complex. Despite the substantial literature (e.g. Richard Webster's massive 600-page *Why Freud Was Wrong*, 1995) documenting in painful detail what the Nobel Laureate Sir Peter Medawar has called "one of the saddest and strangest of all landmarks in the history of twentieth-century thought", the Freud bandwagon rolls on, especially in the USA. In Vienna his consultation room at Berggasse 19 is piously preserved as a museum for true believers.

A now famous letter from Freud to the writer Arthur Schnitzler (1862-1931) is the source of the cliché that Schnitzler uncovered the hidden aspects of the human psyche in his writings that Freud could only achieve by "laborious work on other persons". Schnitzler indeed trained as a doctor, but his huge writing success made it unnecessary for him to practise. He once said "I write of love and death. What other subjects are there?"—a remark that would place him squarely in the Romantic tradition, if his treatment of these two topics were remotely Wagnerian, instead of being the exact opposite. The obsession with sexual pursuit in his novellas and in plays like *Reigen* (La Ronde), *Liebelei* (Dalliance) and the *Anatol* sequence was mirrored in his personal life. The latter is recorded in a diary kept from the age of 17 until his death in which, acting as his own Leporello, he meticulously recorded every orgasm with different partners over half a century (*his* orgasms, not of course the ladies'). He is also cynically candid about the difficulties he gets into through running two mistresses concurrently.

This priapic introspection running through the "games with love and death" with which so many of his stories are concerned underpins the classic view of Vienna's *fin-de-siècle* decadence. However, in Vienna this decadence had become a subject of analysis as much as of indulgence, and the doctor Schnitzler was writing at a time when major advances (but again chiefly in the field of diagnosis) were being made by the Vienna medical school. Unfortunately there were also alarming myths that were still shared by much of the European medical profession. Schnitzler was a huge admirer of Maupassant who rejoiced when he got the syphilis of which he subsequently died, as he believed he would overcome it and thus be immunized from further attacks. While the writer Schnitzler admired Maupassant for his works, the doctor knew better about syphilis, not least because his laryngologist father had given him a terrifying dressing down when he discovered his son's teenage indiscretions. Yet venereal disease, then advancing at a galloping rate, is not the topic of his novels and plays, though his character's behaviour would have led to it. On the other hand "neurasthenia", angst in all its forms and paradoxical psycho-sexual feelings are examined endlessly against a background of *carpe diem* and a lyrical and melancholy metropolitan scene.

Yet Schnitzler was not indifferent to the larger social questions of the day, particularly anti-semitism. One of his greatest plays is *Dr Bernhardi*

(1912), in which a Jewish doctor prevents a Catholic priest from offering the last rites to a patient who does not know she is dying, and whom the doctor wishes to protect from that knowledge. It is a powerful Ibsenesque clash of humanity and dignity against self-interested power hiding behind principle. It caused a scandal, as did the novel *Lieutenant Gustl* (1900), the hero of which refuses a duel, thereby exposing the primitive, corrupt and hypocritical nature of "military honour" (Schnitzler was stripped of his rank as reserve office in the medical corps).

Schnitzler is testimony to the seeming contradiction that all writers of any stature are moralists *as writers*, even though, as an individual Schnitzler was cynical, amoral and mysogynistic. The corrupted ethos of his protagonists flows from the author's ability to lay bare his own psyche. "Dream and waking, truth and lie flow into one another. Safety is nowhere," he wrote in *Paracelsus*. It could have been a description of *fin-de-siècle* Vienna.

The Realists

While the male chauvinist writers were narcissistically examining their souls, three remarkable women writers and two men were drawing attention to the misery of the poor, the irresponsibility of the aristocracy, and above all the exploitation of women and the double standards of a male-dominated society. Ferdinand von Saar chronicled the decline of the aristocracy and the military caste, as well as highlighting abuses of privilege. However, his most popular work, *Viennese Elegies* (1893) reverts to conservative pathos and reads like a melancholy and nostalgic love letter to the city, as lyrically described through the ages and through the seasons of the year.

In his numerous successful plays, Ludwig Anzengruber, dubbed the "poet of the suburbs", supplied a vivid picture of the struggle to survive of the ordinary Viennese in the Vorstadt. Marie von Ebner-Eschenbach took up Saar's social criticism (her first play was panned because it was merciless in dealing with the nobility) and found her *métier* in novellas and aphorisms ("The Wisdom of the Heart"). Apart from their genuine concern for the underprivileged (despite the fact that three of these writers were themselves from the nobility), the realists are remarkable for boldly attacking the oppression of women in a self-satisfied mysogynistic society (an Ebner-Eschenbach aphorism runs: "A clever woman has millions of born enemies: all the stupid men"). Rosa Mayreder was a feminist who wrote philosophical works on the role of women (e.g. *Sex and Culture*, 1923) and founded the first Austrian feminist association as well as an art school for women. But the most impressive campaigner was Bertha von Suttner, a socially progressive Darwinist, feminist and (most famously) pacifist. Her novel *Die Waffen nieder!* ("Down with Weapons", 1889) went through thirty-seven editions and was translated into twelve languages. It catapulted her to fame as Europe's leading pacifist and she received the Nobel Peace Prize in 1905 (she had briefly been Nobel's secretary).

THE COFFEE-HOUSE LITERATI

Richard Webster has written that the Freud-myth has been sustained in the teeth of empirical evidence by the "deep need of countless twentieth-century intellectuals for a system of over-arching certainties and doctrines which could replace the religious beliefs of the common culture they had lost." The coffee-house literati who were Freud's contemporaries reacted rather differently to a similar sense of foreboding and loss; they took refuge in the world of art and ideas, of wit and vicarious living. The coffee-house was not only a refuge from dank and under-heated Viennese apartments, but was an intellectual exchange for ideas and a commercial exchange for picking up commissions and making contacts. The leading denizens of the coffee-houses were the *feuilletonistes*, what we now call columnists, who were adept at dashing off a review, a commentary, a sketch or a quasi-philosophical reflection for the newspapers and journals.

Alfred Polgar has captured the atmosphere of these places, which offered personal privacy in the midst of conviviality: "For ten years the two of them sat for hours every day, quite alone in the coffeehouse. That is a good marriage, you will say! No. That is a good coffeehouse." And further: "A coffeehouse is where you go when you want to be alone, but for that you need to have people around you." Even today, although it has been claimed that psychotherapy has replaced coffee-house therapy, the coffee-house is a place where you can feel the pulse of the city. Each café has its own style and clientele, be it theatre people, politicos, journalists or the professions. In some the waiters are unctuous, in others famously *grantig* (browned off). Time passes differently in the time-capsule of the coffee-house. What is the form of words most frequently heard in a Viennese coffee-house, asks the *Wiener Sammelsurium* satirically? Answer: "My colleague will be with you shortly."

The writer Peter Altenberg (real name: Richard Engländer, 1859-1919) embodied the spirit of the Viennese literary bohemian at the turn of the century, living permanently in the coffee-house and (latterly) a small hotel off the Graben. His impressionistic sketches of city life have a simulacrum in those of Gyula Krúdy in Budapest somewhat later, but in truth they are *sui generis*. Altenberg was a neurasthenic who failed to stick at any job and indeed was finally declared unfit for work. This seems to have come as a relief and enabled him to drift into the life of the café habitué, who survived by sponging off his friends and patrons. His writing was discovered by Karl Kraus, who admired his deft conjuring of mildly apocalyptic encounters, and his microcosmic observations of everyday occurrences in the city. Altenberg evokes the sights, smells and sounds of Vienna in gentle murmuring tones, recurrently spiced with a quasi-aphorism or an oblique insight. Kafka said that Altenberg could discover "the splendours of this world like cigarette butts in the ashtrays of coffee-houses". He became something of a health crank, and indeed his insistence on going about in clogs without socks in all seasons probably hastened his end. His descriptions of women, especially very young women, are romantically erotic, though he was also inclined to lecture them about diet and exercise (his earnest notes to the dancer Grete Wiesenthal on this theme may have improved her bowel movements, but only through the unintended mirth they provoked). His neurasthenia got worse and latterly he was often confined in institutions or clinics, eventually dying of pneumonia induced by recklessly sleeping in damp sheets.

Like few other milieux before or since, Vienna's turn-of-the-century coffee-houses were repositories of wit and wisdom. Not the self-conscious aphorism of an Oscar Wilde or the worked over one-liners of the Hollywood script-writer, but the sort of humour that ambushes the listener slowly. Egon Friedell sent a message to all his friends that read "of all the good wishes I received for my fiftieth birthday, it was yours that delighted me most." The friends may well have been delighted until they reflected that the message was sent on a printed card...

Friedell (1878-1938) was a satirist and scholar whose ambitious and opinionated *Cultural History of the Modern Age* has rather unjustly been ignored by English-speaking readers. It remains in print as an Austrian classic, and should be a worldwide one (Friedell once observed wryly that a list of classics was regarded in the English-speaking world as a guide to

Café Greinsteidl, the meeting place of the Jung-Wien authors, whose main protagonist was Hermann Bahr.

books that should be read, and not, as in German-speaking countries to books that should be avoided). He wrote prolifically for newspapers and journals and can be considered a founding father of the Viennese cabaret, since his skills extended to performance as well.

Yet for all his sophistication, Friedell was capable of naively stating in his *Kulturgeschichte* that "mankind in the Christian era possesses one huge advantage over the ancients: a bad conscience." In fact an era was dawning conspicuous for its absence of conscience, whether one thinks of the ideological gangsters of fascism, Nazism or communism, or the slippery behaviour of Pius XII who put *Realpolitik* above the dictates of conscience in his dealings with Hitler. Friedell's utter helplessness in the face of such a world gone mad was evident from his chosen exit; as Nazi thugs were bounding up the stairs to his flat in 1938, he leapt from the third-floor window. Characteristically he called out a warning to passers-by before jumping...

Curiously enough, Friedell's naïveté was echoed in slightly different form by the "fearless, uncompromising, high-principled, dogged and vindictive" (Harold B. Segel) Karl Kraus. Of Hitler he merely wrote: *Mir fällt zu Hitler nichts ein* ("I can't think of anything to say about Hitler"). And even though this remark prefaced a 300-page polemic denouncing "the new Germany" (*Dritte Walpurgisnacht*, unpublished until 1952), the fact remained that the satire in which Kraus specialized was powerless in the face of brute force. The hypocrisy of jingoistic, drum-beating journalists and writers who propagandized for the Austrian side in the First World War was of a different order to the blunt assertions of thugs who announced what they planned to do and then did it. Kraus' pacifism is expressed in his verbally impressive but virtually unstageable play, *The Last Days of Mankind* (1922), which he himself "performed" in readings that were packed out by admirers. Indeed, the writer Elias Canetti makes the point that the real Kraus was the public speaker whose recitations of Nestroy, Goethe, Shakespeare and Wedekind had just as much impact as his diatribes against the Viennese and Habsburg establishments.

But he was also the Dean Swift of his day, rubbing mankind's nose in its own shit. Pacifist, anticlerical, and a fanatical puritan in regard to language, Kraus was the awkward dissonance, continuously pointing to unclothed emperors. He was the outsider to the cliquey insiders of Jung-Wien. Yet it was one of them, Hugo von Hofmannsthal, who best summed up (in 1893) the turns of *fin-de-siècle* culture in Vienna: "Two attitudes seem modern in our time: analyzing life and escaping from it… one either dissects one's own soul, or one dreams."

SOME SIGHTS ASSOCIATED WITH *FIN-DE-SIÈCLE* VIENNA

The Secession (Friedrichstrasse 12), built by Joseph Maria Olbrich in 1898, was the exhibition hall of the Secessionists, who exhibited their own work here and also that of many foreign painters considered to be modern and pioneering (*Jugendstil* and Symbolist artists in particular.) Klimt's *Beethoven Frieze* is in the basement. The building was largely financed by Karl Wittgenstein, the industrialist father of philosopher Ludwig. Olbrich was an associate of Otto Wagner, but was also inspired by a sketch that Klimt made for the building. On its left façade are the words *Ver Sacrum* ("Sacred Spring") which was the title of the Secession's journal. The motto over the door was supplied by the leading art critic of the day, Ludwig Hevesi, who enthusiastically supported the establishment of the Secession. It reads *Der Zeit ihre Kunst, der kunst ihre Freiheit* ("To the Age its Art, to Art its Freedom"). The Viennese were soon making fun of the exotic new building, calling it the "golden cabbage" after its globe of gilded, intertwined laurel leaves, or the "Assyrian water closet".

Pictures by Klimt and the Secessionists may be seen in the galleries of the Oberes Belvedere (Prinz-Eugen-Strasse 27). Otto Wagner's Jugendstil U-Bahn stations may be seen throughout the city, but two that are near the Secession are on neighbouring Karlsplatz. His famous Kirche am Steinhof (1907) is on the Baumgartner Höhe (Bus 48A from Dr. Karl-Renner-Ring to the penultimate stop.) His magnificent Post-Office Savings Bank (Österreichisches Postsparkassenamt) is at Georg-Coch-Platz 2. It faces the Museum for Applied Art (MAK) diagonally across the Ringstrasse, where Jugendstil furniture and artefacts of the Wiener Werkstätte may be seen.

Josef Hoffmann's Villa Colony for Secessionist artists is in the 19th District (Steinfeldgasse, Wollergasse- Tram 37 from Schottentor to end stop).

The Loos-Haus (1912) by Adolf Loos is at Michaelerplatz 5. A reconstructed Loos interior can be seen in the Wien Museum (Karlsplatz 8), together with works by the Secessionists and Expressionists. His tiny American Bar (or Loos-Bar) is in the Kärntner Durchgang.

Coffee-houses associated with turn-of-the-century literati have been mostly renovated and their interiors are not generally original, but they retain a certain nostalgic ambience: Café Central (Herrengasse/Ferstel Palais), Café Museum (Operngasse) and the reopened Café Griensteidl (Michaelerplatz).

One of Otto Wagner's Secessionist pavilions for the Vienna Stadtbahn on Karlsplatz.

Chapter Twenty-One

REPUBLICS, DICTATORSHIPS AND

WAR

"This city is a pearl in my eyes! I will place it in the setting it deserves…
This city too will enjoy a new flowering."

Adolf Hitler (1938)

The Spanish influenza that swept Europe at the end of the First World War cut a swathe through the Viennese population and weakened many more, making them vulnerable to fatal disease. The year 1918 saw the demise of Otto Wagner, Gustav Klimt, Egon Schiele and the prominent Secession artist, Kolo Moser, to name but a few. A year later, Peter Altenberg died of pneumonia. The Vienna they left behind was a dismal place, the so-called hydrocephalus or gigantically swollen head (its population suddenly 2, 239,000) for a country that no longer had the body appropriate to its size. German-speaking officials expelled from newly independent neighbouring countries arrived looking for jobs that did not exist, as did the defeated soldiers. Austria as a whole wanted to merge with Germany, a move that was forbidden by the Allies who had dictated such harsh peace terms at Versailles.

The "man without qualities", the hero of Robert Musil's novel, had suffered an identity crisis in the sprawling Habsburg realm he dubbed *Kakania*. That disrespectful appellation had been based on the official *k und k* or *kaiserlich und königlich* ("Imperial and Royal") nomenclature of institutions in the Austro-Hungarian monarchy (Franz Joseph was Emperor of Austria but King of Hungary). Now Kakania had been replaced by a tiny "land without qualities", cut off from its economic powerhouse in Bohemia and its breadbasket in Hungary, with hyperinflation until Chancellor Ignaz Seipel succeeded in stabilizing the currency in 1924. There was massive unemployment and a severe housing shortage.

Some intellectuals, like Musil, blamed the fumbling, bumbling monarchy for all their ills; others, like Joseph Roth, looked back with nos-

The most iconic complex of social housing erected under the aegis of "Red Vienna" was Karl Ehn's Karl-Marx-Hof (1930). Half a mile long, it provided virtually everything that working-class families needed from crèche and laundry facilities to a surgery and dental clinic. It operated virtually like a self-contained village. All over Vienna may be found other substantial *Höfe* (blocks of social housing) named after the various officials or politicians at City Hall who inspired a raft of social welfare policies. The idealism and ideology behind their building programme was constantly proclaimed in the rhetoric of Social Democratic politicians. As one of them put it in a speech in 1927: "He who builds palaces for children tears down prison walls." Hugo Breitner, the financial director of Red Vienna, addressed criticism of the crippling tax burden required to pay for the various schemes head-on: "Yes, we levy taxes, but we administer the revenue conscientiously and solely for the benefit of the working people." The radical achievements of Red Vienna in health, education and housing attracted admirers from all over Europe, notably left-wing intellectuals from Britain, who enthusiastically proclaimed the tax and employment model of the city as one to be adopted elsewhere.

talgia to the "good old days" when that same monarchy had provided a kind of stability and (for a Jew like Roth) a workable identity. His sense of loss creates the almost mystical atmosphere of his two greatest novels, *The Radetzky March* (1932) and *The Capuchin Crypt* (1938), which document two generations of a family in service to the emperor. Almost everyone blamed the Allies for imposing a peace at St.-Germain-en-Laye, where the fate of Austria appeared to be almost an afterthought; *L' Autriche, c'est ce qui reste—* "Austria is what is left over" (after the rest of the monarchy had been carved up into "nation states") was the way Clemenceau had contemptuously put it.

RED VIENNA

Into this moral vacuum and spiritual desolation stepped the utopians of "Red Vienna", who set up a quasi-Marxist, but nevertheless democratic, regime in the city. The rich (and even the not so rich) were heavily taxed to enable investment in infrastructure, housing, public services and popular culture. Ironically, the "right-wing" Christian-Social regime of Karl Lueger (d. 1910) had laid the groundwork for many of their measures with his "municipalization" policies. On the principle that "what affects the public interest should also be administered by public bodies," he had taken utilities and transport into public ownership, pushed forward electrification of the city, laid new sewers and built a new gasworks in Simmering, despite a boycott of private capital organized by the banks. (Lueger's solution to that was simply to found a municipal bank.)

Under Lueger the great Otto Wagner had completed his *Jugendstil* Stadtbahn, and built another rail connection called the Vorortelinie linking the suburbs. He also planned the upgrading of the Danube Canal and several hospitals, and designed his studiously functional Steinhof Church (Kirche am Steinhof) as an adjunct to the Lower Austrian mental hospital. On the other hand, the Christian Socials did next to nothing for the working masses who were not voters and, even if they had been, were not their constituency. In particular, the living conditions in the vast *Zinskaserne* ("rent barracks") of the suburbs were appalling and it was no wonder that tuberculosis was known as "the Viennese disease": beds had to be shared, there was minimal sanitation and rents nonetheless ate up to a quarter of wages. Not surprisingly, the first municipal election under a universal franchise in May 1919 was won by the Social Democrats with 54 per cent of the vote and Vienna has remained Social Democratic at every free election held since then. In 1922 the city gained autonomy as one of the Austrian Federal States, but it still had to combat a Christian Social government led by Ignaz Seipel, that was concerned to hinder the socialist "experiment" of Vienna.

The Social Democratic administration worked hard on child policy, schooling, health, education, housing and culture. Adolf Loos, the outspoken functionalist of turn-of-the-century Vienna, was appointed head of the section for new residential developments, but left for Paris in 1924 after all his projects for mass housing were rejected. His architectural achievement in Vienna therefore consists largely of noble interiors for luxury shops and bourgeois villas, even if he was intellectually involved in the social problems of the day. The most famous example of social housing at this time, the Karl-Marx-Hof (1930), was designed by Karl Ehn. In the short civil war of 1934, forces of the "Fatherland Front" bombarded this block, where Social Democratic resisters were holed up.

All over Vienna the great "Höfe" of social housing from the period of "Red Vienna" may still be seen, usually named after one of the leading socialist worthies on the City Council at the time it was built, and often with the rubric "Financed out of the Building Fund Tax" (plus the date) inscribed in red letters across the front. In propagating "workers' culture", *Rotes Wien* adopted decidedly bourgeois methods, encouraging membership of societies like "The Flame" (which promoted cremation, opposed by the Catholic Church on doctrinal grounds), an association of small gardeners, "friends of nature", a "workers' association for sport and physical culture", but also cheap tickets for "classical culture" (concerts, theatre, exhibitions and so forth). It is an interesting feature of Vienna that the nurturing of cultural awareness for its own sake (but with concessions on prices made on an ideological or class basis) went so far that "the working class increasingly aspired to the same culture as that of the middle class."

In the 1930s one socialist writer stands out for his originality, namely Ödön von Horváth. Some of his plays chronicled the lives of the desperately impoverished Viennese working class and *Kleinbürgertum* (petits bourgeois) in a world rapidly being overtaken by Nazism. By no means are these works a sentimentalization of the under-privileged: on the contrary, the characters of *Tales from the Vienna Woods* (1931), *Kasimir und Karoline*

(1932) and *Faith, Hope and Charity* (1932) are brutalized to near-depravity. The plays can be seen as a satirical deconstruction of the Viennese *Volksstück* ("folk play"), whose tradition reached back to Raimund and beyond. The "happy-end" is replaced by Horváth with physical and moral decline, suicide or murder. His dramas are an indictment of the exploitative capitalist dispensation that "Red Vienna" strove to replace; if the old world of dehumanizing impoverishment was symbolized by the plight of the *Bettgeher* (accommodation had been so short for the working class that many beds had more than one occupant, and were serially occupied according to the shifts worked by their users), the new world was symbolised by the *Gemeindebau* (solidly functional social housing.)

The political and psychological dimensions of Horváth's plays vividly illustrate the appeal of fascism to people on the brink and by the same token excoriate the inadequate response of religion (Horváth himself was a lapsed Catholic from the minor Hungarian nobility). The playwright's demise (1938) in his Parisian exile was bizarre, but somehow in keeping with his surrealist dramas. Following a meeting with a director who was contemplating a film of one of his novels, a branch falling off a tree in a thunderstorm killed him while he was walking home along the Champs-Elysées.

PSYCHODRAMA AND THE CONSOLATIONS OF NOSTALGIA

Remarkably, money was still found immediately after the war for traditional, but costly Viennese culture; on 10 October 1919 the premiere of Richard Strauss's *Die Frau ohne Schatten* was staged in the re-branded "State Opera" with *Jugendstil* sets by Alfred Roller and a cast that included Maria Jeritza and Lotte Lehmann. The libretto was by Hugo von Hofmannsthal, the precocious genius originally "discovered" (while still a schoolboy) by Hermann Bahr. He had collaborated with Strauss on several other operas (*Elektra*, 1904, *Der Rosenkavalier*, 1911, *Ariadne auf Naxos*, 1912). For the duration of the military conflict Hofmannsthal had worked in the War Welfare Agency, while other luminaries of Vienna café society—Felix Salten, Stefan Zweig, Alfred Polgar and even the delicate poet Rainer Maria Rilke—had found jobs in the War Archives. These were effectively propaganda jobs and Hofmannsthal was kept busy with the preparation of an "Austrian Library" of patriotic works for which there were few buyers, although twenty-five volumes were published before the series was discontinued in 1917.

Hofmannsthal's old patron, Hermann Bahr, metamorphosed into a militant war propagandist, attracting thereby even greater scorn and contempt from Karl Kraus. The fate of the quixotically conceived "Austrian Library", intended to strengthen the "German-Austrian" identity of its readers by reprinting representative literary, historical and scientific works, is a sign of a wider failure of Austrian cultural politics faced with nationalist pressures. Interestingly, the series began with "Grillparzer's Political Testament," appropriate but hardly reassuring in view of what Grillparzer had written about nationalism; and it ended with the (by then) grotesquely inadequate comfort to be derived from a volume entitled "Schubert among Friends".

Outside Austria Hofmannsthal is perhaps most remembered for his brilliant adaptation of the English mystery play *Everyman* for the Salzburg festival and his libretto for *Der Rosenkavalier*. The latter is the quintessentially Viennese opera of the nineteenth century, as Mozart's *Die Zauberflöte* was for the eighteenth century. *Der Rosenkavalier* (premiered in 1911) mixes nostalgic evocation of *belle époque* decadence with anachronistic Historicism (it is set in the Rococo Maria Theresian era and the Viennese critics loudly complained that its leitmotif waltzes were unknown at the period of its action). While an imperial field-marshal is away at the wars, his wife (the *Marschallin*) indulges in a dalliance with a young nobleman (Octavian) that veers dangerously towards real love. However, when Octavian is chosen to be the "Rosenkavalier" to present the suit of the Marschallin's boorish cousin to the lovely daughter of a *nouveau-riche* war speculator, he falls in love with the intended bride.

The love intrigue and modern take on ambivalent sexuality are heightened by the fact that Octavian is always played by a girl. Add in Strauss' lush, intensely erotic orchestration and we are back to the turn-of-the-century sexual hothouse, but with a dying fall. It is almost as if the Marschallin's dignified renunciation of her claims, the older woman gracefully giving way to the younger, is a larger allegory of an era drawing to a close. It has been said that Hofmannsthal stuffed every Viennese cliché into his libretto—the Viennese love of pomp and spectacle derived from the Baroque ritual of the Habsburg court and the counter-reformatory Church, their Phaeacianism, their easy-going sexuality, their yearning for "happy-ends", even the triumph of *ingénue* love over the class privilege of the elderly Baron Ochs. Yet the Bavarian Strauss also caught in his music the dark obverse of these clichés, the melancholy, the resignation to fate and the nihilistic pessimism behind which lay the astonishingly high rate of suicide among Viennese artists and intellectuals, including Hofmannsthal's own son.

Der Rosenkavalier's anachronistic waltzes were also the end of a musical era. Strauss began to write in a more Expressionistic style thereafter, while the avant-gardists Schoenberg, Webern and Berg were starting to make waves. Bridging the late Romantic and Expressionism was an opera called *Die tote Stadt* by the young prodigy, Erich Wolfgang Korngold, which was based on Georges Rodenbach's Expressionistic novel *Bruges- la- morte* (1892). It was premiered in 1921 and was instantly famous for a duet (*Mariettas Lied*) which is the *ne plus ultra* of late Romantic lushness (or kitsch, according to taste). Korngold went on virtually to invent "film music" in his American exile, while Vienna was being asked to accommodate itself to "modern" music.

If the critics were rude about *Rosenkavalier* ("a hullabaloo that is enough to dissolve the marrow of one's bones" is a representative example), which audiences nevertheless loved, both audiences and critics joined forces to denounce the "New Viennese School" and Alfred Schoenberg's puritanical "twelve-tone system". At a performance in the Bösendorfer Hall in 1907 there had already been a near-riot when works by Schoenberg and Berg were jeered. Mahler, who was present, reprimanded one of the rowdies, who recognized him and said he jeered Mahler's symphonies too. Mahler's companion hit the man, whereupon he pulled a knife and slashed his face. At another concert of modern works in the Muiskverein in 1913 there was full-scale battle between supporters and defenders of the works. The police had to clear the hall.

Of course, the modernists could not be accused of tact in their handling of the public and colleagues—neither Mahler nor Schoenberg had any social graces at all. In the case of an Expressionist artist like Oskar Kokoschka, lack of tact turned into deliberate provocation. His play "Murder, Hope of Women" (1909) dealt with lust, stupidity, hatred and cruelty, and was illustrated by the author with bleak ink drawings that anticipate Picasso's *Guernica* style. Kokoschka was influenced by Otto Weininger, whose mysogynistic and self-hating anti-semitic "Sex and Character" has already been mentioned; but in Kokoschka's piece the influence of Strindberg is felt, while Alfred Roller's light effects and the grotesqueries featured in Strauss' *Elektra* informed the staging and acting. This does not seem to have caused quite the scandal that Kokoschka had hoped (and embroidered in his mendacious memoirs), but it was hardly received with approbation, one critic taking the opportunity to include the rest of Kokoschka's painting in his denunciation of "long dead, mouldering art forms." This was an insult deliberately calculated to undermine Kokoschka's vision of himself as an artistic trailblazer. Of course, he was that, as his pictures in the Belvedere demonstrate, but he needed his patron Adolf Loos to secure portrait commissions, which sometimes caused Loos trouble because of the merciless treatment to which the sitters were subjected. Often they objected strongly to the brilliant but unpalatable end product. A contemporary wrote perceptively that the artist "slit open the souls" of his sitters, and that his "cruel "psychotomies" [i.e. anatomies of the psyche] may be compared to vivisection."

Kokoschka's contemporary Egon Schiele, now regarded as one of the great painters of the twentieth century, showed a similar disregard for bourgeois proprieties, though perhaps more out of naïveté than from an Expressionist desire to shock. On the other hand, he did supply pornographic works on demand to a private patron and got arrested for using under-age girls as models in circumstances that the authorities believed were more than suspicious. Yet the human pain and misery in Schiele's dramatic and moving works is testimony to an artistic vision far more profound than the mere search for notoriety. In his short career, Schiele progressed from the self-disgust of many self-portraits, through the shocking eroticism of *Cardinal and Nun* and the nihilistic despair equally evident in quasi-pornographic drawings or his bleak town scenes, to a stance of humane pity in *The Family*. His friend Toni Faistauer contrasted *The Family* sharply with earlier works ("for the first time a human face gazes out from one of Schiele's pictures") and speaks further of a "body swollen with vitality and organs from which a soul mysteriously looks out." As a confrontation with human suffering and the arbitrary nature of fate, it is ironic that the work appeared just at the moment that Schiele's life was about to be snuffed out. "Everything is living dead," the closing line of one of his youthful poems, had been a leitmotif of his work (landscapes included) up to then. In 1915 it still informed such powerful images as *Death and the Maiden*, where the transience of youth and beauty is evolved from an *ur*-theme of the medieval Dance of Death. *The Family*, however tragic it strikes the viewer, nevertheless features the child who would have been born to the Schieles had not his wife also died of the Spanish influenza.

TOWARDS THE ABYSS

The interwar period was by no means one of artistic or intellectual sterility. Eight Nobel Prizes in science went to Viennese researchers between 1918 and 1938, with later recognition for others then active. In philosophy the scientific empiricism of the "Wiener Kreis" founded by Moritz Schlick was influential throughout Europe between 1924 and 1936. Ludwig Wittgenstein was closely in touch with it, though not a full member, and the British philosopher A. J. Ayer popularized it in his celebrated book *Language Truth and Logic* (1936). Logical positivism provoked a creative reaction in Karl Popper, who published *The Logic of Scientific Discovery* (1934), a ground-breaking work on the philosophy of science. His masterpiece on the "open society", perhaps the single most influential work for conservative politicians and genuine liberals in the twentieth century, was to be produced in exile, but he was born and educated in Vienna.

The great economic theoretician of liberal democracy, Friedrich von Hayek (1899-1992), was also Viennese. He held a post in the Austrian government negotiating the Paris Peace at the end of the First World War that was analagous to that of the English economist John Maynard Keynes; the creative tension between Hayekian and Keynesian economic and political philosophy has marked especially the Anglo-Saxon political discourse, where Keynesianism was dominant until the rise of Margaret Thatcher in the 1980s. Joseph Schumpeter, briefly the Finance Minister of Austria in 1919 and the coiner of the phrase "creative destruction" to describe capitalism's powers of self-renewal, likewise made a distinguished career abroad in the United States. In art history the "New Vienna School", presided over by Otto Pächt and Hans Sedlmayr, was influential, though it lost its way as Sedlmayr increasingly became involved in fascist polemics. Ernst Gombrich, a pupil who reacted against his erstwhile teacher Sedlmayr, went on to be one of the most celebrated art historians of all time, whose brilliant overview, *The Story of Art*, has sold over eight million copies in thirty languages.

The rise of Nazism in the mid-1930s encouraged or drove most of these great thinkers into exile—Hayek in 1931, Schumpeter in 1932,

Popper in 1937, Gombrich in 1936. Moritz Schlick was assassinated on the steps of the university in 1936 by one of his former students who had become a Nazi. Hans Sedlmayr joined the Nazi party in 1932; after the war he worked out his academic disgrace as a journalist on a Catholic magazine before regaining a professorship at Munich University.

After the civil war of 1934, the clerico-fascist regime abruptly ended by the *Anschluss* of 1938, and finally the devastation of the Second World War, Vienna had largely become what Hugo Bettauer's novel *Die Stadt ohne Juden* had predicted: a cultural desert. The best minds had perforce made their careers in exile, but there were exceptions: the few distinguished figures who once again adorned the Vienna cultural scene were often largely unrepentant Nazis, like the conductors Karl Böhm and Herbert von Karajan. After a decidedly *pro forma* "de-Nazification," both *maestri* were quickly back in the saddle and being adulated by the Viennese.

The "Civil War" of 1934

Although Austria's so-called "civil war" lasted a mere four days between 12 and 15 February 1934, it represented the culmination of destabilizing political and economic pressures in inter-war Austria. There were three main "legitimate" political forces at play: the Christian Social-led government, German Nationalists and Social Democrats. The first two acted in an uneasy alliance against the perceived Marxist threat, while the Social Democrats also attracted support from the influential (and substantially Jewish) layer of cosmopolitan liberal intellectuals. From 1930 onwards, the illegal Nazis also began to make themselves felt, starting with disturbances that soon turned into full-blooded terrorism.

Worse, the country was polarized between rival ideologically motivated militias, the *Heimwehr*, which was conservative running to fascism, and the *Schutzbund*, which was Social Democratic running to Marxism. The stronger Heimwehr deliberately exploited events like the burning of the Justizpalast by a mob in 1927 to divide the country further and attack the Schutzbund. One of their more charismatic leaders was Prince Starhemberg, a descendant of the defender of Vienna against the Turks in 1683, who however was an ardent admirer of Mussolini and a protagonist of non-democratic, authoritarian rule.

In March 1933 the three Speakers of the Parliament resigned after a stormy session, and Chancellor Engelbert Dollfuss, who had succeeded Monsignor Ignaz Seipel on the latter's death in 1932, declared that Parliament had dissolved itself. He moved to set up the so-called *Ständestaat* or Corporative State, which was underpinned by a "non-party" Fatherland Front movement. In September 1933 he gave a speech at a mass rally condemning liberal capitalism, Marxism and the terror tactics of the Nazis, but also stressing Christian Social ideas (for example, that the man on the factory floor should no longer be "a mere number or unit of labour, but a human being who should be valued and treated as such"). On 12 February of the following year a Heimwehr provocation led to a socialist uprising in Linz, whereat the Social Democrats called a general strike. A struggle for power ensued, in the course of which the Karl-Marx-Hof and other big tenement blocks in northern Vienna became centres of Social Democratic resistance. They were soon overcome, however, and by the 15th the "war" was over, both in Vienna and Austria as a whole. The Christian Socials, in alliance with the Heimwehr (which acted partly as a political party and occupied important government posts) now consolidated its power. "Red Vienna" was extinguished. As historian Steven Beller describes it, "the culture war between provincial and urban Austria" was decided definitively in favour of the former.

The Ständestaat was patriotic and strongly anti-Nazi in theory, but increasingly forced to make concessions to German pressure in practice (Hitler having come to power in Germany in 1933). A Concordat with the pope, signed in June 1933, greatly increased the influence of the Church in public life and especially in areas such as education. Admittedly this did not sit easily with some of the regime's leading figures, since Starhemberg was already promoting the phrase "Austro-Fascism". Nevertheless, a conservative, Catholic and backward-looking authoritarian outlook characterized the regime's policies overall, while its mixed leadership of Catholics, fascists and crypto-fascists earned it the sobriquet of "clerico-fascism". The stability that victory in the civil war had momentarily bought proved largely illusory against a background of a disaffected working class and ubiquitous Nazi sabotage. On 25 July Dollfuss was assassinated in a Nazi putsch attempt and succeeded by Kurt Schuschnigg, who was faced with the unenviable task of trying to preserve Austria's independence from an ever more threatening and bullying Hitler.

THE ANSCHLUSS AND THE SECOND WORLD WAR

Schuschnigg, a mild-mannered lawyer from Innsbuck, was easy meat for Hitler, who summoned him to his lair in Berchtesgaden in February 1938. The *Führer* spent several hours insulting him and sent him away with demands that would effectively have placed Austria under German control in all but name. Hitler's promise to respect the country's independence in return for these massive concessions was, of course, valueless. Schuschnigg was deserted by the western powers, and by Mussolini, who had hitherto posed as a guarantor of Austrian independence. However, he did manage to rally the country behind him with an emotional speech in Parliament (and even the socialists promised their support at a mass rally in Floridsdorf). His last throw of the dice was to announce a referendum on the question "Are you for a free and German, an independent and social, a Christian and united Austria?" This was forestalled by Hitler's invasion on 12 March (except for one Tyrol village, which did not hear of the cancellation and voted 98 per cent for Schuschnigg). Sigmund Freud had his maid bring in the special edition of the newspaper in the afternoon of 12 March, when he heard the news vendors shouting "Extra! Extra!" in the Berggasse. When he had read it, he wrote two words in his large desk diary: *Finis Austriae.*

The consensus is that some 75 per cent would have voted "yes" in the plebiscite, which makes the rapture with which Hitler was received puzzling to non-Austrians. Partly the jubilation reflected immense relief that the issue was finally solved after years of instability and uncertainty. In this scenario, the Germans played the same role as the barbarians in Cavafy's famous poem, *Waiting for the Barbarians*, in which the people of an exhausted city see the invaders as "a kind of solution" to their no longer viable existence. Partly also it was a genuine enthusiasm for "coming home" to their German brothers and sisters. The Nazi plebiscite surreally achieved over 99 per cent support for the *Anschluss*, though of course "unreliable" elements and all Jews were excluded from the vote, while leaders across the political spectrum from the Church hierarchy to the socialist leader, Karl Renner, urged a "yes" vote.

Hitler was received by near-delirious crowds when he addressed the Viennese on the Heldenplatz. Prominent supporters of the Fatherland Front were locked up (and beaten up), but three-quarters of them suffered only short terms of imprisonment. It was the Jews on whom the Nazis

A worker changes the name of the Rathausplatz to Adolf Hitler Platz after the *Anschluss* of 1938.

focused as symbolic enemies of the new order, and in this they were assisted all too enthusiastically by their new compatriots. During the so-called *Reichskristallnacht* ("Night of the Broken Glass", 9 November 1938) Jewish properties were destroyed and Jews terrorized. A running commentary on the radio described the burning of the Leopoldstadt synagogue in Vienna "as though it were a jolly, Nazi version of Guy Fawkes night" (Beller). Jews who were able to leave Vienna did so, often negotiating their departure with Adolf Eichmann's euphemistically named "Central Office for Jewish Emigration" (Prinz-Eugen-Strasse 22), which stripped applicants of their entire assets before issuing a pass. Prior to the Anschluss there had been more than 200,000 "Jews by race" in Vienna, of whom 170,000 practised the Jewish religion. By the end of the war in 1945 there were still some 5,700 Jews in Vienna, while 2,142 Viennese Jews survived the death camps.

The war was a complete disaster for Austria. Two Austrian divisions were wiped out at Stalingrad, and overall 247,000 Austrians died in Wehrmacht service. There was an Austrian resistance, 2,700 of whose members were executed during the war, while some 32,000 non-Jewish Austrians died in prisons or concentration camps (about half the figure of Jewish victims). In Vienna the Hotel Metropole on Morzinplatz became the Gestapo's interrogation and torture centre. Some Austrians were involved in von Stauffenberg's abortive plot to assassinate Hitler, and towards the end of the war an underground resistance organization known as O5 became active.

In the first few years of the war, Vienna was out of reach of Allied bombing, but that changed in 1943, when the Allies began advancing up the Italian peninsula. The Viennese hoped to have Vienna declared a demilitarized "open city" in order to prevent massive destruction, but Hitler angrily rejected the request, declaring that the city must be defended "to the last stone". It was his ultimate revenge on the city that had humiliated him in his youth. Many prominent landmarks (including the Opera) were damaged or destroyed in a major bombing raid of 12 March 1945. The Opera's final performance before its closure in 1944 had been (appropriately) *Götterdämmerung*; equally appropriately it was to reopen in 1955 after rebuilding with *Fidelio*.

In 1943 the Allied foreign ministers, meeting in Moscow, issued a declaration that described Austria as "the first country to fall victim to

Hitlerite aggression," but warned that her final treatment would depend on "her own contribution to her liberation." Less than two years later Austria was liberated and a provisional government formed under the great political survivor, Karl Renner. Subsequently the country was divided into zones, each under the control of one of the Allies, while Vienna was under four-power control. This was the post-war city made famous by Carol Reed's film of *The Third Man*. Its brilliant script by Graham Greene evoked a seedy, twilight world of criminality and political menace. No film has captured so well the atmosphere of post-war malaise, humiliation in defeat, and black market transactions set in a ghostly milieu of faded Baroque glory and the rubble of war. The last exquisite touch in the film was the zither music provided by Anton Karas, perfectly catching the Viennese tone of sinister cheerfulness, seductive and macabre at the same time. Karas (who could not read music) eked out a living playing the zither in a Sieveringer *Heurige* on the edge of the Vienna Woods until discovered by Reed. He was not even well-known to the Viennese cognoscenti, but had a huge repertoire in his head and "'a speedy thumb', his future hallmark with which he was able to play against the sounds of a full bar." Reed brought him to England to make the soundtrack and drove him to the edge of breakdown with a demanding schedule of composing, of which he had no previous experience. What finally emerged was one of the most original and haunting soundtracks ever made, and it launched Karas on a worldwide career. But all he really wanted was to open his own *Heurige* in Sievering, which he did in 1953.

The Moscow Declaration proved to be a good diplomatic lever with the Russians, who occupied a large portion of Austria and looted what they could from their zone. They raped so many women in Vienna that the Catholic Church informally gave a dispensation for emergency abortions. The "Unknown Soldier" of the Russian Liberation Monument, erected soon after their arrival, was known to the Viennese as the "Unknown Rapist" or the "Unknown Plunderer" (also as the *Erbsen Pepi*, a reference to the dried peas the Russian soldiers distributed to the population, Pepi being a nickname for Stalin). After long and wearying negotiations it was finally agreed that the Allies would withdraw, the price the Russians extracted being a declaration of permanent neutrality by the Austrians.

In the slight East-West thaw between Stalin's death (1953) and the Hungarian uprising of 1956, the Austrian *Staatsvertrag* (State Treaty) was signed in Schloss Belvedere in 1955 to general rejoicing. This enabled the Second Republic to become fully autonomous through the Allied withdrawal from its territory. From 1948 Austria had benefited from the Marshall Plan and materially things now began to improve quite rapidly. However, the difficult legacy of "coming to terms with the past" (*Vergangenheitsbewältigung*) was to last for fifty years and casts its shadow even today.

Heimito von Doderer and the "Second Reality"

The most interesting literary figure to emerge from Vienna's *Götterdämmerung* was Heimito von Doderer, who may stand for those who relatively early made the "Paulite turn" away from Nazism, and after the war suffered the financial consequences for an honest refusal to sanitize their past. Doderer joined the Nazi party in 1933, when it was still illegal in Austria, apparently tempted by an authoritarian alternative to the sterile polarization between socialists and Catholics. However, his experience of Germany from 1936 seems to have disillusioned him and following his return to Vienna in 1938 he entered the Catholic Church in 1940. His period of Nazi affiliation was, to say the least, inglorious: he grovellingly tried to exploit his party membership to secure publication of his works and he divorced his Jewish wife after the Anschluss. He was later to remark that all of his subsequent massive body of writing consisted of "recognizing my stupidity." From this terrible error stem his subtle explorations of human self-deception, for which he developed a theory of the "secondary reality" in which his characters live. Their distorted *zweite Wirklichkeit* "flattens out all the complex, contradictory facets" of the authentic life into some ideology, "a distortion of reality on the psychological, public level."

In his longer fiction, Doderer plots this phenomenon on large canvases of multiple characters and their relationships. His attempted "total novel" escapes from the linear narrative of conventional fiction, and its apocalyptic moments occur when "secondary reality" collides cathartically with external reality; or as Doderer put it "when thought conforms to life" instead of life being forced to conform to thought. It is a metaphysical and literary expression of something similar to the "falsifiability" of Popper's philosophy, the revolt against closed systems of thought that invariably lead to inhumanity. His first big success in this line was *Die*

Strudlhofstiege (1951), which has unfortunately not been translated, although its even vaster pendant, *The Demons* (1956) has been.

The Strudlhofstiege, a well-known and rather lovely *art nouveau* flight of steps in Vienna's 9th District, is the symbolic centre of the characters' upper bourgeois milieu. *The Demons* continues with some of the characters from the first novel and ends apocalyptically with the burning of the Palace of Justice by the mob in 1927, the prelude to civil war. This event was also witnessed by Elias Canetti (he describes it in his autobiography) and inspired his classic work on *Crowds and Power*. Together, the two Doderer novels present Vienna as a stage on which universal passions are acted out. It is ultimately an idea derived from the Baroque *teatro del mundo*, although the realist Doderer supplies finely drawn characters instead of allegorical types. But it is this determination to see the world in the round, to be liberated into complexity, that links Doderer to other conservative Viennese writers like Grillparzer or (through his nostalgic Historicism) to Hofmannsthal.

As Doderer expressed it: "Everything has two sides. Only when you realize that there are in fact three can you begin to understand the matter." This complexity and the need to be familiar with the Viennese context of his work has made Doderer barely accessible to foreign readers, but his significance as a writer who carried the scars of Austria's ideological nightmare is profound. The dismissal of his work as tainted by Nazism is as wrong-headed as it is usually hypocritical, since it is often made by the sort of leftist critics who accept with sovereign equanimity (for example) Jean-Paul Sartre's open embrace of a Stalinism every bit as evil as Nazism. Interestingly, the two leading post-war protagonists of Doderer's literary importance were the writers Hilde Spiel and Hans Weigel, both of them Jews.

FINIS AUSTRIAE—AUSTRIA RESURGENT

The loss to death or exile to Austria of its cultural and scientific elite through the Nazi horror was incalculable. The chastened politicians returned to the stage in 1945, some of them remarkable men like Karl Renner, Julius Raab, Leopold Figl and the Jewish Bruno Kreisky. Even so, the equivocation and ambivalence of the Nazi interlude, its moral contamination, if you like, infected Austrian public life and culture for fifty years or more. The socialist Renner, for example, had warmly advocated a "yes" vote in the Nazi referendum on the Anschluss, while Kreisky (also a socialist) at one point had ex-Nazis (and perhaps not very "ex" ones) in his coalition government. Two, at least, of the "Aryan" conductors, as has already been mentioned, received the lightest dusting of "denazification" and (unlike Doderer) did not seem in the least disposed to recognize the degree of evil they had endorsed.

More equivocally, the popular Viennese poet, Josef Weinheber (author of *Wien wörtlich* in dialect, 1935) committed suicide in 1945, either out of remorse for his earlier endorsement of the Nazi project or in disappointment at its failure. Many ordinary Austrians, who had been encouraged by the Allies to think of themselves as "Hitler's first victims", continued to live in Doderer's "second reality". Most contemptible of all had been the behaviour of the Church hierarchy, notwithstanding that some lay Catholics courageously protected Jews during the war at mortal risk to themselves. The Pan-German advocate and supporter of the clerico-fascist regime, Cardinal Innitzer, had notoriously greeted the *Führer* with a *Heil Hitler!* as he paid his courtesy call to the dictator at the Hotel Imperial after the Anschluss. Subsequently, he appended the same slogan to an appeal to all Catholics to vote in favour of the Anschluss in the referendum. He quickly learned that expediency does not pay, especially when representing the Church whose entire *raison d'être* is to place moral precept above expediency—and which is fond of lecturing its flock to that effect. Seven months later, Nazi thugs smashed up the archiepiscopal residence after some seven thousand young people who had gathered on the Stephansplatz were addressed by Innitzer with the words, "Christ is our *Führer*." It should not be forgotten, however, that for the most part the minority Lutheran Church also tucked itself comfortably into Hitler's slipstream.

After the war the Church made amends with the 1952 *Mariazeller Manifest*, in which (still under the aegis of the great survivor, Innitzer) it renounced intervention in politics. The respected Cardinal-Archbishop Franz König worked hard from the mid-1950s onwards to regain for the Austrian Church the moral high ground it had yielded in the Nazi period. Through him it began to open up to ecumenism, made conciliatory overtures to social democracy and pursued a dialogue with modern artists through the mediation of Monsignor Otto Mauer and his Galerie nächst St. Stephan (director, 1954-73). The necessary *Vergangenheitsbewältigung* ("confronting the past") was also driven forward by lay Catholic scholars like the historian Erika Weinzierl, who became head of the Association against Anti-Semitism and also chronicled the Austrian resistance to the Nazis during the war.

Arguably more effective in penetrating the Viennese "second reality", however, was the work of the satirists. By far the best satirical invention was the time-serving opportunist, "Der Herr Karl", who is a Social Democrat when we first meet him, then a follower of the (quasi-fascist) "Fatherland Front," then a Nazi sympathizer and finally accommodates himself once again after the liberation in 1945. With deadly accuracy, Herr Karl's creators (Carl Merz and Helmut Qualtinger) charted the *vox populi* of the Viennese *Kleinbürger* (Herr Karl works in the store of a food shop), whose superficial *Gemütlichkeit* veils an egotism and heartlessness as chilling as the grave itself. The monologues of Herr Karl were shown on television (initially provoking outrage), and touched just about every raw nerve in an equivocating, half-ashamed, half-defiant population. At bottom it was the old accusation against the Viennese given an especially rancid flavour, that of the genial façade concealing the rotten core. This was ingeniously suggested through Herr Karl's own favoured forms of expression: Viennese dialect for his ignoble personal musings, Hochdeutsch for his lickspittle public persona. His disingenuousness may be summed up in one of his many homespun, insinuating aphorisms: "Austria is a labyrinth in which everyone knows his way around…"

SOME SIGHTS ASSOCIATED WITH "RED VIENNA" AND THE NAZI PERIOD

Social housing from the "Red Vienna" period (1919-34) can be seen all over Vienna outside the Inner City. An excellent comprehensive guide (in German) with detailed descriptions of "Red Vienna's" architecture is by Helmut Weihsmann: *Das Rote Wien: Sozialdemokratische Architektur und Kommunalpolitik 1919-1934* (1985). The famous Karl-Marx-Hof, designed by Karl Ehn, is at Heiligenstädterstrasse 82-92. Public recreation and sports facilities were a high priority. A superb example of such investment is the bathing and recreational facility Amalienbad (Karl Schmalhofer, Otto Nadel, Reumannplatz 9).

The Denkmal der Republik (Schmerlingplatz, to the south-east of the Parliament) features busts of three leading Social Democrats who laid the foundation for the First Republic: Viktor Adler (their leader, who died the day before the Republic was proclaimed), Jakob Reumann, the Mayor of Vienna, and Ferdinand Hanusch, Secretary for Social Security until 1920, who steered through some of the Social Democrats' most important social reforms. Nearby, in the park of the Rathausplatz, may be seen a gleaming metal head of Karl Renner (Alfred Hrdlicka, 1967). Renner became Chancellor in 1918 and was leader of the Austrian delegation at the Paris peace negotiations at St.-Germain-en-Laye. After the Second World War he was the first president of the Second Republic.

Alfred Hrdlicka was also the sculptor of the controversial *Mahnmal gegen Krieg und Faschismus* (Albertinaplatz, 1991). The themes of the three-part monument are the declaration of free Austria in 1945; the humiliation of Viennese Jews forced by Nazis to scrub the pavements clean of the slogans of the Fatherland Front after the Anschluss; and Orpheus in Hades. The Jewish Museum of Vienna in the nearby Dorotheergasse (no.11) frequently holds exhibitions, e.g. of exiled Jewish artists. It has a good reference library located at Seitenstettengasse 4. The Museum of Medieval Jewish Life (Judenplatz 8) features an account of the great medieval pogrom known as the *Wiener Geserah* (1420-21).

The only physical relic of Nazi times are the six great *Flaktürme* round the city, huge self-contained bunkers which it has proved impossible to demolish safely (they are almost 140 feet high and have walls between six and 23 feet thick). One of them now contains the Haus des Meeres aquarium (Esterhazypark).

Epilogue

BERNHARD AND JELINEK

"I don't need to invent anything. Reality is much more atrocious."

Thomas Bernhard

As a new generation of writers and artists has grown up post-war, the reckoning with the "sins of the fathers" has been particularly bitter. Sometimes this took the form of an escape into extreme art as a way of shaking off the cobwebs of a tainted society. The Wiener Aktionismus of the 1960s and 1970s in the arts, and the parallel Wiener Gruppe of writers, pushed the borders of art and literature with "provocations", "happenings" and the like that borrowed also from Dadaism, Surrealism and Expressionism. Art, political statement and ritual combined in an onslaught on the corruption of society, sometimes it seemed on society itself. The old Viennese nihilism resurfaced (in one happening an artist publicly committed suicide). While the movement petered out after 1968, when several of its members were arrested for "degradation of the state insignia", the "Orgiastic Mystery Theatre" of the painter Hermann Nitsch has had an after-life in Schloß Prinzendorf (Lower Austria). This *Gesamtkunstwerk* of music, dance and ritualistic animal slaughter has been taken more seriously by the art critics than much of the ephemera of Aktionismus, and Nitsch's blood-smeared canvases are periodically displayed in Austria and abroad.

The attack on Austrian society has been a feature of the three literary figures best known outside Austria through translation: Thomas Bernhard, Peter Handke, and Elfriede Jelinek.

Neither Jelinek, still less Handke, are really "Viennese" writers, but Jelinek studied at the Vienna Conservatory and her pieces have been performed at the Burgtheater, as have several of Handke's. She became well-known to English readers with her autobiographically inspired novel *The Piano Teacher* (1983) and her receipt of the Nobel Prize for Literature in 2004. The Nobel citation praised her "novels and plays that with extraordinary linguistic zeal reveal the absurdity of society's clichés and their subjugating power." (One member of the committee resigned, however,

Thomas Bernhard, Austria's leading post-war playwright and novelist, who tackled the problem of Austria's Nazi past with a hyperbolic directness that scandalized many.

describing her work as "whining, unenjoyable public pornography" and "a mass of text shovelled together without artistic structure.") There are many who agree.

Jelinek and Handke are, it is true, Viennese figures insofar as they continue a tradition of extreme narcissism (Handke's interminable voyage of self-discovery that may not fascinate readers as much as it does him, and Jelinek's aggressive projection of personal neuroses onto the society she hates, but which rewards her handsomely). The desire to shock a society that reacts by handing out a prize has led to some desperation amongst left-liberal Austrian intellectuals. A Carinthian artist awarded a prize that was to be presented by Governor Jörg Haider of the right-wing Freedom Party built an artificial hand with which to receive the prize, in order to avoid shaking the hand of Haider. He still took the money, of course. A penchant for the limelight may also lie behind Handke's embrace of the well-known humanitarian and promoter of literature, Slobodan Milošević, whom he visited in prison at The Hague and whose funeral address he gave.

The problem with too many of Austria's mostly left-leaning intellectuals in general, and Jelinek in particular, is not only that the society they excoriate is not as bad as they claim (although it isn't), but that they are doomed to the martyrdom of acclaim. One wonders how much they really want to change a society that rewards them so generously (Jelinek has been a communist, but it is doubtful if an intelligent man like Handke really believes in the maligned innocence of Milošević). Handke has to some extent moved on from his self-preoccupation to a more traditional type of narration that he once attacked, and is now even being compared to Adalbert Stifter. Jelinek reacts to her critics by more of the same. She is trapped in her self-referential system, which indeed she proudly proclaims: "Mine is a social intelligence that does not derive from knowledge and experience," as she remarked in an interview for a German magazine. The reaction she expects is applause (confirming her extreme view of Austrian society), while criticism merely proves her point; it is the circular logic of the Freudian diagnosis all over again. She has indeed received most of the major German and Austrian literary prizes. Some of these, at least, were politically motivated, as was almost certainly the Nobel Prize recognizing her virulent opposition to the right-wing Freedom Party entering government. Prizes are indeed the plague of the self-regarding world of German-speaking literature; shortly after his embrace of Milošević, Handke was awarded the Heinrich Heine Prize, though he later refused it after a public outcry.

The most impressive of the post-war writers is Thomas Bernhard, who has played his hand ingeniously with provocation and scandal, but who is also noted for his powerful and beautiful German prose. Bernhard is also in the business of "self-invention", and autobiography underlies many of his narrative voices. Above all, he acts as the merciless chronicler of the national psyche, picking endlessly at the scabs of a nation with a guilty secret. This he does with eloquence and rhetorical aplomb. He has said that love-hatred of Austria is the key to his writings, and this will rapidly become apparent to anyone who reads his works. An interesting aspect of the latter is his relationship to the genre of the *Heimatroman* ("regional novel") an idealization of peasant life serving to build an Austrian identity after the collapse of the Habsburg Empire. There was a blood-and-soil Nazi version of the Heimatroman, transmuted post-war into a sentimental "new dawn" literature that reverted to the Catholic values of the original. Just as Horváth deconstructed the *Wiener Volksstück*, Bernhard deconstructed the Heimatroman, turning it into a dystopian vision of rural life (*Frost*, 1963).

Bernhard's characteristic voice was formed early: the monologues of alienated lone-goers, the gallows humour, the apodictic expression of an outrageous generalization. Like Jelinek, who has an organ diploma from the Vienna Conservatory, Bernhard studied music, and it shows. Both authors heap up repetitions of modal sentences, but Bernhard's have the more distinctive musical quality, like a Baroque fugue. Having suffered from TB as child and from a sarcoid tumour thereafter, death hovers above his long arias, many of which are concerned with mortality, sickness, psychopathy and alienation.

Robert Menasse, one of the few liberal intellectuals in Vienna who is independent-minded enough challenge the *bien-pensant* consensus, alludes sardonically to Bernhard's dying instruction: "The last freedom that remains to me is that of forbidding that my works be performed in Austria." Funny, says Menasse, he had the impression that he enjoyed virtually every freedom in Austria (of speech, of assembly, of publication), but all along he had not noticed that none of these civil rights existed—except that of forbidding performance of his works! Apart from the fact that the prohibition was soon lifted (after all, there was money to be made out of Bernhard), the author himself had always had patrons to get him launched, then an admiring following, and finally the usual meteorite shower of literary awards.

He was, nonetheless, a great writer who lived off what he attacked, like so many other Viennese intellectuals. Ironically, it was an East German playwright whose stiletto wounded where the professional would-be Swiftian authors were most vulnerable: "[Bernhard] writes as if he had been hired by the Austrian government to write against Austria... The disturbance can be articulated that loudly and clearly because it doesn't disturb." What remains is the marvellous music of his prose, the grumbling voice with its black humour, the vulnerable, wounded scorpion who can implicate the reader in his own mortification. And that is great literature.

Further Reading

There are many, many books on Vienna at all levels of sophistication. The selection below simply records some that the author has found stimulating and which might be helpful to someone coming fresh to Viennese culture. Dates of publication are the latest known, which in most cases means a paperback, and may be a reprint of a much earlier edition. No distinction has been made between titles that are in or out of print (and in any case the better books on Vienna have been undergoing a reprint revival in recent years). There is a sad delusion among authors (even this one) and publishers that the "new" book on a given topic is necessarily the better one, which is often only the case insofar as it incorporates the latest research. Ilsa Barea's *Vienna: Legend and Reality* (first published in 1966) remains the best book in English with which to embark on a deeper acquaintance with the city.

General Histories of Austria, the Austrians and the Habsburgs in Europe

Beller, Steven, *A Concise History of Austria* (Cambridge, 2006)

Clearly-written and accessible. A good introduction for those new to the
   subject.

Beller, Steven, *Francis Joseph* (Harlow/ NY, 1996)

Brook-Shepherd, Gordon, *The Austrians* (London, 1997)

Crankshaw, Edward, *Maria Theresa* (London, 1983)

Heer, Friedrich, *The Holy Roman Empire* (London, 1995)

One of the most stimulating (at times maddening) contributions to Austrian
   cultural history is the same author's *Der Kampf um die österreichische
   Identität* (Vienna, 1981), unfortunately never translated.

Kann, Robert E., *A History of the Habsburg Empire 1526-1918*
   (Berkeley/London, 1974)

Rickett, Richard, *A Brief Survey of Austrian History* (Vienna, 7th Edition 1983).

Histories of Vienna and the Viennese: General, Urban and Cultural

Barea, Ilsa, *Vienna: Legend and Reality* (London, 1993)

Beller, Steven, *Vienna and the Jews 1867-1938: A Cultural History* (Cambridge, 1990)

Boyer, John W., *Political Radicalism in Late Imperial Vienna. Origins of the Christian Social Movement 1848-1897* (Chicago/London, 1995)

Hofmann, Paul, *The Viennese: Splendor, Twilight and Exile* (New York, 1989)

Lehne, Inge and Lonnie Johnson, *Vienna: The Past in the Present* (Riverside CA, 1995)

Lichtenberger, Elisabeth, *Vienna* (London, 1993)
> A masterly reference work of urban historical analysis blending history, economics, sociology and ecology.

Morton, Frederic, *A Nervous Splendour: Vienna 1888-1889* ((London/NY, 1980)

Stoye, John, *The Siege of Vienna* (Edinburgh, 2000, corrected edition of this classic work first published in 1964)

CULTURAL PERSPECTIVES: ART, ARCHITECTURE, MUSIC
Culture and Society

Beller, Steven (ed), *Rethinking Vienna 1900* (New York, 2001)

Broch, Hermann, *Hugo von Hofmannsthal and his Times: the European Imagination 1860-1920.* Translated by Michael Steinberg (Chicago, 1984)

Gay, Peter, *Schnitzler's Century: the Making of Middle Class Culture 1815-1914* (NY, 2002)
> This work is about nineteenth-century middle-class culture in Europe, but Gay has chosen the Viennese Schnitzler as his "master of ceremonies".

Gay, Peter, *Freud: A Life for our Time* (London, 1988)
A sympathetic account by a leading cultural historian.

Hall, Peter, *Cities in Civilization: Culture, Innovation and Urban Order* (London, 1999)
The long Chapter 5 of Book One is devoted to Vienna.

James, Clive, *Cultural Amnesia: Notes In The Margin Of My Time* (London, 2007)
> In his "Overture" entitled "Vienna", James notes that: "As a place to begin studying what happened to twentieth-century culture, Vienna is ideal, but only on the understanding that the ideal was real with all the complications of reality, and none of the consolations of a therapeutic dream." The book includes essays on Peter Altenberg, Sigmund Freud, Egon Friedell, Karl Kraus, Alfred Polgar, Arthur Schnitzler, Ludwig Wittgenstein and Stefan Zweig.

Janik, Allan and Toulmin, Stephen *Wittgenstein's Vienna* (NY, 1973)

Johnston, William M., *The Austrian Mind* (Berkeley/London, 1976)
 Stuffed with theory and ideas, some of them wrong-headed, this is a thought-provoking book, but only to be used with caution.

Luft, David S., *Robert Musil and the Crisis of European Culture 1880-1942* (Berkeley/London, 1979)

Schorske, Carl, *Fin-de-siécle Vienna* (NY, 1981)

Timms, Edward, *Karl Kraus: Apocalyptic Satirist* Vols I and II (London, 1989 and 2005)

Wangermann, Ernst, *The Austrian Achievement 1700-1800* (NY, 1973)

Webster, Richard, *Why Freud Was Wrong: Sin, Science and Psychoanalysis* (London, 1995)
 Hugely documented over 700 pages, painstaking and measured, this is a far more devastating demolition of Freudian pretensions than hatchet jobs like that of Thomas Szasz.

Music

De La Grange, Henry-Louis, *Wien: Eine Musikgeschichte* (Frankfurt, 1997) or in the original French edition *Vienne, une histoire musicale* (Paris, 1995) Unfortunately not translated.

Rickett, Richard, *Music and Musicians in Vienna* (Vienna, 3rd Edition, 1990)

Fine Arts

Shedel, James, *Art and Society: the New Art Movement in Vienna, 1897-1914* (Palo Alto, CA, 1981)

Vergo, Peter, *Art in Vienna: 1898-1918* (London, 2nd Edition, 1981)

Werkner, Patrick, *Austrian Expressionism – The Formative Years* (Palo Alto, 1993)

Whitford, Frank, *Egon Schiele* (London, 1981)

Whitford, Frank, *Klimt* (London, 1990)

Architecture

Aurenhammer, Hans, *J.B.Fischer von Erlach* (Cambridge, 1973)

Blaschke, Bertha *et al*, *Architecture in Vienna 1850-1930* (Heidelberg, n/d)

Blau, Eva, *The Architecture of Red Vienna 1919-1934* (NY, 1999)

Craesmann Collins, Christiane, *Camillo Sitte: The Birth of Modern City Planning* (NY, 2006)
 Features a translation of the classic blueprint for historicist urban renewal by

a nineteenth-century Austrian architect.

Loos, Adolf, *On Architecture* (Riverside, CA, 2002)

This anthology of Loos' writings includes one of his most famous polemics, *The Potemkin City*. Another celebrated diatribe, *Ornament and Crime*, is available from the same publisher in *Adolf Loos: Ornament and Crime: Selected Essays* (Riverside, CA, 1997).

Lorenz, Hellmut, *Johann Bernhard Fischer von Erlach* (Zürich, 1992)

Samitz, August, *Architecture in Vienna: 700 Buildings* (Heidelberg, n/d)

Memoirs, Autobiographies

Canetti, Elias, *The Torch in My Ear* ((Vol II of autobiography, London. 1990) and *The Play of Eyes* (Vol III, London, 1990)

Clare, George, *Last Waltz in Vienna* (London/NY, 1981-2)

Metternich, *The Autobiography 1773-1815* (Welwyn Garden City, 2004)

Zweig, Stefan, *The World of Yesterday* (Lincoln, Nebraska/London, 1964)

Travellers' Anthology

Lehmann, John and Richard Bassett (eds), *Vienna. A Traveller's Companion* (London, 1988)

Literature

Bernhard, Thomas

Some fourteen works of fiction, one of memoirs, five plays and three collections of poetry are available so far in English. An introduction might begin with the early *Correction* (NY 1979). One of Bernhard's most delightful works, which contains *inter alia* advice to writers not to equate literary prizes with artistic value, is *Wittgenstein's Nephew* (London, 1986). Of his trilogy on arts and music, the most entertaining is *Old Masters* (London 1989). A fine assessment of his work is: Honnegger, Gitta, *Thomas Bernhard: the Making of an Austrian* (London/New Haven, Connecticut, 2001-2)

Hacken, Richard, *Into the Sunset: An Anthology of Nineteenth Century Austrian Prose* (Riverside CA, 1999)

Useful for getting acquainted with perhaps unfamiliar writers.

Handke, Peter, *Absence* (NY, 1990)

Handke, Peter, *On a Dark Night I Left My Silent House* (NY, 2000)

Jelinek, Elfriede, *The Piano Teacher* (London, 2002)

Kraus, Karl, *No Compromise: Selected Writings of Karl Kraus* Edited by Frederick

Ungar, translated by Frederick Ungar and others (NY, 1977)

Musil, Robert, *The Man Without Qualities* Translated by Eithne Wilkins and Ernst Kaiser, Vol I (NY/London, 1953/ 1965), Vol II (NY/London, 1954) and Vol III (London, 1960)

Musil, Robert, *Young Törless* (Introduction by J. M. Coetzee, London, 2001)

Musil, Robert, *Five Women* (Introduction Frank Kermode, NY, 1986)

Roth, Joseph, *The Capuchin Crypt* (in some translations the title is "The Emperor's Tomb"). A recent edition is available from the Overlook Press, NY, 2002.

Roth, Joseph, *The Radetzky March* (NY, 1995)

Segel, Harold B., *The Vienna Coffeehouse Wits 1890-1938* (West Lafayette, Indiana, 1993)

This book with its commentary, concise biographies of the main protagonists and excellent translations from their Feuilletons, sketches or polemics, is indispensable for understanding *fin-de-siècle* Vienna.

Stifter, Adalbert, *Brigitta* (London/Chester Springs, PA, 1990)

Stifter, Adalbert, *Indian Summer* Translated by Wendell Frye (NY, 2006)

Schnitzler, Arthur, *Vienna 1900: Games with Love and Death* (London, 1985)

Schnitzler, Arthur, *The Road into the Open* (Los Angeles, 1991)

Schnitzler, Arthur, *Lieutenant Gustl* (Los Angeles, 1993)

Schnitzler, Arthur, *Rhapsody: A Dream Novel* (London/NY 1999)

This was the novella on which Stanley Kubrick based his last film, "Eyes Wide Shut".

Torberg, Friedrich, *Tante Jolesch: The Decline of the West in Anecdotes* (Riverside CA, 2005).

Nostalgia and Jewish anecdotes from the pre-Nazi coffee-house culture of Vienna.

Von Doderer, Heimito, *The Demons* (3 Vols., London, 1989)

Von Doderer, Heimito, *A Person Made of Porcelain and Other Stories* (Riverside, CA, 2005)

Commentary and Sourcebooks

Daviau, Donald G., *Austria in Literature* (Riverside, CA, n/d)

Ungar, Frederick., *Handbook of Austrian Literature* (NY, 1973)

Now dated, but still the only comprehensive sourcebook with biographies, criticism and bibliography of major Austrian writers up to the 1960s.

DISCOGRAPHY

A few classic and/or rare recordings of Viennese folk and light music:

Das große Operetten-Wunschkonzert (various well-known singers) (Philips)

Die besten Schrammeln Instrumental: The Best of Schrammel Music Instrumentals – Soul Music of Old Vienna Gefunden von Roland Jos. Leop. Neuwirth (Trikont, Munich)

Historische Stimmen aus Wien A series of commentated audio records that include the voices of artists, politicians and even Franz Joseph himself. These are available as CDs (and can also be downloaded) from: Phonogrammarchiv der Österreichischen Akademie der Wissenschaften (ÖAW).

Kaiserliche Operette Series with various well-known singers (EMI Electrola): Selections include Franz Lehár: *Das Land des Lächelns, Der Zarewitsch, Die lustige Witwe* and *Paganini*. Johann Strauss II: *Eine Nacht in Venedig, Wiener Blut, Der Zigeunerbaron, Ein Walzertraum*.

Strauß, Johann Sohn, *Walzer* Conducted by Willi Boskovsky (EMI Classics)

Wien, Du Stadt meiner Träume Richard Tauber, Paul Hörbiger, Hans Moser, Herbert von Karajan and others (TIM, Hamburg)

Wiener Klänge: A Portrait of Anton Karas (da music, Diepholz, Germany)

Wiener-Lied Edition aus den Kremser Alben: Walter Berry, Heinz Zednik, Angelika Kirchschlager (from CD 7). CD Series 1-3, 1998, 4-6, 1993, 7-9, 1994, and 13-15 1996. (10-12 now unavailable except second-hand.) Produced by ORF Studio Wien.

Wien Volksmusik: Rare Schellacks 1906-1937 (Trikont, Munich)

WEBSITES

www.wien.at

Official website of Vienna: culture, leisure activities, practical information and a city plan.

www.wien.at/english/statistics

The city in figures.

www.explore-vienna.com

Useful for e-mail addresses, telephone numbers and booking details for arts festivals, as well as venues for music, opera, dance, theatre and film.

www.info.wien.at

Comprehensive site for recreational options.

www.wiengv.at/english

Information on current and upcoming events.

www.aboutvienna.org

Fast facts on shopping, nightlife, cuisine, culture etc.

www.webtourist.net/austria/vienna/web-resources.phtml

Worth trying for information on accommodation, but there are many other sites.

www.johann-strauss-gesellschaft.at

A paradise for Strauss fans, it includes full citations for composition dates, commissions, premières and even contemporary press criticism of his works, plus much miscellaneous information.

www.wien-vienna.at.aeiou.at

Illustrations from various sources relating to the history and culture of Austria.

Index of Literary & Historical Names

Index of Places & Landmarks